"At Focus on the Family, we hear from couples every day who are struggling in their relationships and desperately seeking healing in their marriages. Through personal and pastoral experience—along with a keen understanding of biblical teaching—Chip Ingram casts a vision for marriage as God intends it. Better yet, he shows readers how to achieve the kind of marriage they've always dreamed of."

Jim Daly, president, Focus on the Family

"This is not just another book on marriage. Chip cuts through political correctness to get to the heart of Christlikeness by challenging both men and women to greater sacrifice in their relationship with one another."

Kyle Idleman, author, *not a fan.* and *Don't Give Up*

"If you are looking for a practical, biblically based picture of marriage, you need look no further. Chip Ingram has nailed it. I highly recommend *Marriage That Works*."

Gary D. Chapman, PhD, author,
The 5 Love Languages

"A deeply life-giving marriage is not some elusive thing we strive for but can never achieve. To love God and love each other extravagantly is exactly what we were made for. Chip's wisdom and experience are evident on every page of *Marriage That Works*, and our marriages would look radically different if we let these truths change us."

Jennie Allen, author, *Nothing to Prove*;
founder and visionary, IF:Gathering

"My friend Chip Ingram has provided couples with a practical, relevant tool to enhance their relationship to make it all that God intended it to be. You and your mate will be blessed as you live out the principles in this book."

Dr. Tony Evans, senior pastor, Oak Cliff Bible Fellowship;
president, The Urban Alternative

"Chip Ingram writes from the uncompromising biblical foundation of God's design for marriage. His challenges for men and women are strong and yet sensitive, principled but practical. This book is a fresh approach to a continuing need. Each chapter has a set of study questions which will make this book very useful for personal or small group application."

Mark L. Bailey, president, Dallas Theological Seminary

"I quote Chip Ingram frequently. This is one of my favorite quotes of Chip's: 'Marriage is not a debate to be won; it is a dance to be enjoyed.' That's so true! In *Marriage That Works* Chip shows us how to enjoy the dance. His practical illustrations from his own marriage, coupled with the truth of God's Word, will help improve and transform your marriage."

Dave Stone, pastor, Southeast Christian Church,
Louisville, KY

MARRIAGE

That

WORKS

GOD'S WAY OF BECOMING
SPIRITUAL SOUL MATES, BEST FRIENDS,
AND PASSIONATE LOVERS

CHIPINGRAM

BakerBooks
a division of Baker Publishing Group
Grand Rapids, Michigan

Published by Baker Books
a division of Baker Publishing Group
PO Box 6287, Grand Rapids, MI 49516-6287
www.bakerbooks.com

Printed in the United States of America

Library of Congress Cataloging-in-Publication Data
Names: Ingram, Chip, 1954– author.
Title: Marriage that works : God's way of becoming spiritual soul mates, best friends, and passionate lovers / Chip Ingram.
Description: Grand Rapids, MI : Baker Books, [2019] | Includes bibliographical references.
Identifiers: LCCN 2018028803| ISBN 9780801074554 (cloth)
Subjects: LCSH: Marriage—Religious aspects—Christianity. | Marriage—Biblical teaching. | Sex role—Religious aspects—Christianity. | Sex role—United States.
Classification: LCC BV835 .I54 2018 | DDC 248.8/44—dc23
LC record available at https://lccn.loc.gov/2018028803

ISBN 978-0-8010-7469-1 (ITPE)

Unless otherwise indicated, Scripture quotations are from the Holy Bible, New International Version®. NIV®. Copyright © 1973, 1978, 1984, 2011 by Biblica, Inc.™ Used by permission of Zondervan. All rights reserved worldwide. www.zondervan.com. The "NIV" and "New International Version" are trademarks registered in the United States Patent and Trademark Office by Biblica, Inc.™

Scripture quotations labeled NASB are from the New American Standard Bible®, copyright © 1960, 1962, 1963, 1968, 1971, 1972, 1973, 1975, 1977, 1995 by The Lockman Foundation. Used by permission. www.Lockman.org

Scripture quotations labeled NLT are from the Holy Bible, New Living Translation, copyright © 1996, 2004, 2015 by Tyndale House Foundation. Used by permission of Tyndale House Publishers, Inc., Carol Stream, Illinois 60188. All rights reserved.

In keeping with biblical principles of creation stewardship, Baker Publishing Group advocates the responsible use of our natural resources. As a member of the Green Press Initiative, our company uses recycled paper when possible. The text paper of this book is composed in part of post-consumer waste.

19 20 21 22 23 24 25   7 6 5 4 3 2 1

Contents

Introduction

One Thursday night, I got an overpowering whiff of Brut cologne as Dave, my mentor, came down the stairs. Dave had been trained by the Navigators and had launched two successful campus ministries in West Virginia. He was a blue-collar guy who laid bricks for a living, but whose passion was discipling college students.

Dave wore a big smile and a tie and sport coat—clothes I didn't even know he owned.

"What's going on?" I asked him. "Where are you going?"

"I'm going on a date." He grinned.

"With who?"

"Polly, of course. Who do you think?"

I was shocked. Dave and Polly had four kids—two in high school, one in middle school, and one in elementary school. I had never seen my or anyone else's parents go on a date unless they had to chaperone a dance. My folks loved each other, of course, but they did not look at each other the way Dave and Polly did even after twenty years of marriage.

I had been around Dave and Polly for about five years, moving with them to a new city after college graduation to help them launch a campus discipleship ministry. While Dave worked, I taught high school, coached basketball, and lived in the garage apartment behind Dave's house.

I had eaten more meals at their table than I can remember. I had seen their struggles. And I knew they really loved each other. But the picture of Dave coming down the stairs anticipating a date with his wife had an impact on me. It redefined what a marriage could be.

The Marriage God Wants for You

This book is about having that kind of marriage. Whether you and your mate are newlyweds or have been married for decades, God has designed this unique relationship to, over time, produce best friends, passionate lovers, and spiritual soul mates.

> *Best friends, passionate lovers, spiritual soul mates. That is the kind of marriage God wants for you and your mate.*

Best friends, passionate lovers, spiritual soul mates. That is the kind of marriage God wants for you and your mate. This is not hyperbole. It isn't idealism. It's a real possibility, regardless of where you and your spouse find yourselves.

Don't get me wrong. This isn't easy. It will require some *knowledge* that most people don't have, some *skills* everyone can learn, and a lot of *grace*, which God promises to provide.

It will also require setting aside some assumptions you've made about marriage, as well as mustering up the courage to honestly examine where your marriage is—and where you want it to be.

Paying a High Price

If you're thinking I'm one of those pastors from a long line of wonderful ministers who have had wonderful marriages and wonderful children—someone who has never had any problems, can't understand your marriage or your issues, and just wants to tell you how to do things the right way—you need to know that's not the case.

The kind of marriage I have with my wife is far better than I ever dreamed, but the price has been higher than I ever imagined. I don't mean to sound harsh about that; I'm just being honest.

Like many couples, Theresa and I carried a lot of baggage into our marriage. I came from a semifunctional alcoholic family, a background that is fairly common to those whose fathers served in World War II. Theresa's experience was even more severe, and it was complicated by an early marriage as an unbeliever to another unbeliever who found it more profitable to sell drugs than work—and more appealing to run off with another woman than to provide for his infant twin boys.

9

Theresa and I both came to know Christ in early adulthood, met a couple years after her husband left, were involved in a campus ministry in addition to having full-time jobs, were friends for about a year, dated for about a year, then married and left for seminary with two four-year-old boys. We had no premarital counseling and no money. I went to school full-time *and* worked full-time so she could care for the children. By God's grace, I adopted the boys a year later. Also by God's grace, one of my professors was Dr. Paul Meier, founder of the Meier Clinics, when less than a year into our marriage the wheels were falling off.

Theresa's and my journey has involved counseling, marriage exercises, reading books together, going to conferences, forgiving each other (again and again), learning to communicate, resolving anger, and figuring out how to get on the same page with money, values, in-laws, sex, parenting, and most of the big decisions of life, many of which we've disagreed on. Other than that, it has been pretty smooth!

Learning God's Design

How did we make it? I could tell you it was all by the grace of God, but as true as that is, it's too generic and not very helpful.

I could also tell you we got some very good insight from counselors and friends who helped us understand the issues from our pasts and our families of origin and who gave us some tools we needed to work on our marriage. That's true too, and I don't want to discount any of it.

But the fundamental reason we are still together and have the kind of marriage I always dreamed of—still with normal struggles like every couple has—is that we *learned God's design for the marriage relationship and committed to follow it.*

The Larger, Overarching Plan

This book is not a personal story, and I'm not a psychologist. I'm a pastor who has worked hard to have this kind of marriage and has spent thirty-five years counseling and observing Christians and non-Christians struggle, settle, and—far too often—quit.

The world doesn't need another marriage book that will give you psychological inventories, inspiring stories, and conventional advice. Plenty of those resources exist, and many of them are excellent. I have read, studied, and benefited from quite a few of them, both in my own marriage and in my ministry.

> *The world doesn't need another marriage book that will give you psychological inventories, inspiring stories, and conventional advice.*

What we do need in this day of sexual confusion, pop psychology, and addiction to narcissistic personal fulfillment is some very clear biblical truth from the Author of marriage—the One who created and designed it. And we need practical application of that truth.

God has communicated what marriage is, how it works, the roles and responsibilities for husbands and wives, and why his instructions are so important. He did this not only for the sake of marriage but also for his larger, overarching plan to reveal Christ's love to the world and his commitment to the church. That's why this book exists.

In the pages that follow, you will discover the power of making a covenant with your spouse. You will read some things that in today's culture may be considered politically incorrect. But they are foundational for a husband loving his wife well and taking responsibility for his God-given assignment. You'll read some challenging thoughts about how a wife must trust God and overcome fears of her husband's inadequacies.

Most of all, you will experience the beginnings of a spiritual, psychological, emotional, and physical oneness that you and your mate were both designed to enjoy.

With that in view, let's begin this journey together to discover God's design for the marriage you long to have.

1

God's Design for Marriage

Submit to one another out of reverence for Christ.

Wives, submit yourselves to your own husbands as you do to the Lord. For the husband is the head of the wife as Christ is the head of the church, his body, of which he is the Savior. Now as the church submits to Christ, so also wives should submit to their husbands in everything.

Husbands, love your wives, just as Christ loved the church and gave himself up for her to make her holy, cleansing her by the washing with water through the word, and to present her to himself as a radiant church, without stain or wrinkle or any other blemish, but holy and blameless. In this same way, husbands ought to love their wives as their own bodies. He who loves his wife loves himself. After all, no one ever hated their own body, but they feed and care for their body, just as Christ does the church—for we are members of his body.

"For this reason a man will leave his father and mother and be united to his wife, and the two will become one flesh." This is a profound mystery—but I am talking about Christ and the church. However, each one of you also must love his wife as he loves himself, and the wife must respect her husband.

—Ephesians 5:21–33

The early years of my marriage to Theresa were rocky, and there were times when I wanted to bail. But we stuck together and got professional help, and it was the best money we ever spent. Everyone has troubles; that's just part of marriage. What you do with them makes the difference.

Now, more than three decades later, we connect early in the day. We're early risers, and whoever gets up first makes the coffee. Maybe a half hour later, depending on the day, we talk about what's going on in each other's life, what the day looks like for each of us, what's coming up, where we're feeling pressure. It doesn't happen every day; sometimes one of us needs some alone time first. Often, I'll grab her hand and we'll talk to God together about what we're facing.

It took us some time, but we realized long ago that there is a design for this relationship. It works when we align ourselves with the design, prioritize each other's needs and fulfillment, and honor each other's uniqueness and relationship with God.

It's a lot like owning a high-performance car. You know it took years of planning, creating, and refining by the finest engineers and that it functions at its best only when you tune it to certain settings, use the highest-quality gas and oil, and are meticulous about maintenance. Marriage is like that.

The Master Designer of marriage has given us a manual for optimal performance. Marriage isn't easy to maintain, but neither is anything else that is valuable or worthwhile. His blueprint tells us how things work, and if we don't follow it, we will experience the consequences—as many in society are finding out nowadays. But unlike the instructions for high-performance machinery, these come from the loving heart of a Creator who wants his people to have deep, meaningful relationships with him and others. His Word tells us how.

One of the clearest pictures of marriage in Scripture is in Ephesians 5:21–33, and it works for every married person, even for those who are coming out of a dysfunctional past. It tells us about the role of a husband and a wife, how they should relate to each other, and what the higher meaning of their union actually signifies.

In this passage, Paul is writing to the Ephesians. He has just explained how they can be filled with the Holy Spirit and allow God to control their lives. He talks about the transformation in attitude that occurs when we are living by the Spirit's power. It's a beautiful and inspiring passage, but it begs a question or two: What does this spiritual life look like in real-life situations? How does it affect our relationships? Verse 21 begins with an explanation. Here's what a Spirit-filled marriage looks like. And it starts with a very unexpected statement: "Submit to one another out of reverence for Christ."

Words like "submission" are not received well in a culture that demands political correctness. They upset a lot of people. I can understand that, especially in light of the ways some of those concepts have been abused in the past. Whatever reservations you have about them, however, I want you to put them on hold for a bit.

We are going to explore what submission really means and the context in which it is to be lived out. I think you will find that the demands on each of us as marriage partners are equally challenging, stretching, and even impossible to accomplish in our own strength. God's instructions will not appear fair at first glance—until we realize the example he set for us and how the roles of husband and wife are both reflections of his extravagant love.

It Starts with Mutual Submission

There are three important initial observations about the Ephesians 5 passage, and being subject to one another is the first and foremost. Mutual submission is the only way a marriage can work.

First and foremost, each partner needs to understand that God is in charge of a marriage and that it should reflect his nature—his love, his concern, his radical sacrifice. It requires a selfless relationship because God is selfless. Marriage is not about fulfilling your own wants and needs; it's about fulfilling someone else's. If you enter into it thinking it's about you and getting your needs met, you're rejecting the design. Marriage is about honoring God and receiving from him whatever your spouse needs to get from him through

Mutual submission is the only way a marriage can work.

you. That isn't easy. I understand that. But above all, it requires mutual submission to God and to each other.

Second, marriage won't work unless you learn how to love your mate not as you define love but as *God* defines it—and as your mate is designed to receive it.

As a husband, that means I am given an absolutely impossible job of loving my wife as sacrificially as Jesus loved the church—that I would actually give up my life for her, that I would nourish and cherish her and be sensitive to her needs. We husbands need to create an environment in which our wives will flourish. We can't do that on our own. We need divine help.

And wives are given the seemingly unreasonable commandment to do for their husbands what the church is to do for Christ: devote herself in service; partner with him in a degree of intimacy that stretches her level of trust; and respect him in ways that build him up, strengthen him to be the man he was created to be, and encourage him to do what he has been called to do. She can't do that without divine help either.

Third, this passage assures us that marriage has an even bigger purpose than our own happiness. Our joy, pleasure, and fulfillment are important to God, but they are only lasting within a larger context. According to this passage, marriage is a picture of an eternal relationship between Christ and the church. That is the blueprint behind the blueprint of marriage and family. God designed family to be a stable environment for offspring and a fundamental unit of society, yes. But it flows out of the eternal relationship designed for Christ and his bride, the church.

Demonstrating God through Your Relationship

One of the greatest opportunities you have to demonstrate the reality of God in your life is in your relationships, especially in how you get along with your marriage partner. In my experience the number one reason given for divorce is irreconcilable differences. In other words, "We just can't get along." People who do get along—who communicate well enough and compassionately enough to build each other up, even when they have differences—stand out.

Theresa and I once had a neighbor who got to see the good, the bad, and the ugly in our relationship because a next-door view provides that window into your life. Our kids and hers played together, we would occasionally talk in the yard, and sometimes we would invite her to church or to dinner. She was never very interested in spiritual conversations, but when she was getting ready to move, she said something I'll never forget.

"I've always been turned off by religion, and I'm not sure I believe in God, but over the years I've watched you and your wife. If I were ever going to be a Christian, I'd want to be one like you."

She was not saying that because she had seen a perfect marriage—not by a long shot. We made a lot of mistakes. But I think what she was trying to say was that she saw a man and a woman who loved each other through all of life's ups and downs. She saw commitment in a world that doesn't have many examples of it. And that made an impression about the kind of God we serve. In some way, our marriage was a reflection of the heart of the Master Designer.

God's Blueprint for Marriage

In the world of design and engineering, seeing a blueprint is necessary before you can implement a design. We can see the blueprint of marriage in the lives of those who are doing it as Scripture defines it. But an even simpler picture might help us envision how it works.

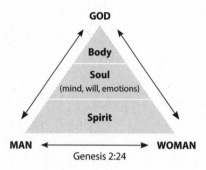

This equilateral triangle represents the basic premise of biblical marriage. God is at the top, of course. He created men and women in his image and designed us for the kind of relationship that embodies his nature and Christ's relationship with his people.

Marriage is his idea. That's really important to remember. Marriage is not just a social construct, one idea out of many others that developed in ages past as a good option for our society. No, it is written into the DNA of this world as God's normative pattern for the growth and development of humanity.

At the bottom of the triangle is a verse that points to the nature of marriage, established from the very beginning. Genesis 2:24 identifies the goal of marriage as oneness, or intimacy. "That is why a man leaves his father and mother and is united to his wife, and they become one flesh." When God created marriage, he said, "It is not good for the man to be alone" (Gen. 2:18). He designed it to address the problem of loneliness or isolation. A God of love by nature shares who he is; those made in his image are created to share themselves with someone else. The goal of marriage is for two beings—male and female—to be united as one, with hearts and minds and bodies that connect at every level.

From all I've observed about human nature over the years, that oneness is a basic human desire. Nearly three out of four Americans believe in the idea of a soul mate, according to a 2011 study. The largest group of true believers are under 30 (80 percent) or 30–44 (78 percent). The percentages drop for older folks, but still, 72 percent of those 45–59 and 65 percent of those 60 and older think soul mates exist.[1] Whether there's one Mr. Right or Mrs. Right for each person on earth is debatable. But there's no debating that we've been created to experience—and long for—an intimate, lifelong relationship.

Your Spiritual Connection Is the Foundation

Back to the triangle. Inside it, you will see three levels of connection—oneness in spirit, soul (mind, will, and emotions), and body. A biblical "soul mate" is fundamentally spiritual. It includes your relationship with God as well as your spouse's relationship with God. It is a triangle of unity, three spirits knit together in deep intimacy. The soul (mind, will, and emotions) and the body are certainly part of that. But the spiritual aspect is the biggest and most foundational part of what it means to be a soul mate.

There is a closeness in that process of
growing in spiritual intimacy that ranks
as high as sexual union. When spirits come
together before God, he does something to
draw a married couple together. It can be
very awkward at the beginning, but later
it's as natural as eating and breathing.

> *Spiritual oneness with God and each other is meant to be the foundation of a marriage.*

Spiritual oneness with God and each other is meant to be
the foundation of a marriage.

Sharing Your Soul: Your Mind, Will, and Emotions

In addition to spiritual oneness, God also wants us to have
soul oneness. He wants you and your mate to be best friends.

Many married couples started out that way but are now just
living as roommates; the mind, will, and emotional connections are not what they used to be. The goal was never
for both of you to get absorbed in your jobs or for the husband to hang out with the guys all the time while the wife
hangs out with her girlfriends. Too many couples spend their
"together" time in the same room but with faces glued to
a screen or a book. There's nothing wrong with reading
or watching TV. But separate lives absorbed with separate
activities undermine the connection, and it eventually goes
away. That was never God's plan.

God wants soul mates to talk together, walk together, pursue
hobbies together, and have some fun. Life will not always be
just like it was when you were dating—that would be completely unrealistic. Many couples are disillusioned when the

21

joy of dating fades away underneath the responsibilities of adulthood. But when you continue to date your spouse, it stirs those special feelings and excitement about being together—like my mentors you met in the introduction, Dave and Polly.

Soul oneness requires communicating and injecting some fun into the routines of your lives. Best friends support each other with the bonds of friendship—empathy, comfort, and affection. That kind of connection is at the heart of God's design for marriage.

The Bonding Power of Physical Union

As the icing on the cake, God designed physical oneness not only to fulfill the "be fruitful and multiply" (Gen. 1:28 NASB) command but also for our enjoyment. He wants married couples to be passionate lovers.

God designed men and women to bond in the sexual experience, not only physically but also emotionally and spiritually. The brain secretes the hormone oxytocin during and after sex, causing couples (especially men) to want to open up and share what's going on inside. The physical chemistry enhances the connection at every other level. God has wired that bonding into his creation and his design for marriage.

Historically, some Christian leaders have had trouble with the idea of passionate sex as a gift to married couples and have taught against it. Unfortunately, a consequence of that faulty teaching was to provide unhappy and unfulfilled people an "excuse" to seek physical fulfillment outside marriage.

Hebrews 13:4 tells us that God wants the marriage bed to be undefiled—sex is holy.

One of the biggest problems with society's perceptions of marriage is the separation of sex from the rest of the relationship so that people are led to believe that the best sex is outside of marriage. Ironically, secular studies have found that the best and most fulfilling sex in America is happening not in the singles scene or in extramarital affairs but in monogamous couples who are deeply committed to one another with high moral values.[2] I'm convinced from the way we are made that the physical relationship is meant to be the culmination of a foundational spiritual relationship and a mind-will-emotions relationship that flows out of the spiritual. Sex is the physical expression of a deeper union that serves its purpose only in the context of love and commitment.

Our culture has separated sex from love, which leaves people unfulfilled on both counts. Pornography, romantic fantasies, and illicit relationships are all examples of false intimacy that grow out of a society that does not understand the multiple connections of real intimacy. I recently read a statistic suggesting that more than two-thirds of people who get involved in extramarital affairs begin the relationship on social media.[3] If you're having struggles in your marriage and you connect online with an old flame from high school or college, it's easy to see where things might go from there.

I'm not suggesting that married couples delete their Facebook accounts or ignore old friends, but I am suggesting that we tend to treat our marriages too casually. And it isn't working out for us, is it? False intimacy in any area of life undermines unity in our homes, harms our children, can have devastating effects on our finances, and leaves us unfulfilled. It contradicts God's plan for our lives. He wants oneness for us at every level.

Closer to God, Closer to Each Other

I want you to try a little exercise with the triangle graphic.

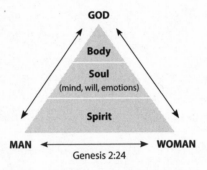

Put a finger on each of the corners that say "man" and "woman," and then slowly move your fingers up the sides to the point that says "God." Where are your fingers in relation to each other? They are closer, right? The point is simple, but it's also profound. The closer you grow to God, the closer you and your spouse grow to each other.

God designed marriage in such a way that it does not work as it should apart from him. It's true that many people who don't know him would say they are happily married, and I wouldn't argue with them. But are they as connected physically, emotionally, mentally, and spiritually as they could be? I don't think so.

And neither are many Christian couples. Just being a Christian doesn't change the dynamics very much. But I promise you that growing in intimacy with God changes everything despite our baggage and struggles. It was this passionate pursuit of Christ, which both Theresa and I were committed to, that saved our marriage. The greatest thing you can ever do for your marriage is to live as a committed, passionate follower of Jesus. You become like whomever you spend time with. When you spend time with God, he revolutionizes your heart and mind, and a new person shows up in your marriage. Only he can give you the power, freedom, and grace to give your mate what you could never give on your own.

> *The greatest thing you can ever do for your marriage is to live as a committed, passionate follower of Jesus.*

I married a selfish person. So did my wife. If you're married, there's a very good chance you married one too. All of us are innately self-centered until we mature. That's because of the sinful nature we inherited, and it can be remedied only by God's work in our lives.

The "satisfy me" urge in marriage never ends unless we make a radical decision to lay our own lives down, just as Jesus told his disciples to do. A husband lays down his life for his wife, and a wife comes under her husband to serve—not with the expectation that the other will respond but with the commitment to live sacrificially even if the other doesn't.

If that doesn't seem fair, it's because it isn't. But we aren't trying to work out what's fair, are we? We are trying to have a great marriage. And that's the only way to do it. That ends the cycle of selfishness and draws us close to God and to each other.

Spiritual Oneness, Deep Friendship, Physical Intimacy

After more than three decades of marriage, a lot of hard work, and plenty of struggles along the way, Theresa and I have found ourselves in a relationship in which we get what we need from each other because we are more focused on giving the other person what he or she needs rather than on seeking our own fulfillment.

I don't get up in the morning and read the Bible to cross an item off a list of spiritual requirements. I do it because I'm a desperate man in need of power and grace to give my wife what I would not otherwise be able to give her. She does the same for me. The result is a deep spiritual oneness, an ever-growing friendship flowing out of that, and then an intimate physical union that has produced a relationship beyond what words could ever express. That's God's design.

The blueprint for marriage as it is spelled out in Ephesians 5 tells us what marriage ought to look like. But underneath that blueprint is an even deeper truth about what marriage actually is. It is one thing to know what the blueprint is and another to know how to make it a reality in our lives. Ephesians 5 points us to the answers to that question of "how," and its truths may seem a little surprising, especially in today's world. But they are timeless truths that really work.

When we get a handle on these truths, we approach marriage in an entirely different way than our culture does, and we begin to discover and experience the crucial components of success.

_____ **Questions for Reflection and Discussion** _____

1. Why do you think most people identify a fulfilling marriage and family as something they want to experience in life? If this is such a strong desire, why do you think so few people are actually experiencing it?

2. Did you have realistic expectations when you first got married? Why or why not?

3. According to Ephesians 5, what does marriage illustrate? What bigger purpose does it serve?

4. Why doesn't being a Christian couple automatically imply having a better marriage? What must happen in any marriage—Christian or not—for a couple to grow closer to each other?

5. If you are married, which level of the relationship—spirit, soul, or body—has been the most fulfilling for you? List three things that originally attracted you to your spouse. Share those three things with your mate in a card or over coffee this week.

6. What one thing could you do this week to improve your marriage?

2

Is There a Man in the House?

Submit to one another out of reverence for Christ.

Wives, submit yourselves to your own husbands as you do to the Lord. **For the husband is the head of the wife as Christ is the head of the church, his body, of which he is the Savior.** Now as the church submits to Christ, so also wives should submit to their husbands in everything.

Husbands, love your wives, just as Christ loved the church and gave himself up for her to make her holy, cleansing her by the washing with water through the word, and to present her to himself as a radiant church, without stain or wrinkle or any other blemish, but holy and blameless. In this same way, husbands ought to love their wives as their own bodies. He who loves his wife loves himself. After all, no one ever hated their own body, but they feed and care for their body, just as Christ does the church—for we are members of his body.

"For this reason a man will leave his father and mother and be united to his wife, and the two will become one flesh." This is a profound mystery—but I am talking about Christ and the church. **However, each one of you also must love his wife as he loves himself, and the wife must respect her husband.**

—Ephesians 5:21–33

L ittle boys dream big. Ask them what they want to be when they grow up, and you'll get all kinds of fascinating answers: astronauts, presidents, athletes, superheroes, and even some pretty realistic professions that may or may not ever work out. If you ask them who they want to be like, they can come up with some big names—people who have made a name for themselves and an impression on their young audiences. And every once in a while, you hear one say something much more touching: "I want to be like my dad."

Those words come more easily for young boys than older ones. As boys grow into young men, the sentiment gets rarer. Perhaps their fathers have let them down, or maybe they've just seen a larger world of role models to choose from. Whatever the reason, of all the young men I have counseled or mentored over the years, only a few have ever pointed to their fathers as the men they most want to be like—as a Christian, a father, a husband, a man of integrity. It is an extremely high compliment that only a few men ever receive.

At a church I pastored, we had a gifted young staff team, and we often teamed up to teach the weekend services. Father's Day was coming up, so I casually asked around the room, "Who had a great relationship with their father?" Most of us on the team had major struggles with our fathers. There were eight of our key pastors in the room and each of them told their story. Out of that leadership team, there was not a single man in the room who could point to a positive relationship with his father. That's when I realized this is a really big deal.

Beginning with Mutual Submission

We are going to look at a picture of what a real man is, and we will see that genuine masculinity, as defined by God, does something life-changing in the people around us. It powerfully affects a man's wife, his children, and his friends. They become better people just by being with him. And it's never too late to become that kind of man.

Redefining manhood in marriage and in the home always begins with mutual submission. That's the umbrella concept covering the entire Ephesians 5 passage about relationships. Before Paul talks about the mystery of marriage and the roles of husbands and wives, he gives an instruction that precedes every other detail: "Submit to one another out of reverence for Christ" (Eph. 5:21).

This is really important. It provides the context for statements that trip people up when they read them in isolation.

The passages that follow Ephesians 5:21 explain roles not only for husbands and wives but also for parents and children and masters and servants (which we often apply today to the workplace). Whatever responsibilities and attitudes Christians are to have within all these relationships, the overarching attitude must be a sense of walking with God and putting other people first—expressing love and looking out for the best interests of others in all our relationships.

That alone should defuse a lot of the controversy surrounding the masculine and feminine roles Scripture describes for marriage. There are roles, but they are secondary to the context of mutual submission in the relationship.

The most important question, then, is not about who does what but about what mutual submission actually looks like. What does it really mean?

In the original Greek, the word "submit" that is used in this verse is *hupotasso*, and it is often used in a military context. It is a compound word: *hupo* meaning "under" and *tasso* meaning "to be in order or rank." It is the opposite of self-assertion. It urges subjection or submission to one another. Another way to think of it is a mutual desire to get less than one's due.

When both partners are engaging in mutual submission, it becomes a contest to see who can outdo the other in love and good works.

Think about what that means. What would it look like to be in a relationship with your mate in which, rather than each of you trying to get your way, each of you make it a goal to get less than your due in order to serve the other's interests? That's a different way to approach marriage than most people experience.

The issue is no longer which person is in control; the issue is which person is responsible. Mutual submission is the embodiment of a spiritual attitude that turns control over to God's Spirit and considers the person you are married to more important than you. If this sounds odd or even crazy to you as a man, I understand. God's design begins with him, and mutual submission to Christ and each other is where it all begins.

Learning the Dance

Mutual submission in marriage is like a dance floor. It is an open space where you have the freedom to move. It requires that the man and woman, each in a relationship with Christ as their Lord, come to each other not to take control but to serve. Each one asks, "How can I help you be successful? How can I express my love for you?" In this dance, the issue is not who takes the first step. It's the beauty of the movement itself.

Male chauvinism and female manipulation find no place on this dance floor. They have disappeared even before the first steps. Each person recognizes the importance of the other— this was never meant to be a solo act—and of the choreographer. They realize that every step honors the relationship and reflects well on the One who orchestrated it all.

If you have ever watched an elaborate dance routine, whether it was in a TV show like *Dancing with the Stars*, an ice-dancing competition, or a classic Fred Astaire and Ginger Rogers movie, you may have noticed that all the lifts and catches require a lot of trust. If the partners are not at the right place at exactly the right time, somebody could get hurt.

Dancers look at the dance differently than viewers do. Every step, every lift, every turn, every nuance has been choreographed ahead of time and rehearsed to perfection. They put in hours upon hours of work and years of preparation to create what appears to be a seamless piece of art.

Viewers, though, just see beauty and rhythm and flow. We don't have to know the discipline and technique behind all the steps and movements. We are looking at the whole.

That's like marriage. You have to know the choreography, you have to put a lot of practice into it, you have to trust— and the focus is not which person took the first step. You hear the rhythm of the music, see the movements, and try to absorb the beauty of it all. The attention is on the overall picture and how you move together as a unit.

An Ideal to Strive For

For the rest of this chapter, we will look at some of the ways men can make the dance more beautiful for their partners. In the book's following chapters, we'll also focus on how women do that too. But it all takes place on a dance floor of mutual submission, where, instead of being confining or restrictive, the divine "choreography" allows room for each partner to be at his or her most creative.

For the dance of marriage to be beautiful, God gives men and women different roles and movements. Those roles and movements have nothing to do with either partner being more important or whether the partners are equal. Rather, they have everything to do with function.

The man's role in the dance of marriage is as the one who leads. The bar is high for this role. For many men, it will take a lot of practice and retraining to step into it. But when you do, the woman in your life will feel loved, cherished, and completed. You will enable your family to move in the right direction at the right time for the right reason. Your children will grow up thinking you are the greatest man in the world, and they will have a healthy self-image and strong moral values. You will create a context for your loved ones to grow into their true selves as God designed them.

A word of warning, however. Sometimes a man's first reaction to this standard may be one of guilt. When I was taught the concept of true leadership early in our marriage, my response was, "Are you kidding? How could I ever possibly live up to this?"

> *God's instructions are meant to instill hope, not regret.*

That is not the intention here. God's instructions are meant to instill hope, not regret. The point is not to cover us with shame or give our wives yet another reason to tell us what we *should* be doing.

Instead, we're going to look at an image of true, God-designed masculinity for us to grow into. It is an ideal, not something for us to beat ourselves up over if we fall short. Rather, it is a clear target we should aim for and be fully committed to pursuing.

Choosing to Love Unconditionally

The marriage dance is described in Ephesians 5:22–33. You'll notice in that passage a role—"the husband is the head of the

35

wife" (v. 23)—and a responsibility—"love your wives, just as Christ loved the church and gave himself up for her" (v. 25). You'll also notice that the word "love" comes up quite a few times. It is not the love of friendship (*phileo*), romance (*eros*), or family connection (*storge*). It is agape love. What's the significance of this?

Agape love is not, in its essence, an emotional love, though it may have emotions that come along with it. Agape love is choosing to give another person what they need the most when they deserve it the least, at great personal cost.

> Agape love is choosing to give another person what they need the most when they deserve it the least, at great personal cost.

Paul makes it clear that this is how Jesus loved us. When I was in sin, I didn't want God's help, and I certainly didn't deserve it, but Christ died in my place anyway. He did that to offer forgiveness and salvation to whoever would believe, allowing the Father to place our sin on him. Was any emotion involved in that sacrifice? Absolutely. We are told very clearly that Jesus did it "for the joy set before him" (Heb. 12:2), and he did it in spite of the agony that nearly overcame him as he prayed in the Garden of Gethsemane, "Not my will, but yours be done" (Luke 22:42).

Jesus's sacrifice was motivated by the kind of love that goes deeper than immediate feelings and is grounded in commitment and obedience to the Father's plan for our deliverance. This kind of love is a choice. That is the same kind of choice a husband is meant to make every day for his wife.

It is a wonderful thing when I treat my wife well, am sensitive to her needs, care for her, and respond to her in godly ways because I feel good about her. But if I do those things only when I feel good about her, we have a problem. I need to love her in the same way when she hurts me or acts in ways that distance me.

Agape love means giving her what she needs the most when she deserves it the least, at great personal cost. That isn't just hard to do. It's impossible—apart from the Spirit of God working in our hearts.

To Present Her in All Her Glory

Some might argue that Jesus's love for the church is different from a husband's love for his wife in some pretty significant ways. After all, according to the passage, Jesus gave himself up for the church in order to cleanse her and present her holy and blameless. A husband can't do that for his wife, can he?

If we demystify the language, "make holy" simply means "to set apart as special." A man can set his wife apart and honor her as special. Jesus did that for us, and the role of a man is to help his wife become the special person God intends for her to become. Jesus did it by the "washing with water through the word" (Eph. 5:26), the spoken word (*rhema*), speaking life into his church. A husband has the opportunity to speak life into the soul of his wife through affirmation and encouragement.

> A husband has the opportunity to speak life into the soul of his wife through affirmation and encouragement.

37

Ephesians 5:27 refers to Jesus presenting a "radiant" church to himself. Another Bible translation uses the phrase "in all her glory" (NASB). A husband is to make his wife radiant—to bring out the brilliance and glory that God has put within her. Nearly every woman has experienced some kind of rejection, and many struggle with deep insecurities about their real worth.

Theresa was rejected by her father and then her first husband. It amazed me how a beautiful woman like her could look in the mirror and see someone ugly. I learned early that my job as a husband is to help her see how beautiful she is, from the inside out, and how radiant, gifted, and valuable she is.

And I found that as I learned to love her and began to see her transform, she started responding in ways that met my deepest longings as a man. In loving her, I was actually doing something really good for myself.

No one is in a better position than a husband to help his wife overcome her sense of rejection by accepting her just as Jesus has accepted us. A man is to bring out the radiance and glory of his wife so she can be the woman God created her to be. It's been the most difficult but rewarding aspect of our marriage.

Nourishment That Grows a Marriage

A husband is commanded also to "feed and care for" his wife as Christ feeds and cares for the church (Eph. 5:29). Another word for this concept is "nourish." In the context of a relationship, it implies being devoted, providing for needs, and promoting the development and maintenance of health. A husband is created to develop, maintain, and help his wife—mentally, spiritually, emotionally, and relationally—become all that God created her to become. That's the kind of nourishment he provides.

This was a foreign concept to me when Theresa and I got married. I thought marriage meant being attracted to your mate, falling in love, making a commitment, having some kids, and letting things work out. I would play softball and basketball, help some with the kids, and hope everything would end up okay. That's all I knew. But as I grew as a Christian, I began to realize God had created my wife with one set of needs and created me with another set of needs, and we were created to be the instrument to meet each other's needs. We were designed for mutual nourishment. That's an entirely different approach to marriage. It has to be other-focused, a selfless expression of agape love.

The word for "care for" in this passage literally means "to keep warm." Relationally, it involves communicating in ways that make sense to each other. A husband is to give his wife a sense of safety and comfort.

When a woman says, "Let's talk," a caring response would be to open up and let her know what's going on inside. A lot of men don't understand the need in this area, and a woman probably won't explain it. Most women will begin a conversation not to fix a problem or share superficial information but to connect. She wants to know how her husband is feeling, what his fears and concerns are, and how he is processing them. She may want to pray together about what's going on inside. In contrast, men typically want to exchange information, get something done, and have conversations that have a transparent purpose and solve problems.

Navigating Our Insecurities

Remember the bigger picture here. A woman is looking for a man who will assume the same kind of responsibility for his wife that Jesus demonstrated for the church, even to the point of sacrificing himself for her. She wants a man who embraces his devotion to her by nourishing and cherishing her, a man who sees his God-given role as provider not only for her external needs but also for her heart. That's a real man from God's perspective.

Most of us men never saw that as we were growing up. Our role models taught us that real men make a lot of money, play hard, live their own lives, and maintain their marriages by taking care of their wives' external needs. A few men have seen great examples of biblical manhood up close, but most of us have had to piece together this picture of real masculinity as we have grown and learned what Scripture says. It can seem so far over our heads that we may wonder if we can ever pull it off. But if we ask God to help us be that kind of man, regardless of which stage of life we are in, he will answer. And when he does, some fantastic things begin to happen in our relationships.

One of the reasons we men have difficulty being successful leaders in our homes is that we can be very insecure about our role there. We don't always come across that way, but beneath the surface, we struggle with how to care for a woman's heart. Many of us do not navigate the inner world very easily because whenever we encounter a problem, we want to fix it, and some of the deep inner workings of the human heart are not quick fixes.

Sometimes that isn't even the goal; women often want to have a conversation not for the purpose of problem solving but just to be heard. We don't always know what to do with that. We know how to do our jobs, shoot a basketball, and fix a faucet. We're comfortable in those worlds. But to help our daughters grow in their femininity? Discipline a child with sensitivity to whatever is going on inside him? Pray with our wives? Those are different matters. They pull us into areas where we are unskilled, untrained, and most insecure.

But it doesn't have to stay that way. As we learn to make these things our priorities and get to know God and understand how he has designed us to serve our wives and families, real change happens.

Five Diagnostic Questions

Answering these questions will tell you who is leading your home.

Again, the purpose of these questions is not to induce guilt. It is to make you aware.

In the first two years of our marriage, my answers to most of these questions would have suggested that Theresa was the leader in our home. I needed to become aware of my lack of leadership and by God's grace take responsibility.

That's the point of this exercise—awareness that leads to change through a process of growth and grace. Read the following questions with that purpose in mind.

1. **Who initiates spiritual growth in your home?**

   Who says, "Let's sit down and talk about this. Let's see what the Bible says about it. Maybe we need to spend some time praying about it"?

2. **Who handles the money?**

   This question is not about who makes the most money; that isn't the issue at all. Some wives make more than their husbands, and that is no indication of who is exercising leadership in the marriage. But which one of you is assuming the responsibility for making sure bills get paid on time? If the wife is managing money and writing checks, is she doing that as a function of her gifts or because her husband is neglecting his responsibility and leaving it to her?

3. **Who disciplines the children when you are both at home?**

   Each parent will need to discipline a child at various times and in different situations, but when the problem behavior is relevant to both spouses and you are both present to deal with it, which one of you takes the lead?

4. **Who initiates talking about problems, future plans, and areas to develop?**

   For example, how do you decide how many kids you want to have? What school they should go to? What kind of jobs you and your spouse should take? When you should retire? What the course of your life together will look like?

5. **Who asks the most questions in your home, and who gives the most statements?**

   Who is the one who is always asking what to do for dinner or about the decision you need to make about next week's plans? Whichever person is asking those questions is the one who feels the weight of responsibility for them.

None of these questions are meant to prompt a legalistic standard in your marriage. Women will often see issues that men don't see, so they will naturally be the ones to bring them up first. There's nothing wrong with that. Many women are gifted with making plans and orchestrating schedules in ways that their husbands are not, so it is perfectly normal for them to contribute their gifts in those areas.

The real question is, Who is carrying the weight of responsibility in the marriage? Many women have to initiate discussion, make plans, and ask the big questions because their husbands do not. These men don't want to shoulder the responsibility for making life work. They let their wives carry the burden. When this happens, wives do not feel cherished, nurtured, and protected. In other words, they are not getting what God designed for their husbands to give them.

That is what these diagnostic questions are getting at, and if they reveal a pattern of neglect, some of the dynamics in the relationship need to change.

How to Love Your Wife: Step Up

Let's get down to the nitty-gritty. Ephesians 5:33 calls men to love their wives as they love themselves. How do you do that? As a man, how do you get out of unhealthy patterns to free your wife's heart from the burdens you were meant to carry? How do you grow deeper into true manhood? If marriage is a beautiful dance, a man needs to step up—in leadership and in love.

You might hear the same language from a coach anytime the star player goes down with an injury. Everyone else on the team will just need to "step up." That is a great way to express God's design for a man in his marriage and his family relationships. We men need to step up in leadership and step up in love in order to fulfill our God-given role.

> *If marriage is a beautiful dance, a man needs to step up—in leadership and in love.*

I believe there are three specific ways to love your wife the Ephesians 5 way that will change the nature of your relationship: (1) love her sacrificially, (2) love her intentionally, and (3) love her sensitively.

43

Love Her Sacrificially

Paul's instruction to husbands to love their wives sacrificially is clear from Ephesians 5:25. The kind of love Jesus has for the church cost him something. The kind of love a husband has for his wife should cost him something too.

One of the ways you can love your wife sacrificially is in how you demonstrate your preferences. When you choose her over the other "loves" in your life, you make a statement about her value to you.

Years ago when our kids were young, I was just learning about how marriage is supposed to work. I was watching the Slam Dunk Contest of the NBA All-Star Game, and my boys and I were rooting for the players and screaming at the acrobatic dunks. These were some of the greatest players in the game, and I had been waiting all year to watch this. But I happened to look over at Theresa across the room, and she wasn't mad or upset—there was nothing disapproving about her countenance at all—but I got the feeling that not everything was right in her world. Something was bothering her.

I had a thought that could have only come from God, because I never would have thought it myself. A voice inside my head said, "Chip, why don't you get up and ask Theresa if she wants to go on a walk. Find out what's going on inside." My first reaction was to push that thought aside. We could take a walk anytime—the contest was going on right then. But I usually don't have promptings like that, and this one was persistent.

So, amid the bewildered looks of my sons, I walked over and asked her how she was doing. She said she was fine and told me to go ahead and watch the game, but I could tell something was still not right. I told her I would catch it later on a replay. So we went for a walk.

She started opening up, and I realized there was a lot going on inside her. We ended up getting a cup of coffee afterward and talked a little bit more. Going on a walk with Theresa wasn't a huge sacrifice, but she turned to me and said, "Chip, I feel so loved right now."

"Why? I didn't do anything." We had just walked around, I asked a few questions, but mostly I listened for about an hour. Like most men do, I was thinking we hadn't really accomplished anything. No problems got fixed.

"I know how much you love sports. And for you to leave that behind to talk to me really sent a powerful message," she said.

I had made a choice—not even a very big one, in the grand scheme of things—that reflected my preference for her over other things going on in my life. It wasn't a huge sacrifice, but it meant something to her. It made a statement about her value to me.

Before we go on, what would that statement look like in your life this week? What small sacrifice would say to your wife that she matters more than that "something else" in your life?

Another way to love your wife sacrificially is to invest time in her. A lot of men work long hours during the week, and on their one day off, they spend five or six hours on the golf course or pursuing some other hobby independently of the family. If this describes you, not only does that leave your wife with very little of your time, but one day when your kids are grown, you'll want a lot of those hours back, and you won't be able to get them. Your golf game will be a little better, but your children will grow up with some emotional voids in their hearts. That is not a good trade-off.

You do need to have hobbies, to connect with other men, and to get some exercise. Those things are important for a balanced life. But to step up as a leader in your home and to love your wife sacrificially, you will need to adjust your priorities and invest your time in her and your children.

It took me some time to learn how to do this, and I wasn't good at it initially. But we developed a habit in our family of eating dinner together at 5:30 five or six nights a week. I was leading a large church, and I certainly had demands on my schedule before and after that time, but my family knew I would be there at 5:30 to eat with them. After eating, we would push our plates to the middle of the table and just talk. We laughed, joked, talked about school and friends, and communicated what we were hearing from God and the challenges we were experiencing. Sometimes we would pray together, other times we would read a passage, or we would simply talk.

Then, at least a couple nights a week, I would take over the kids' bath time and tuck them into bed. I didn't want Theresa to get all the fun in connecting with them. That requires time, but believe me, it's worth it. Your wife and your children will treasure your investment in them.

For most of the years of our marriage, I have had a weekly date with Theresa. Since I had never seen a married couple have a date when I was growing up, it was a foreign concept

to me, but it was one way I could show her she was important to me. So every Friday, my day off, we went to breakfast
together. For three or four hours, she knew we were going
to hang out together. And those times shaped our marriage.

We have read books and listened to CDs and discussed them
together. I didn't know what I was doing as a father and husband, and she was learning how to be a wife and mother, but
we realized a lot of people had gone before
us and learned some good lessons about
marriage and family. So we would read
their books or listen to them and try out
whatever might work for us. Theresa was
very cooperative and encouraging; she had
a lot of patience toward me. And over time,
we have grown in more ways than I could have imagined. But
it takes time, and it costs something. It requires sacrificial love.

> *Your wife and
> your children will
> treasure your
> investment in them.*

Another cost of sacrificial love is rejection. When we come
out of denial and deal with some of the problem areas in the
home—a rebellious child or a harmful behavior pattern—it
causes some friction. Sometimes the kids don't want to sit
down and have a meal together. You can be passive and let
them do what they want to do or you can take the lead and
say, "Here's what we're doing." And you just might experience some rejection. A father who intentionally leads his
family has to be able to handle that.

Leaders change things, and not everyone likes the change. Some
people prefer the status quo. Sometimes the kids will take a
smart-aleck tone and say, "Who do you think you are? You
don't run my life." And if it really escalates, you will have to

impose discipline, which is never fun for anyone involved. The stakes get higher as the kids grow older. It goes from "time-out" to "hand over your car keys" faster than you ever thought it would. But as a leader and a parent, you do have control.

I'm always amazed at fathers who say they don't have any control over their children. "They just go to their room, slam the door, and play video games." But whose house are they living in? Whose food are they eating? Whose cars are they driving? A short-term loss of privileges is far better than a long-term lack of discipline or character. And some kids, even though they will never show it, are des-perately hoping for someone to place bound-aries around them and demonstrate the love of discipline. Women may have a harder time expressing that kind of authority, especially with adolescent boys—that's one reason so many boys have big problems when there isn't a man in the house—but your manhood gene was given for both the soft and hard sides of fatherly love. Enduring the rejection that comes with fulfilling your responsibility in the home is not easy, but it is worthwhile. Your kids will eventually come back to you and say, "Thanks, Dad." And they will grow up to become that kind of parent too. Sacrificial love endures the cost of the moment for the sake of the big picture.

> Sacrificial love endures the cost of the moment for the sake of the big picture.

Love Her Intentionally

Ephesians 5:26–28 tells us that Jesus had a plan for his church. He purposefully sanctified her, cleansed her, and sought the best for her. You will need to do the same for your wife.

Have you ever asked her what her dreams are? What spiritual gifts God has given her and how she wants to use them in this season of life? How you can help her do what she feels like God created her to do? You are not only her leader; you are also her facilitator. God has given her to you to help support you in your God-given mission in life, but loving her sacrificially means doing the same for her. One of your greatest opportunities in marriage is to purposely seek to develop your wife's beauty and gifts and to help her grow spiritually, emotionally, and physically.

Imagine your wife as a flower. You can't make her grow and bloom, but you can create the right conditions for her to do so. You can be an instrument in the hands of God to help her grow into the beauty she was created to display. To do that, you will need to be her number one cheerleader and encourager, to recognize gifts in her that she doesn't even see, and to call out the treasures that God has placed inside her. Though only God can cause growth, you have a huge role in creating the right environment.

Soon after we got married, Theresa wrote our first Christmas letter to friends and family. I had been writing all kinds of papers in seminary, but I read her letter and thought, *She writes so much better than I do*. I told her so. "You're just saying that because you're my husband," she replied. I had to work to convince her because, as many women do, she minimized her gifts.

Later, I heard her explaining something to someone, and I thought, *Wow, she really communicates well*. And, of course, she denied it. But in our first church, a group of about a dozen ladies asked her to speak. Theresa didn't think she could do it, so I encouraged her. We went over her outline together. It was a little terrifying for her, and she felt sick for days before the event, but she just needed someone to believe in her. She needed someone to say, as often as necessary, "You can do this. You have a gift for it."

Twenty years later, she taught a series called "Precious in His Sight" at a women's retreat, and it helped women so much that we made it part of the *Living on the Edge* radio broadcast. People loved it. Her series actually had a greater response than mine. Some husbands might feel threatened by that, but I remembered all the years of dreaming that Theresa would grow into her gifts and that God would use them. She was blooming in ways I had always wanted to see her bloom.

I remember when Theresa was entering into the early part of midlife and thinking of all the health issues that can affect women as they get older. She wanted to be proactive about them. But she had no athletic background. I love working out—I would do it twice a day if I could and it would not feel like a discipline—but Theresa didn't even know where to begin. She mentioned her concerns when we were on vacation one year, so I suggested we start walking together. We've been walking ever since, and some of the best times of our marriage have come out of the conversations we have had on those walks.

Theresa also mentioned how she had always been intimidated by gyms. So I rearranged my schedule for two years so that during my lunch hour on Mondays, Wednesdays, and Fridays we could work out together and I could show her how to use the machines and lift weights. It made a huge difference to her. It was a sacrifice, but a small one in light of the payoff. When you love your wife intentionally, the benefits always far outweigh the costs.

This never ends. You will always be in a position to help your wife develop into the person God created her to be. Loving your wife intentionally is a big job, but you will never regret it. She will grow spiritually, emotionally, physically, relationally, and in every other way as you encourage her and help her see what she may not have seen in herself.

Love Her Sensitively

Little things can be big things for women. As you nourish and cherish her, don't always look for the big gestures.

Little words of encouragement make a huge difference. Calling when you have no reason to call touches her in a way most men will not understand. Planning a date and working out all the arrangements makes her feel secure and loved. Noticing what needs to be fixed around the house, the stresses you can relieve for her, and the plans that need to be made will make her life a little bit easier and her heart a lot fuller.

It's what many women call "sensitivity." It means being aware of what's going on in her life and being willing to meet her there.

I have a set of faded index cards that I have had since the early '80s. I had been married about four years, and I was

51

learning many of the principles in this book. But they weren't sticking. I would be a good husband for about a week, then default back to the habits and patterns I had developed growing up. So I decided to write down on these index cards the kind of husband I wanted to be, thinking that if I read them over and over again each day, eventually my new identity as a husband would stick.

It's a little embarrassing to read them now, but my "Life Goals with Wife" look like this:

- *My goal is to love Theresa sacrificially in a way that makes sense to her.*

    I wanted to remember what my job was, so that was number one.

- *My goal is to be the leader and initiator in our family that God wants me to be.*

    I had not seen that modeled for me as I was growing up, but I wanted to be different.

- *My goal is to get away with Theresa alone three times each year.*

    I don't think I ever accomplished that when we had young children, but we usually got away at least twice. Compared to before—which was "never"—that was a huge improvement.

- *My goal is to make our home a beautiful place to live, within our priorities financially, as a gift to Theresa.*

I didn't notice a lot of things she noticed. We had an old dishwasher that leaked water, so she would always have to put towels underneath it. Our kids' rooms had old windows, so she put towels under them to absorb the rain when it came in. She would tell me about these things, and I would just think of how much money a dishwasher and new windows would cost. Towels seemed like a pretty good option. But I realized that our home was her domain, the environment she spent most of her time in. That's the place God designed her to oversee. I needed to cooperate with him. So without being extravagant and living beyond our means, I learned to do whatever I could to create a good environment for her to live and work in.

- *My goal is to read with Theresa once a week.*

    That did not work every week, but we have read dozens of books together in the years since I wrote that goal.

- *My goal is to pray seriously with my wife once a week and briefly each day.*

    That doesn't sound like a big deal, especially for a pastor. But when I've spoken at pastors' conferences, I've asked how many do this, and very few hands go up. It doesn't happen if it is not intentional.

- *My goal is to give my wife what she needs instead of what she wants.*

    As a leader, you need to do what is best. One of the dangers is to think that a loving husband will say yes to whatever his wife wants, but that can produce codependency. Your goal is to do what is best for her, for your marriage, and for your family. At times, that will mean saying no to something because you can't afford it or you don't see it fitting into long-term goals. You might experience some conflict and rejection over that. But showing up as a man in the relationship has a powerful effect that is good for you, her, and the family as a whole.

What Loving Sacrificially Does *Not* Mean

After about a year and a half of trying to fulfill all of Theresa's desires, I read a book on codependency and realized that it described me perfectly. I needed to make some adjustments.

Being a loving husband does not mean giving your wife whatever she wants or satisfying her every desire. Ultimately, God is the fulfiller and satisfier. A husband creates the conditions that give God room to work. As a man, you will often be God's instrument in her life, but you won't be everything for her.

Loving her sacrificially also does not mean that you can never have a life of your own. You need male friends, hobbies, and time to be alone. You need to plan some times to get with other men, have fun, and be refreshed. Your wife will need to understand your need for healthy activities alone and with other men and cooperate with that so you can bring your best self to her.

But this needs to be balanced. Some men will spend much more time cultivating a world of their own and then entering the worlds of their wives and children only occasionally. You need to be able to find a balance and do both.

Loving your wife sacrificially also does not mean that you make her dependent on you. She needs to have her own self-identity too. Sometimes you will take care of things for her; at other times, you will encourage her to do things on her own. You don't want to smother her; you want her to grow.

Theresa came from a town of about two hundred people, so when we first moved to Dallas, she didn't know what to do with six lanes of traffic. I would always drive whenever we had to go downtown. But I realized this was reinforcing her dependence on me, and it was really limiting her. She had to call me every time she needed to take one of the kids to a doctor's appointment downtown. So despite her early objections, I made sure she got behind the wheel and grew in confidence with cars zipping in and out and around her. Pretty soon she could drive anywhere because she overcame her fears. Sometimes we need to give our wives room to grow and express by our behavior that we have confidence in them.

Many men will recognize a potential no-win situation here. If you do a lot of those things for her, she may accuse you of believing she can't do anything for herself. If you back off of some of the things she wants you to do and leave them for her, she may get upset because you won't help her out.

That dynamic prompted another index card: "Father, give me the wisdom to know how to give my wife what she needs, not what she wants, so that I love her the way you love her."

I had to get to a point where I realized not all conflict is bad. It can help both spouses grow. But the goal is always to empower our wives, not to avoid responsibility. We have to learn the difference.

Finally, *loving sacrificially does not mean calling all the shots*. That is not biblical manhood. It means you talk together, you pray together, you get God's counsel together, you work as a team, and at the end of the day, you do what you're called to do. You lead so you can dance together, not so you can be the featured performer.

Meant to Make a Difference

Unfortunately, many husbands are living in a way that is slowly killing them. You were made to lead, to be strong, to have courage, and to make a difference. Somewhere between the false extremes of dominance and negligence is a kind of leadership and responsibility that involves sacrifice and sensitivity. You were made to feel the responsibility and joy of watching your partner bloom and develop and, if you have children, to watch them bloom and develop too. You matter, you are valuable, and you can do this by the grace of God.

You will notice that your efforts to love your wife sacrificially are not only personally challenging and will require you to overcome some past habits and attitudes. Your efforts will also be challenged by a culture that does not embrace these values or give you many good examples of how to live them out.

There are reasons so many men have to learn what it means to be the kind of husband God calls them to be. We will explore some of those challenges and how to overcome them in the next chapter.

————— Questions for Reflection and Discussion —————

1. What are some of the pitfalls and misunderstandings of the word "submission" in biblical descriptions of marriage? How does the idea of mutual submission address these misunderstandings?

2. Why is the metaphor of dance such an effective picture of marriage? What elements of a dance do you think help clarify the roles of men and women most?

3. Why is clarity of roles important in marriage? What happens when marriage partners are not clear about each of their roles?

4. If you are a man, which aspects of sacrificial love seem most challenging to you? If you are married, what immediate practical steps can you take to love your wife more sacrificially, intentionally, or sensitively?

5. If you are a woman, what attitudes and actions do you think will most help the man in your life grow into his role as the Bible defines it?

3

The Evolution of the American Man

I f you feel overwhelmed, maybe even downright inadequate, after reading the last chapter, welcome to the club. Everything in that chapter was completely foreign to me before I got married. In fact, it was foreign to me in the early years of our marriage, as evidenced by the need for counseling and the deep struggles and dissatisfaction we both had, despite loving each other deeply.

You may feel as if the ideals presented here only give your mate more ammunition to point out where you don't measure up, but that's not what this book is about. And it certainly isn't about pouring more guilt on the secret wounds that most of our wives have no idea we carry. The chapters for men are for guys like you and me who really want a great marriage but don't know exactly what that looks like and how to make it happen. So let's review and tackle this God-sized assignment with his power and grace.

In the last chapter, we learned that God has called us men to *step up* and give our lives to lead and love our wives and families in the context of Christlike mutual submission. I outlined three things that God commands husbands to do:

- We must love our wives *sacrificially*.

- We must love our wives *intentionally*.

- We must love our wives *sensitively*.

What husband doesn't want to be this kind of man? But why is it so hard?

Why is this model of biblical leadership within marriage such a different paradigm from what most of us saw in our own homes growing up?

What forces today are working against us as we try to become that kind of man and that kind of husband?

And, most importantly, how do we break the habits learned in the past to become the men we long to be, the husbands our wives need us to be, and the models our children are desperate to see?

I want to take you on a journey that will help you understand the problem, perhaps like never before. I want you to understand how and why the depiction of manhood has changed drastically in the last five or six decades. I call it the evolution of the American male. It's why we don't know what it looks like to step up as men.

The Evolution of the American Male

Perceptions of expectations for men and women, and marriage, have changed more in the last fifty to sixty years than in the previous two thousand. Those of you who have lived fewer than, say, four decades have grown up entirely inside the dynamic of today's culture. You may not realize how all of today's television, movies, books, social media, and marketing messages are opposed to the God-given design for marriage.

That's a dramatic statement, isn't it? We need to understand where we came from and how we got here to see the direction of our culture and thus be able to push back and live biblically.

Trends since at least World War II have eroded the concept of manhood—with devastating consequences.

In the early 1950s, American soldiers had recently come home from World War II, the "baby boom" was expanding families, suburbs were flourishing, and the vast majority of young boys and girls had both a father and a mother in the home. They were building the American dream. Divorce wasn't unheard of—movie stars were getting them, and occasionally it would happen to someone closer to home—but for the most part, it was a rare occurrence. That doesn't mean every couple was happy, but they usually weren't looking for overt, legal ways out of the marriage. The family unit was a pretty stable anchor for society.

That changed in the '60s. The Vietnam War and widespread restlessness over issues of race and justice combined to cause

61

people to question all social norms, including sexual moral-ity. For many people, existentialism became not just a Euro-pean philosophy but an American way of life. Truth became relative. Authority (of any sort) deserved to be questioned, undermined, ignored, or destroyed.

The rallying cry was "Make love, not war." Sex, love, and marriage became separate categories. They no longer had to go together. Sex did not imply any commitment of love and certainly not of marriage. Men could openly be biological fathers without embracing any responsibilities of father-hood. The stability of the family began to disintegrate.

The radical feminism of the late '60s and '70s went well beyond the important issue of getting equal pay for equal work. It not only aimed to put men and women on equal footing, but it also aimed to erase any differences in stan-dards for the way men and women behave and the roles they have in society. It denied differences to the point of emasculating men.

By the 1980s, people began to tire of sexual issues and fo-cused on themselves: the "me" decade. The emphasis on af-fluence and greed—living as if the goal in life were to acquire more and more—naturally led to an epidemic of workahol-ism. Many fathers (and mothers) turned their attention away from their families to focus on careers. Many single-income families turned into two-income families, as rising costs and changing work dynamics stretched family expenses beyond past income levels.

By the 1990s, society was no longer grounded in any coherent understanding of family norms. Confusion disoriented an entire generation. Sex roles were blurred, open homosexuality increased, the family unit was redefined, and the culture began to normalize behaviors that were once considered marginal. By the 2000s, "diversity" had become the only "norm" that anyone could identify as a consistent standard for families.

The effects on children of fathers being absent from the home are staggering. In America, 23.6 percent of children (24 million) lived in father-absent homes in 2016,[1] and 63 percent of youth suicides are from fatherless homes.[2] Children living in fatherless homes have a poverty rate of 47.6 percent, over four times the poverty rate of children living in married-couple families.[3]

Many people will never have a clear understanding of why marriage is even desirable. If it doesn't work, why keep doing it? The majority of young couples live together before they get married, if they ever do, which actually undermines the marriage before it ever starts. The emotional fallout in this generation is not hard to see.

To be fair, much of the social change that has come since the 1950s has been positive. Social expectations sixty years ago pushed many people into conventional careers and family situations that were not fulfilling or suited to their gifts or interests. Women were rarely treated equally or even taken seriously. The "normal" roles people played were often a veneer covering a much more complex reality. My parents and Theresa's were "doing family" right in the middle of that generation, and clearly, they were wrestling with some pretty serious issues. Not everything was rosy.

But the positive changes have come at a significant cost and with a lot of negative baggage. Those of us who have been around for a while have seen the fracture and fragmentation of an entire culture, with numerous damaging side effects.

Dumbing Down Dads in the Media

If you want a visual picture of how society has changed and how our perceptions of manhood have been redefined, look at the iconic TV fathers over the last few decades. If you're much younger than I am, you may not remember Ward Cleaver, although you may have come across reruns of *Leave It to Beaver* (1957–63). Mr. Cleaver had a good job, provided and cared for his family, and was always there for paternal discipline and wise guidance if Beaver or Wally ever got into trouble (which they did, every episode). He was the voice of reason and an anchor for his family. If you're even older than I am, you might recall earlier popular shows like *The Adventures of Ozzie and Harriet* (1952–66) and *Father Knows Best* (1954–60).

The next generation of TV introduced us to *The Brady Bunch* (1969–74), where the father handled a blended family of six kids in partnership with his wife, but still with the kind of paternal wisdom portrayed in traditional father roles. Then in the late '70s and into the '80s, things began to change.

We saw a movement away from family units in entertainment: *Three's Company* (1976–84) pushed the boundaries of television standards and played with expected gender roles. *Murphy Brown* (1988–98) represented feminism at its peak, as the lead character managed to have her career and be a single mother without any need or desire for a man in her life. In the '90s, *Friends* (1994–2004) showed us what an extended adolescence looks like—how to sleep with whomever you wanted to sleep with and move in and out of marriages as needed. And don't even get me started about the dysfunctional *Married with Children* (1986–97), which presented the antithesis of a real man and a godly marriage.

The Simpsons (launched in 1989) has shown us the absolute lowest point of fatherhood in Homer Simpson, a bumbling, know-nothing fool who earns plenty of laughs and no respect. He may be an extreme example, but if you think through all the family sitcoms that have been produced in the last couple of decades, you'll find very few examples of strong manhood and quite a few examples of husbands and fathers who are either tolerated or beloved for their quirks while their wives really run the family.

You would be hard-pressed to find a representation of a strong, compassionate, sensitive, courageous, providing, protective man in recent TV shows or movies. The days of *Father Knows Best* and *Leave It to Beaver* are gone.

We know, of course, that those shows were idealized pictures of family life; few families in the '50s and '60s actually functioned like that. But the ideals of an age are significant. They demonstrate how Americans wanted to perceive the role of the man at home, and those desires and expectations have almost completely deteriorated over the years.

In addition to television and film role models, our heroes have changed. They are no longer warriors or strongman characters (which, admittedly, were sometimes over the top);

they are athletes and entertainers, whether actors or singers. There's nothing wrong with appreciating what celebrities do, but competing and entertaining are jobs, not courageous acts of manhood. Actors pretend to be other people. Singers and musicians make music. Athletes play. They get a lot of money too, and many of them are incredibly talented. But their accomplishments have little to do with character and integrity, as we have seen again and again.

Unfortunately, though, they're our children's role models. A young boy used to say he wanted to be a fireman or police-man or even the president. Now it's more likely to be an NBA player or a rock star. What does that mean for how the next generation views manhood?

Absent-Father Families

We live in a culture that devalues true manhood and mar-riage. One of the consequences is families without fathers or those whose fathers are passive.

I dated a girl in high school and went over to her house one day to meet her mother. After the usual small talk, I noticed a picture on the mantel of a man in a military uniform. He was a good-looking guy with a nice smile on his face. I asked who he was, and my friend said, "That's my dad."

"Oh, is he around?" As soon as I asked, my friend's face fell and the room got quiet.

Her mother filled in the story. "Her father has been missing in action in Vietnam for a number of years now. We don't know if he's alive or dead. We pray every single day that he'll come back home one day, but we don't know. We just wait."

That had to be an incredibly difficult situation, through no fault of my friend or her mother. Nobody had made bad decisions to break up this family. But the effects were just the same. It became apparent as I got to know them that there were some real deficits in their lives—a girl growing up without experiencing her father's love, a woman who was missing what a husband has to offer. There was a huge gap in their lives because there was no man in the home.

I've researched families and especially the role of the father in the family for my master's thesis. I grew up in a typical but dysfunctional situation. Dad was home, and he was a good guy—a great athlete, a strong masculine figure—but he wasn't emotionally or relationally "present." In addition to his issues with alcoholism, he took a passive approach to being a husband and father. He became so dependent, my mom had to pick out what clothes he would wear to work. My mother ran the home.

I remember coming home after school one day, and I could tell Dad was really ticked off.

"What's wrong?" I asked.

"I'm hungry!"

"Isn't there food in the refrigerator?"

"Well, yeah, but your mom isn't here to fix it for me."

All I can remember thinking is how pathetic that was—that a grown man was paralyzed by the fact that no one was there to pull some food out of the fridge and fix it for him. But over the years since then, I've realized that, in less dramatic ways, that isn't unusual. Men are missing in action in a shocking number of homes.

I don't mean that as a slam against anyone in particular. It is a large cultural trend that has been building over the last several decades. I understand that life is hard and that it isn't easy to stand firm against shifting social dynamics. But there is a profile of manhood in Scripture that men are called to live out, and it builds up women, children, and the family unit as a whole. When men fit into that biblical portrait, they become the strength of society.

> When men fit into that biblical portrait, they become the strength of society.

I see absent-father families as one of the two major consequences in this evolution of the American male. The other is the impact of these changing roles. Whether for reasons no family can avoid (like war or illness) or because of bad decisions and dysfunctional relationships, the absenteeism of American fathers has left a huge hole in the lives of many children.

The negative impact on families caused such concern that the US government conducted a study on child development called Code Blue. In its evaluation of adolescents, it stated: "Never before has one generation of American teenagers been less healthy, less cared for, or less prepared for life."[4] This observation was followed with the note that this situation occurred "in one of the most affluent and privileged nations in the history of the world."[5]

Another study concluded that boys suffer more than girls from the absence or noninvolvement of a father. They are twice as likely to drop out of school, twice as likely to go to jail, and four times as likely to need treatment for emotional and behavioral problems as boys with engaged, at-home fathers.[6] Harvard psychologist William Pollack, author of *Real Boys*, says divorce is difficult for all children but particularly for males. "The basic problem is the lack of discipline and supervision in a father's absence and his unavailability to teach what it means to be a man."[7] So homes with absent or disengaged fathers beget homes with future absent or disengaged fathers.

Sociologist Peter Karl notes that 80 percent of a boy's time in his childhood years is spent with women. "They don't know how to act as men when they grow up. When that happens, the relationship between the sexes is directly affected and men become helpless and more like big kids."[8]

My mental picture of that dynamic is the man who dons a backward baseball cap and the jersey of some twenty-five-year-old star athlete to play fantasy football. His manhood comes from playing and pretending. And why not? He may have never been around a man who leads, provides, and lives with courage. Somewhere between *Friends* and *Homer Simpson*, he never got a picture of what it means to be a man. The roles have blurred.

Not Missing, but Present

If you are a woman, you may wonder if it is even possible for your husband or son to learn how to be a "real man."

He genuinely may have never been given a picture of biblical manhood. That's a legitimate concern, and much of this book will aim to address it.

A psychologist and author in San Francisco, Pierre Mornell recognized the same concern in many of his clients nearly four decades ago. He was amazed at how many wives of powerful men in the financial districts of San Francisco were coming to see him for counseling. The book recounts multiple stories of wives whose husbands drove into the city daily to lead major financial institutions where they exercise power, strategy, and focus to achieve multimillion- and even billion-dollar deals. Yet they returned home only to be couch potatoes or bury their faces in the *Wall Street Journal*.

Mornell writes, "A man who is passive at home is often extremely active at work. On the job he is energetic and assertive. Indeed he may be absolutely dynamic. And yet as the old saying about the salesman goes, 'He may be a tiger in the territory, but he's a mouse in the house.'"[9]

> Just because a man is in the home does not mean he is in the home in a meaningful way.

He described this phenomenon in a best-seller called *Passive Men, Wild Women*. His thesis was that this behavior in men creates "wild," frustrated, angry women. I would suggest that it also creates very confused children. Men in that situation may not be as absent as the MIA father of the girl I dated in high school, but they produce similar results. Just because a man is in the home does not mean he is in the home in a meaningful way. Boys and girls need fathers who are not missing in action.

Avoiding the Two PCs

At this point, if you're a man and feeling discouraged, or a woman and feeling discouraged *with* men, I want to remind you that trust is powerful. God has always redeemed people groups through the hands of a few committed men and women who choose to believe, obey, and swim upstream. Later we'll discuss practical ways to turn the tide, but let's be careful to avoid the common pitfalls.

Society has tried to compensate for MIA men, and it has come up with two extremes we want to avoid. I call them the two PCs.

One is the modern politically correct image of manhood, which says anything goes—any lifestyle, any family unit, any alternative. In light of what we have seen from Scripture and research, I think we can agree that this PC definition of manhood is not an effective one. It doesn't work.

The other PC is pseudo-Christian. It's a knee-jerk reaction to politically correct manhood, and it shows up as the image of a narrow-minded, bigoted, I'm-in-control, I'm-the-head-of-the-house, Bible-thumping stereotype. The old chauvinistic caricature of the "man of the house" who has to insist on his authority and make everyone else submit to him is not a biblical image. If you have to thump your chest and tell people you're in charge, you aren't. If you have to demand respect, you don't have it. That picture of manhood is absolutely not what the Bible teaches.

I grew up without knowing what it meant to be a man. I just did what my father had done. I figured out how to be a good athlete and pretend to be a man. Then I became a Christian.

71

I had to completely relearn manhood, and in some ways I started from scratch. It's a lifelong process, and it goes against the grain of our culture. But the blueprint has been there for a long time: it was perfectly embodied in Jesus, and it is explained in Ephesians 5.

We can even become the examples and role models for the next generation that we wish we would have had in ours.

In chapter 2, we saw what real manhood looks like; in this one, we've seen the enormous obstacles standing in the way of our ideals. But those obstacles are not insurmountable. In fact, with an admission that we can't do this in our own power and a resolve to trust God's promises and encourage one another, we can overcome them. We can even become the examples and role models for the next generation that we wish we would have had in ours. We just need a few tools and a lot of encouragement.

Bringing It Home: Now What?

By and large, we are the product of the significant people in our lives. Modeling is the most powerful influence in human development and behavior. We all grow up in certain homes, and without exception, we speak, eat, form traditions, get perspectives, and develop identities very much as our parents did. The way we look at the world is shaped by the key influencers in our lives. Unfortunately, it's rare to meet men who say something like, "I want to be a godly man like my dad."

So for those of us who didn't grow up as believers and didn't have a strong, godly father, what are we to do? Let me give you a few key suggestions that have helped me become the kind of man described in Ephesians 5.

Find a godly mentor. More is caught than taught.

In my early years, coaches filled the role of a father figure when my dad was absent. They taught me the disciplines of manhood and believed in me. After trusting Christ, I met Dave, the bricklayer I wrote about in the introduction. He discipled me during college and modeled what it looked like to date his wife, love his kids, and practice biblical priorities. Since that time, I've prayed for, looked for, and found men in every season to help me become the kind of man who loves his family well.

Start or join a men's small group. It's impossible to make it on your own.

Our wives can be wonderful friends and companions, but they don't fully understand how we think, where we struggle, or the fears that hold us back. From those early days until now, some four decades later, I've committed to doing life with a group of men. These have been honest, raw, gutsy, biblical, heart-to-heart relationships of love and support, and they have been safe places to share my biggest failures and strong places to give me the kick in the rear I needed whenever I started to drift.

Renew your mind. You are the product of your thought life.

Don't just read the Bible and great books on manhood and marriage. You should be doing that anyway. Every day we are bombarded by messages—on sports talk radio, on the financial page, in movies, in video games, and in certain negative relationships—that constantly work against our desire to become the men we long to be. To be a man of God, you have to stop the negative flow that creates desires and temptations that pull you away from God and from your efforts to love your wife sacrificially, intentionally, and sensitively. You have to replace that input with positive and inspiring thoughts about the rewards of a great marriage. You can fill your mind with those kinds of thoughts through books, movies, and relationships that inspire you and encourage you to be an Ephesians 5 man and husband.

Tools for Becoming an Ephesians 5 Man

With that in mind, here are some practical tools to help you.

The Daily Walk Bible is the easiest and clearest Bible I've found that provides context and understanding for those who don't know much about the Bible or who want to grasp the overall message and meaning. For the first fifteen years of my Christian life, I read it every year, and I have dipped back into it multiple times since.

True Spirituality: Becoming a Romans 12 Christian is a book I wrote about my journey in understanding what it means to be a disciple of Christ and how to practically follow him in the five key relationships of your life. The greatest gift I have ever given my wife is becoming more like Christ, but for years I didn't really know how that worked or how to go about it. I think some of these lessons from my own journey may be a great help to you. This content is available in multiple formats: free MP3s, CDs, or videos at

truespiritualityonline.org.

The Five Love Languages: The Secret to Love that Lasts by Gary Chapman is a perennial bestseller I believe every man should read tomorrow if he hasn't already. It's a very simple and quick read, but it will open your eyes to the way your wife and other people think. For years, I nearly drove myself crazy trying to love my wife in ways that didn't connect with her. After I read this book and learned her "language of love," tons of frustration turned into positive emotions. I learned how to make deposits instead of constant withdrawals in the love bank of our relationship. It greatly improved how we relate to each other.

Those resources can help every man become a better husband, but, of course, this book isn't only about how men can make their marriages better. We have focused on the roles and characteristics of men in the preceding two chapters because men have the ability to set the tone for everything else in marriage and family relationships. But men and women are in this relationship together. The roles and characteristics of women are just as critical to the beauty of the dance. In the next two chapters, we will explore the wonders and opportunities of biblical femininity.

_____ Questions for Reflection and Discussion _____

1. In what ways have you seen the definition of manhood change during the course of your lifetime?

2. Think of one man you have looked up to as a model of manhood. What characteristics does he have? Where does he fit in the cultural evolution of masculine ideals? How well do you think he embodies the biblical idea of manhood? Why?

3. In what ways, if any, have you experienced or witnessed absentee fatherhood? What about passive fatherhood? What effects of this phenomenon have you observed?

4. If you are a man, what is your response to the examples and research presented in this chapter? Do they discourage you? Confirm your beliefs? Motivate you to make any changes? Why?

5. What next step do you sense God would have you take to become the man and husband he has designed you to become?

6. Who could help you on this journey? What man or men would be willing to be a "band of brothers" with you as you move toward biblical manhood?

4

Is There a Woman in the House?

Submit to one another out of reverence for Christ.

Wives, submit yourselves to your own husbands as you do to the Lord. For the husband is the head of the wife as Christ is the head of the church, his body, of which he is the Savior. Now as the church submits to Christ, so also wives should submit to their husbands in everything.

Husbands, love your wives, just as Christ loved the church and gave himself up for her to make her holy, cleansing her by the washing with water through the word, and to present her to himself as a radiant church, without stain or wrinkle or any other blemish, but holy and blameless. In this same way, husbands ought to love their wives as their own bodies. He who loves his wife loves himself. After all, no one ever hated their own body, but they feed and care for their body, just as Christ does the church—for we are members of his body.

"For this reason a man will leave his father and mother and be united to his wife, and the two will become one flesh."

> This is a profound mystery—but I am talking about Christ
> and the church. However, each one of you also must love
> his wife as he loves himself, and the wife must respect her
> husband.
>
> —Ephesians 5:21–33

It's an age-old stereotype, isn't it? Men are in charge, and women are supposed to submit to them. Some have claimed that to be Christian teaching. But as we have seen, it is really a distortion of what the Bible says. It's an abuse of Christian truth that ignores context and focuses on only a few isolated, misinterpreted phrases. Men and societies with an inflated sense of patriarchy have for centuries exploited Scripture to control women.

The fact that counterfeit teaching has been around for a long time, though, should not keep us away from the real thing. The truth is that mutual submission is the background of our entire discussion of male and female roles. Both men and women look to God to say, "I'm going to submit to you and do life your way, according to your Word." Then they turn to each other and say, "I'm going to seek your needs and your well-being above my own." In God's economy for human relationships, this mutual submission is where everything begins.

Marriage is never about establishing your own rights or telling your mate what he or she is supposed to do. God's words to men are directed toward men, not toward women to use as a weapon against their men; and God's words to women are directed toward women, not toward men to use as a weapon against their women. When each person takes the words directed specifically at them to heart, beautiful things happen. When we cross lines and direct those words at each other, we stir up conflict.

The questions to ask your spouse are, "How can I make you more successful? How can I love you more deeply? How can I serve you well?" Those questions fit under the umbrella of mutual submission. We are given a vivid picture of it in Philippians 2:3–4:

> Do nothing from selfishness or empty conceit, but with humility of mind regard one another as more important than yourselves; do not merely look out for your own personal interests, but also for the interests of others. (NASB)

This teaching is not addressed specifically to men or women. It is written to all the members of the church at Philippi. In Christian thought, submission is not an exception or for one group of people; it is the norm. This is how everyone should treat each other. In fact, the following verses (Phil. 2:5–8) command us to have this other-centered attitude toward everyone just as Christ did. We, like Jesus, are to take up the role of servant, and applying this to the marriage relationship should not be surprising at all.

As unto Christ

We saw a couple chapters ago that this Christlike attitude is where the dance of marriage begins, and it started with the man stepping up. But the dance requires some more clarity of roles. What is the woman's role? How does she make the dance beautiful?

Let's look at the choreography again, this time specifically with an eye on what it says to women:

> Wives, submit yourselves to your own husbands as you do to the Lord. For the husband is the head of the wife as Christ is the head of the church, his body, of which he is the Savior. Now as the church submits to Christ, so also wives should submit to their husbands in everything. (Eph. 5:22–24)

The word "submit" is not a negative word. We will see that it has nothing to do with inferiority or inequality and everything to do with function, structure, and roles. As the church is subject to Christ, wives ought to be subject "to their husbands in everything" (v. 24). If a man loves his wife as Christ loves the church, it is not difficult to submit to him, in the true sense of submission.

Submission does not mean saying, "Yes, dear," to whatever your husband says. Scripture does not tell wives that they need to be *passive*. That is an extreme reaction to trying to be in control, and it goes too far in the opposite direction. A wife is to step into the marriage relationship—not step over her husband—with strength and respect. She is an equal partner. A partner who submits to the righteous leadership of the other partner—her husband.

Equal Standing, Different Roles

What exactly does this mean? First, couples must understand that marriage is not a fifty-fifty proposition.

Every organization—whether it's a business, the military, a school, a club, or even a small group—has some sort of structure and leadership. Ultimately, someone is responsible. That does not mean members are not equal as human beings or that some members are more valuable than others. It does mean, however, that some people carry more weight of responsibility than others.

This applies to marriage too. God says that just as Christ is the head of the church, the man is head of the family—spiritually, emotionally, relationally.

Again, this has nothing to do with value or equality. We know this because the same principle is discussed in 1 Corinthians 11:3, where Paul writes that "Christ is the head of every man, and the man is the head of a woman, and God is the head of Christ" (NASB). Jesus submitted himself to the Father, but the Father, the Son, and the Spirit are equal in essence and in value. There is no higher or lower in the Trinity, but there are different roles and functions.

Christ, being equal to the Father, chose to submit to him because of their different roles. Likewise, a wife first must submit to her husband, not because of any difference in value or importance, but because of the distinction of their marriage roles.

Second, a wife must voluntarily support her husband from the heart as an act of obedience to God. The key word is "voluntarily." This is not a burden to bear; it is a choice that comes from a joyful heart. When a woman believes that God has put this man in her life ultimately for her good, she doesn't have to worry that he might mess everything up for her. Ultimately, it's God, not her husband, who's in control and sovereign over her life.

Third, a wife must believe that submission—responding as a skillful dance partner to her husband's initiatives rather than competing against him—is her greatest ally in bringing about positive change. It is her way of cooperating with God's design in choreographing the steps of her marriage and her family.

R.E.S.P.E.C.T.

After Paul's words on marriage and the responsibilities of the husband, he concludes the passage in Ephesians 5 with the wife's response to her husband's selfless love: "The wife must see to it that she respects her husband" (v. 33 NASB). The Greek word for "respect" in this verse comes from the root word "phobos," from which we get our word "phobia," but it doesn't have the same connotation. It means reverence, not fear.

Many women do not realize how deeply men need to feel honored and respected. A man feels loved when he is encouraged—when his wife steps into his life and communicates by words and actions, "I believe in you." When she willingly supports and encourages his leadership, she is making a profound statement that will resonate deeply in his heart. She is acknowledging the position God has put him in and respecting his God-given role. Even though he may feel that he has been given an impossible standard to live up to, she is on his side to help him be successful.

When a man loses the respect of his wife, he will shut down, be passive-aggressive, bury himself in his fantasy teams or his work, and have no idea what's going on in the hearts of his wife and children. It is devastating for a man not to be honored and respected.

If this has been a problem in the past—if he had a father who did not affirm him or a history of relationships in which he has been torn down—he may no longer believe in himself. He will seek affirmation wherever he can get it—by driving a hot car, getting a scholarship, dating a beautiful girl, getting degrees, making a team, nabbing a high-salary job, acing a project, and on and on.

> *Every man has a desperate need for his wife to step in and believe in him.*

Affirmation feels like love, but it isn't, and it doesn't fill a man up. A husband will be on a never-ending search for it unless he gets it from his wife. Every man has a desperate need for his wife to step in and believe in him.

His Insecurity, Her Strength

The fear of failure is one of the greatest fears every man secretly lives with. That's one reason men are such experts at overcompensating. We focus on the things we know we can be good at, like our work or sports or hobbies. We know what we are doing there.

But if you ask the average man how his family is doing spiritually, you may get an awkward response. The same is true if you ask him how sensitive and caring he is in guiding his children through their challenges. We men can be awfully insecure on these points, even though they are part of our God-given design.

Women often respond to that insecurity by taking the reins of the family and trying to control their husbands and children. This ultimately sabotages the marriage. So God tells wives to submit—not because the husband is inherently better or more important, and not because he is more capable or qualified, but because her submission to him builds him up and empowers him to lead.

Where men are to *step up* in the dance of marriage, women are to *step in* with support, affirmation, and encouragement, building up their husbands with strength and respect so they can lead their families in righteousness.

Antiquated Thought?

You can imagine how well this goes over in some circles, especially in light of today's social and political climate. Imagine meeting a woman at a coffee shop and having a conversation with her about this:

"What are you reading?" she asks.

"A book about marriage."

"What are you learning?"

"Well, the past few chapters have been pretty cool. They say my man is supposed to step up, lead, provide, and even lay down his life for me."

"Wow, that's great. Maybe I should read it too."

"Well, you should see what it says about women first," you warn.

"Really? What does it say?"

"It uses the *S* word."

"Huh?"

"'Submission.' My husband is responsible to be a servant leader, and then I bring all my strengths and gifts into the relationship. We talk and share our opinions. But if we get to an impasse, I'm supposed to defer to him and submit."

"Wow, that is so antiquated. I can't believe there are still people who think that way."

And it's true that this is extremely politically incorrect—if we look at it through the lens of the twenty-first century.

But imagine being a man who has grown up in an ancient culture about the time Paul was writing. If you're a new Christian, you may be nicer to your wife than most men of this era are to theirs, and perhaps you have a pretty good marriage. But you've grown up thinking women are just a step up from slaves or are primarily objects of pleasure. Many of the people you know have been divorced numerous times, and it's not considered a big deal. So imagine how shocked

85

you would be when you go to a church in Ephesus and hear a letter from a well-known apostle being read to the congregation, and it starts talking about mutual submission—not to a friend or colleague but to your wife. A woman.

This apostle actually considers her to be a coheir of God's grace and an equal in God's eyes. You are supposed to love her sacrificially and maybe even lay down your life for her. Paul comes across as incredibly progressive, very liberal, and downright radical. It's hard to believe someone would elevate women to a status equal to yours as a man.

Do you see the difference perspective can make? At the time, Paul could be considered a liberator, just as Jesus had been a few years earlier. The Bible elevates both partners. When it talks about submission, it is always in the context of a sovereign God who created roles that fit together. When each person does his or her part, they form a rich and healthy relationship.

Taking Control Alone

Our culture today has distorted that perspective. A woman wants to feel secure and protected. When she doesn't, fear takes over and she seeks control. As we will see in the next chapter, radical feminism exploited injustices—many very real ones—and embraced the desire to control to the point that many feminists not only believe they no longer need men but also hate men and blame them for most of society's problems.

That theme still runs pretty strongly through some areas of our culture, and I've seen some very bright, well-educated women buy into it unconsciously and start down a path that ends with them hating their own lives. That distorted perception of men does not lead to a healthy place or a rich and fulfilling relationship.

I sat next to an extremely intelligent young woman on a plane recently. She was in her late twenties, spoke five languages, and was flying into Atlanta to interview with an airline for a very high-powered position that would require her to travel all over the world. We had a great conversation. She said she had been married for about a year and a half, so I asked her what her husband thought about the possibility of her traveling so much. She said he was excited about it. I asked how things were going to work in their marriage if she was gone two or three weeks at a time. "Oh, it will be fine. We only see each other for half a day each week now," she explained.

"What do you mean?"

She told me about his job, which paid him a lot of money but kept him on a tight schedule. Then she told me about her job, which also paid a lot of money but kept her busy. "So he has later hours, and I work an early shift, so we only see each other for about a half day on Saturday anyway, and we're both pretty tired."

That's the kind of living arrangement their choices had led to, and it's hard to believe anyone would make that kind of arrangement on purpose. But they had both unconsciously bought into the cultural ideal of making a lot of money, moving up the ladder, and squeezing in a marriage on the side. I suspect she will wake up in about fifteen years and question it all. If this couple has a child, she will experience all the natural pangs and urges of nurturing and motherhood, but those urges will have to compete with years of investing in a high-stakes career, a two-income lifestyle, and the status and self-image that go along with that life. It's going to be difficult to manage that crisis. And tragically, the promises of happiness that wealth, power, and travel make will never satisfy the deepest yearnings of her heart.

Intentional Choices

You have to be clear on the identity God has given you and what really matters. That will mean making some hard decisions. Some women are able to pursue a career for a while and then embrace marriage and motherhood with ease. Some choose never to go the marriage-and-family route. But for those who are trying to do it all, it can be very stressful and often unfulfilling.

A couple needs to be very intentional about who is going to work in which seasons of life and know how to live out their God-given roles. They need to ask the hard questions of how their relationship will play out practically in terms of jobs and raising a family. The best scenario for fifteen years down the road is not having parallel fast-track careers that allow you to see each other once or twice a week; instead, the best scenario is having a rich and rewarding relationship that is stable and secure and satisfies your needs at the deepest levels.

And if that scenario includes children, providing a stable and secure environment where they can also experience love and deeply secure relationships becomes part of the equation. You want your children to grow up and still desire a relationship with you, to be able to look back and appreciate the sacrifice and investments you have made for them. But couples who try to balance it all without making any major sacrifices are going to end up making the biggest sacrifice of all. They are going to miss out on the fullness of what marriage and family can be. It's no accident that attempting to "do it all" and "have it all" among Christians and non-Christians alike has resulted in fractured families and painful, life-altering divorces.

As a pastor, I've never done a funeral that focused on how many languages the deceased spoke, how many promotions he or she got, or how much money that person made. The letters behind the names, the stock portfolios, the professional accolades—none of that comes up when everyone is sitting around talking about this person who is no longer with us. People talk about two things: relationships and love.

I've also never heard of people on their deathbed talking about their professional regrets. It's always about how they wish they'd spent more time with their family, parented their children differently, or appreciated their spouse when they had the chance. At the end of life, relational issues come to the forefront and all the other pursuits fade into the background. People finally realize what's important. Sadly, sometimes they realize too late.

God has a plan for that—for men and women to relate to each other in the healthiest and most satisfying ways and to share the love between them with the next generation by raising children in that same nurturing, fulfilling environment. Part of that equation is for women to step into the marriage relationship to support, affirm, and encourage their husbands with strength and respect so that their husbands can lead their families in righteousness.

The Power of Submission

For that to happen, women need to take a huge step of faith and believe that submission is actually their greatest ally in seeing the change they want to see in the men they love. Most women I know would like for their husbands to be more romantic, or more responsible, or more intentional in the way they lead, provide, and communicate. They already know that nagging doesn't work. Neither do arguing or passive-aggressive moods.

What if God said, "If that's what you really want to see in the life of your husband, try submitting to him and see how he changes"? Would you be able to trust him on that—not for a day or two, but over enough time to see genuine change?

The issue is not whether your husband deserves your voluntary, joyful submission; there are plenty of days when he does not, and he probably knows that. Nor is the issue that he will make better decisions than you; he may not. This is a trust issue with God, who blesses marriage and has, in one way or another, put you and your husband together in a committed relationship.

When a man feels honored, respected, affirmed, and encouraged, something happens inside him. It may take time, but

God begins to work in his heart. The change you are looking for begins to take shape.

Theresa's Three Truths

I can interpret Scripture and teach these principles, but obviously I've never been on the other side of this teaching—listening to it as a woman. I know the truth, but I don't really know the practical implications.

So I asked my wife how a woman perceives this teaching. She pulls this off beautifully, without being a pushover or being manipulative. What goes on inside a woman's mind when she tries to apply this "outdated" concept in real life? How does it work in her heart? Here's what Theresa said:

> This hasn't always been easy for me, but I've found three things that have really helped me live out submission in the biblical sense.
>
> First, I feel secure because I trust Chip to have my best interests in mind. I certainly don't believe he's perfect; I know his flaws better than anyone, and I will not hesitate to disagree with him. But I also know his heart and that he's on my side. I know that he will give careful thought and prayer to every decision.
>
> Second, I love the Lord and his Word, and it is my heart's desire to obey God. I ask God to shape my heart, I lean on his strength, and I claim the promises from his Word when I don't understand and don't feel like submitting. I am convinced that God will take up my cause because he cares for me.

The third thing is clear communication. It gives me great confidence to know that Chip and I will talk through everything. In our marriage, we have worked hard on this. We talk nearly every day, share our thoughts, struggles, dreams, and how we are processing decisions we need to make and issues we need to deal with. I'm confident, even though we may go through significant conflict, that I'll really be heard and that I can trust Chip's heart.

> I am convinced that God will take up my cause because he cares for me.

I believe that these three concepts, if embraced by both husband and wife, will help women accept their role in a biblical marriage. It's been a real journey and a process for me to understand what it takes to build a safe environment in which Theresa and I can work through difficult issues and come to resolutions that we can both live with.

Stating Her Case Strongly

Theresa and I have had some pretty big areas of tension over the years, as nearly all couples do. One of ours was how to discipline our children. Another has been taking care of the home—maintaining and repairing the physical environment. We've had major challenges with in-laws, communication, frequency of and perspective on sex, and where and how we spend our time. We see these things very differently, and Theresa is very honest about how difficult it has been to submit sometimes, especially when she considers something to be a major issue and I consider it a minor one.

Some of these issues have evaporated as we've matured, but every couple has ongoing issues. The most difficult for us have been those rare times when we've had major decisions to make and didn't see eye to eye. We have moved a lot, and we haven't always agreed on where God was leading us (or if he was leading us somewhere different at all). Like many wives, Theresa likes to feel settled. Both men and women may experience this, but I believe women are more often reluctant to leave friends, schools, and other social connections behind.

She has cried out to God more than once to claim his promise in Romans 8:32: "He who did not spare his own Son, but gave him up for us all—how will he not also, along with him, graciously give us all things?" She knows that wherever we are and however uncertain life seems to be, God is going to freely give her what she needs.

I cannot express how much I value Theresa's willingness to be supportive and encouraging as she follows my lead, but I equally value her willingness to express how she feels, raise the difficult questions, and state her case with passion and strength.

That does not feel threatening to me because I know if she buries her true feelings, they are going to come out sideways in other areas. Resentment will grow and eventually come to the surface. It isn't easy for her to follow along when she is concerned I may be doing the wrong thing, or to have a good attitude in the process, but she gets there. She trusts my heart, and she trusts God to be sovereign over every human decision.

What Happens If He Does Not Lead?

When women don't trust their husband's heart, or fear that he is not leading well, they face a formidable challenge. Ideally, a wife follows a husband who is loving her sacrificially as Christ loves the church and is always praying and seeking godly wisdom as he leads. But what if he doesn't? How do you follow from a place of insecurity? How do you let go of the reins when you fear that things will fall apart as soon as you do?

That's a really difficult situation, but it isn't beyond God's provision.

Women have a very natural desire to run their homes and families well, but that desire often turns into a sense of control. This issue of submission is one area in which God will allow that sense of control to be tested and challenged.

Are you willing to let go and trust God? That's the real issue, and it isn't an easy one, but it is important. Remember that in any situation, God cares for you. He is ultimately your defender. He will take up your cause in whatever situation you find yourself in if you submit it to him.

Prayer is your best strategy in any area of life, especially this one. Pray for your husband, knowing that God can change his heart. Pray with the expectation that God will change circumstances if necessary.

And then, in faith, give God room to work in your husband, in your circumstances, and in your own heart. Sometimes people pray for change and then allow no space for it to happen. They keep acting as the agent of change even when their intervention is not helping. Give God space, time, and your trust, then wait to see what he does.

You might be surprised how hands-on he can be when you determine to be hands-off and trust him. We'll talk about how to do this in a later chapter, but for now,

Are you willing to let go and trust God?

purpose in your heart to refuse to live in fear of what "might happen" if you entrust your husband and his role to Christ. At times it can be really hard to discern, especially if your husband isn't currently walking with Lord, what is wise to submit to and what is not. The appendix in this book is written by a friend who specializes in helping women who find themselves in difficult situations.

Wanting the Best for the Marriage

Theresa's motto for her approach to our marriage is from Proverbs 31:12: "She brings him good, not harm, all the days of her life." Behind every discussion and every decision, she is asking, "Am I doing him good, or am I doing him harm?"

Sometimes doing good for me means submitting to something she doesn't necessarily agree with. Sometimes it means refusing to take responsibility for something that is really on my shoulders.

But in every case, she wants the best not only for our marriage and for herself but also for me. And, of course, I want that for her. When all those steps come together, the dance can be a beautiful experience. But remember, as we learn to dance, we often step on each other's feet. In the next chapter, we'll take a look at how this works out in real life.

_____ Questions for Reflection and Discussion _____

1. How have abuses and distortions of the concept of submission made it difficult for a woman to function according to God's design?

2. In what ways does the context of mutual submission make a wife's submission to her husband more reasonable than many people assume?

3. In what ways does a wife's role meet her husband's needs? What can a husband do to create a safe environment for his wife to fulfill her role?

4. If you are a woman, what is the most challenging aspect of your role as described by Ephesians 5? What mental shifts would you need to make to trust God's process and your part in his choreography?

5. If you are a man, what changes do you need to make to help your wife step more fully into her role in the relationship?

5

The Evolution
of the American Woman

Before we go any further, I want you to know I'm deeply aware that the preceding chapter may have been difficult to swallow. If you're thirty-five or younger, it may have sounded like a foreign language from another planet. No matter how diplomatically and sensitively I present it, and no matter how much biblical support I use to communicate a woman's role in marriage, it still comes across as counter to our culture's pervasive beliefs. It is difficult for many women to fathom.

So I asked my wife to share her perspective and experience in living out a role that is so at odds with today's cultural values.

Over the past several years, I have had the privilege of leading a Bible study in my home called *Five Aspects of Woman: A*

Biblical Theology of Femininity, written by Barbara Mouser. It has been around for many years but is not very well known. We do an in-depth study of what the Bible says about the feminine gender. Every time I go through it, I become more aware of how wonderful it is to be a woman in the way God created us to be. God did not create us to be servants or to be used and abused. He created us in his very own image with a much bigger picture in mind of who we are. We are the crown of his creation, and we are made to reflect the relationship that Christ has with his treasured church. God has given us the authority and responsibility to nurture, rule over, and bear fruit in what he has entrusted to us.

God's truth about femininity is the same for every woman. In my group right now, there are young singles, older singles, young married women, engaged women, career women, stay-at-home moms, and grandmothers. We come from all over the world, and we have varying levels of education. Some of us come from very difficult backgrounds, and some come from great Christian homes. We are all made in God's image, he loves us dearly, and we all have a purpose to fulfill in this life that will bring glory to him.

In our first Bible study session, one of the questions is, "Do you like being a woman?" I am always concerned when many group members respond that they do not necessarily like being a woman. They believe that men, throughout history and still today, have had more opportunities, more pay, and more recognition, and they have taken advantage of and oppressed women. Many women are fed up and get mad and fight back, as the radical feminist movement encourages us to do. Those of us who are not radical also feel the tension and challenges of being a woman in the twenty-first century.

Yet as women study God's truth about what it means to be a woman and they begin to get the "big picture" and the "right picture" of who they are—as they see themselves through God's eyes and understand his great plan for them—many learn to fully appreciate being a woman. We are not door-mats for men to wipe their feet on! We are made in the image of God with gifts and abilities, women who have been given responsibility, capability, and authority to change our world and bring great glory to him.

I am amazed by the stories Theresa shares with me about the transformation in these women's lives. They are wrestling with the big questions that women face in the twenty-first century: "What am I supposed to do with my life? I have so many voices and so many expectations about what it means to be a woman. How does a woman know what is most important, what to give her life to, and why?"

As their identity gets rooted in who God made them to be, they begin to have a new confidence. As they embrace what makes a woman flourish and discover what she needs to get and what she needs to give, they peel away old paradigms and prisons of external expectations. People from liberal and conservative backgrounds surrender their preconceived no-tions and get a fresh, new vision of what it means to be a woman. The positive changes that follow in them and in their relationships are amazing to behold.

So before we talk about practical ways to be an Ephesians 5 wife, I think it will be helpful to discuss the evolution of the American woman. As with the changes men have expe-rienced, the cultural transformation that has occurred in the last fifty to sixty years with regard to women has made biblical marriage more difficult than ever before.

The Evolution of the American Woman

While I was researching material for this book, I had a conversation on an airplane with a young woman—a different one from the woman I talked with in chapter 4. She had been thinking a lot about what to do with her life. She had just finished grad school, was already pretty far along a successful career path, and was about to get engaged. "But," she said, "there are so many voices in my head, I just don't know what to do."

"What do you mean?" I asked.

"Well, I've finished school, spent all this money on a degree, and have a great career, but I want to be married and have kids. I'm already thirty-two, and if we get married and wait three or four years, I'll be in my midthirties when I have children, so we probably won't have many. And I really want to be home with my kids to raise them, but my friends tell me that I'd be wasting my education. I'm not sure my fiancé and I are on the same page. My mom says one thing, my aunt says another, and then I read about people and the choices they have made—it's like all of a sudden, I'm wondering what it means to be a woman. What am I supposed to do with my life?"

I think a lot of women have similar thoughts, though many may not articulate these feelings as clearly as this young woman did. She was right about the voices speaking to her;

they come from all directions, and some of them are pretty critical of motherhood.

I've encountered an attitude, I think especially common in Europe—motivated by concerns about boosting national economies—that undermines mothers staying at home. In fact, I remember hearing the term "waster" applied to mothers who don't work outside the home. It seems that struggling economies in some countries are more important than strengthening families.

Wasters? That attitude is blind to the noneconomic factors of a woman staying at home with her kids.

A stay-at-home mom is there for the first six to eight years of a child's life, when 80 percent of a child's brain and personality is being formed—how they feel about themselves, their confidence, their moral values, their sense of identity, their understanding of their place in the world.[1] Some people would encourage women to completely outsource their childcare during those critical years—to pay someone else minimum wage to handle the most critical years of a human being's life. I'm not saying it is wrong for women to work outside the home or to expect men to share in the parenting load (unlike in generations past). My point is that we need to recognize the almost universal devaluation of motherhood and its impact on the family and society. And all I want to say is, "How is that working?"

To understand how we got to this point, we need to look back at the bigger historical picture and especially the last few decades. Womanhood has its blessings, the miracle of childbirth and motherhood among them. But womanhood also comes with its own set of challenges, many of them deeply embedded in cultural biases and perceptions. In this case, we're going even further back in time to examine some of the roots of the negative perception of women. And I'll begin not with the Bible but with the contexts it came from—ancient Jewish, Greek, and Roman cultures.

The Old Testament is not disparaging toward women, but Jewish culture during the time of Jesus had a pretty low view of them. Women were often viewed as servants or property. At every stage in life, a woman was considered to be under the care and supervision of a man—a father, a husband, or a son—and those who weren't (e.g., widows, especially childless ones) were considered especially vulnerable. Women were not considered in Jewish law to be valid witnesses—one of the main subthemes behind the disciples' doubt over the testimony of the women who had come back from Jesus's empty tomb. One attitude of men during that time, expressed in Jewish prayer books in later centuries (and even today), is reflected in a daily prayer in which a man thanks God for not making him a Gentile, a slave, or a woman. As much as men may have valued their wives, they considered them lower in status.

The Greeks were often worse. Marriage was arranged, divorce was easy (for the husband), and women were generally forced into one of three roles.

> We have courtesans for pleasure, we have concubines for the sake of daily cohabitation, and we have wives for the purpose of having children legitimately and being faithful guardians of our household affairs.[2]

As this quote from a fifth-century BC Athenian orator suggests, men found their pleasures outside of marriage: fornication and prostitution were rampant. Greek men had a wife for housekeeping and bearing legitimate children, another woman for meeting sexual and companion needs, and access to prostitutes when they wanted to satisfy urges at other times.

When Paul writes in 1 Timothy 3:2 that an overseer must be the husband of one wife, he is not talking about men in a second or third marriage after their wives have died. The phrase he uses literally means "a one-woman man" because many Greeks were three- or four-women men, having relationships with several women even when they were married to only one.[3]

Among Romans, divorce was much more common. Jerome, translator of the Bible into Latin in the AD 400s, wrote of one Roman woman who was married for the twenty-third time, and she was her husband's twenty-first wife.[4] That was by no means standard, but neither was it uncommon. To some, marriage was nothing more than legalized prostitution.

Of course, injustice toward women is not confined to ancient times or traditional cultures. Historically, the world has not been a great place for women. Rights and freedoms have not been fair or equitable between the sexes at most times and in most places. That's a historical fact. Women could not vote in the United States until 1920; in Switzerland, they could not vote until 1971. In 1960s America, a woman who wanted to rent an apartment or get credit had to have a male relative sign for her. Apparently, women were not considered responsible enough to pay their bills.

103

As you know, we have experienced a huge cultural trans-formation. Women have gone well beyond voting and pur-chasing on credit; many run businesses, serve in legislatures, invent new technologies, run for president, and excel at law and medicine. In fact, there are more women than men in medical school in the United States right now.[5] Women's movements have accomplished a lot in a relatively short time.

Feminism versus Radical Feminism

"Feminism" is not a negative word. It may be a controver-sial one, depending on your perspective, but it is not bad. *Merriam-Webster's Collegiate Dictionary* defines it as "the theory of the political, economic, and social equality of the sexes." People may argue over the application of that defi-nition, but the core principle should be well accepted. Equal-ity between men and women is a good thing.

But feminism and *radical* feminism are two different things. Somehow the movement for women's rights transitioned in the '70s from gaining equality to labeling men as the source of all injustices. A magazine playing on the acronym for the National Organization for Women once declared that "NOW is the time to take back control of our lives. . . . NOW is the time to drop the boot heel in the groin of pa-triarchy, NOW is the time to fight back. No god, no master, no laws."[6] Women's studies programs were birthed in the '70s at women's colleges such as Wellesley and Smith as well as at larger universities, where they are now common. Though women's studies itself is certainly a legitimate field of inquiry, many programs originated with strong agendas.

One author suggested that some women's studies programs should publish the following warning label as an honest expression of their intent:

> We will help your daughter discover the extent to which she has been in complicity with the patriarchy. We will encourage her to restructure herself through dialogue with us. She may become enraged and chronically offended. She will very likely reject the religious and moral codes you raised her with. She may well distance herself from family and friends. She may change her appearance, and even her sexual orientation. She may end up hating you (her father) and pitying you (her mother). After she has completed her reeducation with us, you will certainly be out tens of thousands of dollars and very possibly be out one daughter as well.[7]

Some brands of radical feminism certainly come across that way. In other words, men are the problem behind everything.

USA Today cited a study spanning the '70s, '80s, and '90s that examined how women's values had changed over time.[8] In 1920, only one out of every five women worked outside the home. By 1990, between 75 and 80 percent did. But something happened in the 1980s. Women in the survey felt that they had two full-time jobs—one outside the home and one at home, with no time for pursuing other personal interests or relationships. Juggling a career and motherhood was perhaps manageable for some, but most found it overwhelmingly stressful.

Contrasting the world of 1920 to today, violence is up, divorce is up, test scores are down, teen suicide is up, and depression is up. Many of these trends can be traced to the absence of fathers in the home, but the unavailability of mothers and the breakdown of traditional family models are contributing factors. Women felt liberated for a time and in many ways still do, and much worthwhile progress has been made. But side effects have accompanied that progress, and not all of them are good.

We have seen how the changing definitions of family have led to the disintegration of this foundational social unit. Incomes have risen dramatically for men and women as both genders have sought multiple jobs and higher pay, and some families have ended up with two, three, or even four incomes. But that comes at a cost.

Parents with such strong career-oriented drives have little time left over for parenting. And as we have seen, research shows that 80 percent of a child's personality—moral values and sense of identity—are formed in his or her first six to eight years. Too many children have been entrusted to caretakers outside the family at early ages because cultural trends have brainwashed women into believing they are not valuable unless they have a certain career or earn a certain income. Despite wonderful exceptions of believers living out their faith in family life, the culture of our day is characterized by kids who are under-nurtured, confused, and prone to depression and addiction.

Is It Better or Worse Now?

Let me be absolutely clear that the inequalities of the past had to change. Feminism has accomplished a great deal in establishing justice and equality for women. But the extreme positions and the blaming that radical feminism encourages have had destructive effects, and they compel us to ask a fundamental question: Are women's lives, marriages, and families better in the aftermath of all our politically correct experiments, or are they worse?

To answer that question, I think we have to address the core issue: What kind of life will actually lead to a woman's maximum fulfillment? Women would address that issue in a variety of different ways, and a successful career may well be the right choice for some. But if we're looking for God's design in the marriage relationship, we need to explore what embracing biblical femininity looks like and to address questions of how much energy a wife and mother needs to devote to her marriage and family.

God's blueprint leaves plenty of room for options, but it also gives us the key to making marriages work and being good parents. He has created us with certain needs that can only be satisfied in certain ways, and the only way to reach our full potential and find ultimate fulfillment is to honor his design.

God's Design for Wives

How does God define womanhood in our marriages and homes? His design has not changed along with our cultural trends; it does not go up and down, rising and falling with every movement or study or philosophy. I think we can acknowledge that as much as biblical masculinity has been distorted throughout human history, biblical femininity has been distorted even more.

The idea of womanhood has been twisted and abused and turned against the very people it should honor. That has been true from ancient times until today, though the abuses have taken various forms at various times. But we have to acknowledge that today's culture is hardly any better at defining womanhood than past cultures have been because families are disintegrating, divorces are commonplace, children are confused, and the social consequences related to the breakdown of the family—addictions, poverty, and crime, to name a few—are still a huge problem. We have missed God's design for deep, intimate marriages that are satisfying to both partners, that create homes where love and security flourish, and that remain stable over time.

We have explored God's design for womanhood and how women fit into the dance of marriage God has choreographed for our maximum fulfillment, but in no way am I trying to turn back the clock to a time when women were controlled by men and confined to the home with few options of their own.

> *We can point to Scripture and say that it contains the key to understanding how God created us as men and women.*

We cannot point to any era in the past and say that was when things were done right. What we can do is point to Scripture and say that it contains the key to understanding how God created us as men and women, and that his plan for women is far better than any definition society has given us in the past.

So what does it look like for a wife to submit to her husband in a biblical marriage?

Early in our marriage, one of my less than loving behaviors was causing regular conflict between Theresa and me. Because I was working and going to school full-time, I felt entitled to a little pickup basketball after work. Sometimes, if I would get on a good team, we would keep winning—and if you win, you get to keep playing. I would lose all track of time, would not call Theresa, and would arrive home after our family supper.

She was understanding until it became a regular occurrence. When my apologies and promises to change (or at least call) were followed by the same habitual behavior, it became a source of constant conflict in our marriage. In my mind, I was entitled to a little fun and she was being unreasonable. In reality, I was habitually insensitive, defensive when confronted with my behavior, and unwilling to change.

The results were predictable. Theresa and I would have a fight. She wouldn't talk to me for two days, we would roll opposite ways in bed, I'd stuff my anger, she would be cold and unaffectionate, and I would quote verses to her about what a wife is supposed to do.

This became a chronic issue. I learned quickly that a good offense is better than a bad defense, so sometimes when I came home late, I would find something wrong and get on her about it right away before she had a chance to condemn me for missing supper. Yeah, we had some pretty dysfunctional ways of dealing with conflict, but we were young and didn't know any better.

I still remember the turning point. It was when Theresa applied this principle of a submissive spirit. I came in from playing basketball (late as usual). There were two candles on the table and I was waiting for the backlash. I knew the routine. But this time it was different.

She said, "If you want to sit down, your food is in the oven. I kept it warm for you." There was no hint of anger in her voice.

It felt like a trap, but I didn't say anything. I just began eating.

"Do you like it? I hope so. I worked all day. I just had thoughts of how much I love you, and I spent all day making this meal for you because I really wanted to communicate how much I care about you."

Part of me wanted her to step up and fight, because deep down I knew I was wrong. But it felt way better than our usual fight. So I kept eating as the candles burned about halfway down, and she kept saying kind and loving things. She calmly addressed the situation.

"I know we have our differences. But I feel deeply hurt when I spend all day doing something to express my love for you and then you just miss it. It feels like you don't love me."

That was like a dagger in my heart. I had never made the connection between our meals and her love for me. Not once. I had only thought about my rights, my time, and my need to work out. And she had only nagged me about her expectations, which always led to a fight.

Now, her willingness to love me and share her hurt with a submissive, tender spirit made me see the imbalance and gave her the opportunity to express her feelings in a way I understood. In that moment, with tears in my eyes, I looked at her and realized that if these meals meant love, I would be there for them. When I saw that I was hurting her, which I would never want to do on purpose, I made a decision. She changed my heart.

The way she got through to me was not by insisting that I see things her way but by doing what God said. When you relate to your husband with a gentle and submissive spirit, there is power. By contrast, when a woman sounds more like a mother than a wife with words like, "You ought . . . you should . . . you always . . . you never . . . ," men respond poorly.

> When you relate to your husband with a gentle and submissive spirit, there is power.

Nothing good happens when grown men hear their wives talking to them like their mothers did. (That works both ways, by the way; no woman wants to hear her husband telling her what to do like a father would.) That's a certain recipe for all kinds of problems, especially with regard to intimacy and sex. It creates a dynamic that alienates and deepens the conflict.

Theresa's attitude spoke to my heart and accomplished something that nagging or complaining never could. It was her greatest ally in bringing about the change she wanted.

What Submission Does *Not* Mean

Because the idea of submission comes with so much baggage, many people attach negative meanings to it that just aren't there in the biblical context. In the last section, we discussed what submission does mean, but I also want to caution you about what it does not mean.

It does not mean you are to be passive or feel inferior.

Submission does not imply being stepped on. Being a doormat is not God's design for your life; that isn't in his blueprint.

My wife at times gives people the impression that she is very sweet and agreeable, and she is. But there is a strength underneath that not everyone sees. When we have a disagreement, she brings it. She is respectful, but she is strong and powerful. She has deep convictions and important opinions and presents them in a calm but persuasive manner. She does not say, "Whatever you think, dear." She brings up her objections, points out my contradictions, and does a great job of expressing her thoughts and reasoning. Her submission comes after we have hashed out a lot of details and thoroughly talked through an issue. There is nothing passive about her approach, yet it is solidly biblical and it works. A good leader wants his wife to bring her strengths, thoughts, gifts, and even her best arguments to the table.

> A good leader wants his wife to bring her strengths, thoughts, gifts, and even her best arguments to the table.

It does not mean submitting only when you think he is right.

Submission is not the same as agreement. The test of submission is when you think to yourself, *This may be one of the dumbest things he has ever done. I've made my case, laid out the evidence, passionately argued, and he still thinks he is right and that this is what God wants him to do.* Are you still on board then? That's submission.

And all you can do in that situation is ask God to protect you both from bad mistakes and to work all things together for good, which he has already promised to do anyway.

I remember making a decision that Theresa disagreed with. It wasn't necessarily the wrong decision, but the way I did it and the timing of it was not wise. Theresa said, "I will go with you because the Bible commands me, and I will choose to have a good attitude. But I don't want to, and I don't think it's wise. In fact, I think it's pretty unwise. Nevertheless, I'm with you."

As it turns out, it *was* a dumb idea, and we paid a pretty big price for it. Graciously, Theresa never said, "I told you so." She gave me room to grow, learn, and continue to lead.

It does not mean you violate Scripture, reason, or morality to support your husband.

If your husband is leading you to lie, cheat, be unethical, be immoral, or anything else that clearly violates godly character, you submit to God and his Word rather than to your husband.

Some men come up with some pretty bizarre ideas and in-sist that their wives follow their leadership, but there is a difference between following your husband's bad idea and following his sinfulness. The percentage of adult Christian men who regularly view pornography has in some research topped 50 percent.[9] It would be logical to assume that these men, if married, might increasingly view their wives as an object to satisfy their lust—rather than a precious partner to cherish. Like Abigail in the Old Testament who wisely and strongly opposed her carnal and evil husband Nabal, wives at times must strongly stand against any kind of abuse or behavior that is demeaning or unwanted in the sexual relationship. First and foremost, you submit to a higher authority. If God has forbidden something, you should not let your husband lead you into it.

It does not mean you use submission as a tool to get your way.

It is possible to fake submission for a time in order to get your way in the end. I've had more than a few men share with me over the years that their wives can be really sweet and submissive at times only to discover their hidden agenda that involved remodeling the kitchen or changing their husbands' minds about a previous roadblock. (Men, of course, are guilty of the same false servanthood and leadership to get what they want.) Submission is not a tool to get your way. In fact, it has much less to do with your relationship with your husband than it does with your relationship with your heavenly Father.

Bringing It Home: Now What?

For better or worse, women, like men, are in many ways the product of their environment. The primary role model for a girl is her mom. You may have had an amazing, kind, godly mother who had wonderful priorities. She may have been a stay-at-home mom or one like mine who worked and still had the energy to be emotionally available, supervise the household, and be the glue for meals, family activities, vacations, and conflict resolution.

I would encourage you to take a minute to list the top four or five qualities you most admire about your mother. You might also list two or three things you don't want to emulate. My point is simply to get you to think about what you have consciously and unconsciously picked up from your family of origin with regard to the roles of being a woman, wife, and mother.

On the other hand, your mother may not have been around or available as often as you would have liked, or she may have been emotionally distant, preoccupied with her own issues, or focused on her work or a husband other than your father. Family life has become very messy in recent times, and the increasing number of divorces and blended families has created significant confusion for young and not-so-young women as they work through their identities. In confusing or unusual situations, how can a woman grow into the kind of woman described in Ephesians 5?

Tools for Becoming an Ephesians 5 Woman

The tools listed at the end of chapter 3 for becoming an Ephesians 5 man—*The Daily Walk Bible*, *The Five Love Languages*, and *True Spirituality* (on the kind of discipleship described in Romans 12)—are just as relevant for women. Wives will find that these resources can revolutionize the ways they relate to their husband. The following tools and practices are recommended by Theresa. They've proven to be extremely helpful to women in their spiritual and relational journey.

- Read and meditate on God's Word. Scripture promotes its own role in your life again and again: "Your word is a lamp for my feet, a light on my path" (Ps. 119:105); "You are my refuge and my shield; I have put my hope in your word" (Ps. 119:114). Many other verses declare the benefits of immersing yourself in biblical truth. Whether you use a tool like *The Daily Walk Bible* or another Bible or reading plan, the daily practice of reminding yourself of truth is life-changing. Make it a priority.

- Barbara Mouser's *Five Aspects of Woman*, an in-depth study on biblical femininity. It can help reorient your perspective to understand God's design and resist the distorted messages about femininity in today's culture.

- Affirmation cards from the series that Theresa taught entitled "Precious in His Sight." These principles provide the foundation of a positive, biblical self image. (livingontheedge.org/marriagethatworksresources)

- Here are three other regular practices that will help you become the woman God designed you to be:

  (a) Join with other women to study God's Word and pray for one another.

  (b) Pray for your husband daily.

(c) Pray for yourself. Ask according to Proverbs 31:12 that you would bring your husband good, not harm, all the days of your life.

Up to now, we've talked a lot about the roles of men and women in the marriage dance and what each partner is supposed to do. But knowing what to do and how to do it are two different things. In the remaining chapters, we are going to dive deeper into the "how" and develop a picture of what the choreography of this dance looks like in practical terms. We will move from the big picture to the real-life application—and a more fulfilling marriage and family life.

_____ **Questions for Reflection and Discussion** _____

1. In what ways do you think traditional definitions of womanhood have fallen short? In what ways do you think modern definitions of womanhood have fallen short?

2. What are some of the challenges women face in modern Western culture?

3. If you are a woman, in what ways have you experienced tension between the desires for career and family? How have you balanced those desires?

4. How would you answer the fundamental question of whether women's lives are better because of the "politically correct" experiments of recent times?

6

What's a Man to Do?

Imagine being one of several men chosen for a critical mission. Part of your preparation means entering US Marines special-ops training. It's a nine-month course, and on day one, the commander introduces the program.

"Men," he says, "you are about to go through the most difficult training of your life. Your commitment to stay on track and have each other's back will determine whether you live or die. If you are successful, you will save tens of thousands of lives. If not, you will die. So will those tens of thousands of lives."

The pressure is on. It's time to step up. Envision it: treading water for an hour nonstop with clothes and boots on, running twelve miles carrying forty-five pounds of gear, being dropped into extreme conditions that demand survival skills, mastering battle and marksmanship skills, and more. You and your band of brothers have to make quick decisions, keep your commitments, and stretch yourself far harder and deeper than you ever thought you could go. But in the process, you will change the world.

A God-Centered Worldview

That's the spirit in which Moses pulled together the next generation of leaders after enduring a forty-year trek through the wilderness and watching many of his companions fail. Many died out of disobedience. They thus did not fulfill the mission or keep their commitment.

So in his last words to the assembled tribes of Israel, Moses spoke bluntly to their leaders, their men. He reminded them of the commandments God had given and how those decrees were to be instilled in their children and their children's children. He described what it means to fear God and how God rewards obedience with long life and fruitfulness.

These instructions would be essential to remember because the people of Israel would be entering a land filled with diverse gods and goddesses, blatant idolatry, and rampant perversion. So Moses assured the people that there was only one God, and this God's desire for his people was all-encompassing: "Love the LORD your God with all your heart and with all your soul and with all your strength" (Deut. 6:5).

Then he gave them a picture of what that kind of devotion should look like. They were to teach God's ways to their children, formally and informally—to provide instruction and then to impress it on their hearts by talking about it when they got up, when they lay down, and when they went about their business.

Far more than giving them information, God, through Moses, was giving his people a worldview to shape their lives. Why? So he could bless and prosper them as expressions of his love.

The temptations in the land of prosperity would be great; the human heart tends to drift away in times of abundance. But there would be consequences because God is jealous for the love of his people. To bring them back, he would allow them to experience hardships that would make a Marine's special-ops training look like a walk in the park.

Your God-Given Assignment

That scenario in Deuteronomy, when Moses was preparing the people for the special mission of entering into the Promised Land and serving God faithfully, highlights principles that are extremely relevant for us today, especially for men as leaders in their homes. In this chapter, we are going to explore what God wants men to do. We have already looked at a description of the role and discussed what it means to *be* a real man, but here we learn what a man is to *do*—his responsibilities.

Men, you need to know that your God-given assignment can be extremely rewarding but also pretty intense. It requires commitment, and you can't do it alone. You may not have many role models to look at for inspiration; not many of us do. I got the Marine part of a father, not the Christian part, as I was growing up. But if you are willing to embrace a picture different from what our culture teaches, you will be richly rewarded.

> Men, you need to know that your God-given assignment can be extremely rewarding but also pretty intense.

You will become the kind of man who attracts the kind of woman you dream about and helps her grow into the woman of your dreams. You will become the kind of man that your sons want to emulate and your daughters want to marry. You will learn to walk with the integrity and character that reflects the nature of God and prepares you to receive his best for your life.

Show Me the Box Top

I have a friend near Lake Tahoe who often lets me get away to his A-frame house to spend some time with family or to focus on study. Once when I was visiting him there, I walked in to see a coffee table covered with a beautiful picture. I looked a little closer and realized it was made up of thousands of separate pieces that had come out of a box sitting nearby.

I have never been very good at puzzles. "If my life depended on it," I told him, "I could never do something like that."

"Oh no, Chip, you really could," he assured me. "Here's the key. You just have to have the box top. If you can see the picture, all you need to do is take it a step at a time."

He walked me through his process of finding all the border pieces, then grouping the remaining pieces by color and piecing them together bit by bit. "If you do it little by little, have a lot of patience, and realize it's a journey, you could put that whole thing together yourself. It all depends on looking at the box top."

That's exactly the advice I want to give men in this chapter. You are going to get the biblical equivalent of a special-ops Marine box top in the next few pages—the job description Scripture gives you for being a man, a husband, and a father.

If you look at it as a to-do list or something you need to accomplish in a few weeks, you will lose heart and give up. But if you see it as a pathway, a journey toward being the man you were created to be, with a marriage and a life you were created to have, you will grow into the picture you see. You will become what you envision, and in that transformation you will make a difference in your home, your work, your neighborhood, and everywhere you have influence. You will fulfill your mission.

My father did the best he could, given his life experiences. I've told you a little of his story—how he struggled with alcoholism and his memories of the war, and how he came to Christ at the age of fifty-five. His dad died when he was thirteen, so he didn't have a clear picture of fatherhood to grow into, and he didn't know how to give me a clear picture either. So when I married Theresa, who had been abandoned shortly after her twin boys were born, I was immediately a husband and father of four-year-olds at the same time; and I had no idea how to fulfill either of those roles.

I have been in special-ops training for more than three decades to progressively become the kind of man that my sons would want to be like, that my daughter would want to marry, and that my wife would want to tell her friends about. They are all aware of my flaws and know I have a lot of growing to do, but I want them to see the heart of God in my love for them. And I want them to pass that same heart down to future generations.

Finding the Right Picture

Knowing your role as a husband is one thing; living it out is another. What exactly are you supposed to do? What does your leadership look like in your marriage and your home? What does it mean to step up in love? What do real men do?

Society does not give us the right box top for this puzzle. We get all sorts of images of manhood, but as we have seen, most are unreliable, and even the good examples are often mixed with distorted elements. We get pieces of the puzzle, but we need the picture on the top of the box to show us how to put it together.

> Knowing your role as a husband is one thing; living it out is another.

You have entered into the dance, which we discussed in chapter 2. You have stepped up in love. What does that look like for a real man? Scripture tells us that you need to provide, protect, and nurture.

That covers a lot of territory. Most of us men understand the financial-provision part of this instruction, but we tend to struggle more with the spiritual and emotional parts. But the biblical picture covers all of it.

This is a comprehensive calling into manhood, and it flows out of sacrificial love as demonstrated by Christ's love for the church and depicted in Ephesians 5. We are going to look at these three specific areas—providing, protecting, and nurturing—through the lens of some other verses of Scripture that fill out the picture for us. What we're going to see is that the New Testament version of being a nonconformist, like the picture Moses gave the Israelites in Deuteronomy, requires a heart commitment and skills that can change the course of a whole family's destiny.

We'll continue our discussion of a man's responsibility in the following three chapters, each with questions and resources to help you digest and think through the implications of God's design for you in your marriage.

7

Stepping Up as a Man: *Provide*

As a man, you are to provide financially for your family. That does not mean that your wife must always stay at home and never have a job. It also does not mean that you are less of a man if you go through a period of unemployment or struggle in your path toward financial security.

It does mean, however, that the burden of responsibility for providing for the physical needs of your wife and children, of making sure the bills get paid, and of staying out of unreasonable or unwise debt is on your shoulders.

"But if anyone does not provide for his own, and especially for those of his household, he has denied the faith and is worse than an unbeliever" (1 Tim. 5:8 NASB). The translation of that verse is that the welfare of the home is the man's moral responsibility.

You are the family's chief financial officer, the CFO. If the numbers don't add up, you can't blame the accountants. You're the man. If there is not enough money to go around or if your debt ratio gets too high, it will be on your shoulders, and you will be the one who has to address the underlying issues and implement changes.

Your wife can certainly help out, but there may be times when her family responsibilities don't allow her to earn income. Your job is to take the pressure off her and declare that you own the moral responsibility to provide food, shelter, and clothing not only now but also in the future.

Please don't translate the last paragraph to mean you're all alone in this or that you need to make all the decisions or handle all the finances; what we're talking about is who holds the moral weight and responsibility for the finances. As I outline the five major financial objectives for your finances, know there are a number of practical ways to accomplish these that will vary from family to family based on skill and giftedness.

Five Financial Objectives

The following five specific objectives go along with financial responsibility:

1. Do honest work.

2. Honor God first.

3. Live within your means.

4. Prepare for the future.

5. Train your children.

1. Do honest work.

The first objective starts with you. Your wife and children need to see your example of what it means to work hard and work well, with diligence and integrity. No shortcuts, no cheating. "Whatever you do, work at it with all your heart, as working for the Lord, not for human masters" (Col. 3:23).

When you apply diligence and integrity to your career responsibilities as well as household tasks, you are setting an example of someone working primarily for the Lord rather than human beings. In a very real sense, your work is ultimately an act of worship. One of the

> *In a very real sense, your work is ultimately an act of worship.*

greatest gifts you can pass on to your children is a strong, clear work ethic. It will change their lives. So do your work with excellence.

2. Honor God first.

You are the steward of your finances. You may get a paycheck once a week, twice a month, once a month, or only on commission. However it looks for you, your income came from the hand of God before it passed through the hands of your employer or your clients. You are the manager of his money, the steward of whatever he has entrusted to you. You need to live and handle money and possessions with that mindset.

The clearest way to maintain that stewardship mindset is to give your first and best back to him. When you do, you make a statement that he is the one in control and that you trust him.

In the Old Testament, the first and best was usually the pick of your livestock or the first of your harvest. In a money economy, that became a 10 percent tithe—not an afterthought after all the bills are paid, but right off the top. That number is not a maximum and it's not a legalist "bill" to pay. It's a statement of faith and step of obedience; as you get older and your income increases, you can increase your percentage to give even more. And yes, in times of financial crisis, God may give you different specifics to be able to honor him while still making ends meet.

But in general, this is a foundational way that you express your love and trust to the One who has provided you with the means to earn a living and support your family. You are the CFO of your family, but God is the CEO of the universe, and his blessing comes to those who trust him. It takes a step of faith to model that perspective for your wife and children. And God promises to provide for your needs (Phil. 4:19) and bless your life in ways far beyond money (Luke 6:38).

3. Live within your means.

Make sure you have more money coming in than going out. That may make things really tight sometimes, and that's okay. Most families look back on lean times with fondness because they know they accomplished something difficult together.

The alternative is much worse. Indebtedness can enslave you. At the very least, it limits your freedom later. The average college student is $28,950 in debt;[1] many of them file for bankruptcy before they ever start their careers. They have learned from their parents and their culture that debt is a way of life, and they have not yet learned to discipline themselves. Because of their debts, many young adults are not able to follow God's leading into careers like ministry and missions, or they are forced to delay marriage or begin family life with extraordinary financial pressure. Their debt has taken their freedom. Fathers are strategy number one for preventing that tragedy, and it begins by modeling for the family how to live within your means.

I made my way through seminary by selling insurance and investments. I regularly met people who made six- and seven-figure incomes but had cash-flow problems. The issue was never their amount of income; it was discipline in managing their expenses and lifestyle choices. Most people figure out how to spend their income easily, and then they stretch beyond it just a little bit. Pretty soon, they are wrestling with overwhelming debt, even though their income was good to begin with.

We live in a culture that teaches us to buy now and pay later. As the financial managers of our families, we have to set the pace and go against the trends of the culture. Real men, godly men, live within their means.

4. Prepare for the future.

I've read that the average American today saves only around 2 percent of his or her income, and many don't save anything at all.[2] The days when most families saved for the future are gone. You need to have a savings plan, even if you start with what seems like an insignificant amount. When Theresa and I started saving, we had three kids and I was making only $1,800 a month as pastor of a tiny church. But we put away $50 each month for retirement. Developing the practice and the discipline is far more important than the amount.

In addition, you really do need to have a will. You need life insurance. Someone needs to know where your savings and investments are. You may need a financial planner to help. Perhaps you expect to live a long life (I hope you do!), but the majority of Christian men have not made provisions for their families in case of their deaths. It's one of those things we keep procrastinating on that just has to get done. Preparing for your family's future with or without you is your moral responsibility as leader of your home.

5. Train your children.

Many faith-based financial trainers have taught us about the beauty of compound interest. They recommend a simple formula to help our children learn the basics of financial management. It's the 10/10/80 principle: give the first 10 percent to the Lord, save the next 10 percent, and live on the last 80 percent.

If we as adults modeled this basic plan and taught our children the same, we would avoid some of life's biggest problems. Most, though, have not been taught to do this (see point 3, "Live within your means"). Marriages end over issues like this. Many people get divorced not because they stop loving each other but because they don't have enough money and start arguing about whose fault it is.

But when we step up as men and put our family's financial security on our shoulders, we change the destructive patterns that many in our society never overcome. It can be extremely difficult at first, and it may have to begin with very small steps. That was certainly true for me, but the payoff has been way beyond the pain. Looking at how my grown children handle their money and the pitfalls they missed because of that make all the challenges seem minor today.

It's easy to get caught up in the details of what to do and what not to do as you live out these objectives, so I want to turn our focus to the core values behind them. Being a man is not a legalistic list of details to remember; it's an expression of who you really are and what you really believe—the true you God designed you to be. It's about letting Christ transform your nature and then living out of your true identity.

The objectives I've listed will help you get started and measure your progress, but they are simply the outcomes of the core values you embrace. Let's take a deeper look at the root of these objectives.

Your Core Values as Provider

One of those values is a Christlike work ethic. Beyond just owning this value for yourself as you approach your work, it is critical for you to instill it in your children. Theresa and I started when our children were very young.

We showed them how to make the bed and take out the garbage. When they got older, we let them help out with cooking, dishes, and laundry. We gave them an alarm clock so they would learn to get themselves up and ready for school.

Feed your children more responsibility, in appropriate measures, so they become more independent from you and more dependent on God. Yes, it takes time and it's far easier to just do things for them. But it's in this process that they form positive habits and gain confidence and strong self-worth. As you live out the work ethic you want your children to emulate, you're preparing them for success in whatever God calls them to do.

Another core value is stewardship of time and money. This means more than giving a portion of income. It is a mindset, an attitude, a biblical worldview that you're seeking to help your children develop. We began teaching our kids the 10/10/80 principle when they were about two years old. We put three jars on each of their dressers. Each had a label: one said "Giving"; another, "Saving"; and the third, "Spending."

> Feed your children more responsibility, in appropriate measures, so they become more independent from you and more dependent on God.

Early on, they would get ten pennies for picking up their toys or doing some other basic task, then we increased it to dimes, quarters, and dollars as they grew. It was a visual picture of how they would eventually structure their budgets as adults. They learned that everything belongs to God and that there were always opportunities to be generous—with a visiting missionary, a sponsored child whose picture we put on our re-frigerator, a fund-raising drive, or the church offering plate. They also learned that the longer they saved, the more they could buy—the gift of delayed gratification. If they wanted to splurge on something like designer jeans or expensive sneakers, we would contribute what we would have spent on normal jeans or shoes and let them earn the rest. We set the pace for them to follow.

How you use money is just a symptom of a mindset, but it reflects your true values. It is a good indication of how you view your stewardship. You have to be a little more creative to teach your children how to manage their time, but the principle is the same: it all comes from God, and we want to learn, and we have to be responsible in how we use it.

Jesus talked more about money than about heaven and hell combined, not because God needs our money but because our hearts will be wherever our treasure is. He also talked about time—using it wisely to be fruit-ful and be ready for his return—because that's a reflection of our values too. It is a matter of stewardship, of responsibil-ity, and of personal discipline. These are challenging things to practice, let alone teach our kids, but they are important issues in God's economy. And as a man, it's my responsibility to make them important issues at home.

> *How you use money is just a symptom of a mindset, but it reflects your true values.*

Finally, stewardship isn't all about discipline and self-denial. God actually commands us to celebrate and enjoy the good gifts he brings into our lives. Paul warns against putting too much hope in riches, but he also tells us that God gives all things for us richly to enjoy (1 Tim. 6:17). Sometimes you need to go out for an amazing meal or have a great vacation.

God actually commands us to celebrate and enjoy the good gifts he brings into our lives.

Plan for those things, and don't go into debt for them. But don't be afraid to enjoy the gifts God has given you. Live with joy and generosity, and your children will grow up with a healthy understanding of the goodness of God.

There's a lot to process here. Let me encourage you to willfully set aside some time to let this content sink in. I've developed some questions and resources to help you with that.

————— Questions for Reflection and Discussion —————

1. What was most helpful in this chapter for you? Why?

2. Which of the five practices discussed in this chapter do you find come most naturally to you?

3. Which of the five practices do you sense needs some additional attention or focus from you? Why?

4. What's the biggest barrier or challenge you are facing in providing for your wife? Your family?

5. Who could help you take those next steps to provide for your family the way you want and need to?

Recommended Resources

Master Your Money, by Ron Blue

The Treasure Principle, by Randy Alcorn

Sermon audio, book, and Bible study: "The Genius of Generosity," by Chip Ingram (livingontheedge.org/marriagethatworksresources)

Sermon audio and Bible study: "Balancing Life's Demands" by Chip Ingram. This series unpacks how to develop biblical priorities with your finances and time. (livingontheedge.org/marriagethatworksresources)

Sermon audio: "Download—Passing On What Matters Most," by Chip Ingram. (livingontheedge.org/marriagethatworksresources)

8

Stepping Up as a Man: *Protect*

Many men see financial and material provision as their primary, or *only*, responsibility in the home. But husbands also hold the crucial responsibility for the spiritual development and protection of their families. In essence, you are not only the family's CFO, you are also the spiritual leader.

That is not how it works in most homes; women often find themselves providing the spiritual direction for their husbands and children to follow. But God has appointed us as men to take responsibility for the spiritual welfare of our families.

That does not mean fathers do everything for their families spiritually. Each member has his or her own relationship with God. But a man who serves as the spiritual leader for his family will take his wife's needs, hurts, fears, and struggles to God on her behalf and ask for wisdom and guidance to provide spiritual direction and encouragement to his wife. I actually pictured myself as a family priest: one who brings God's Word and heart to my family and my family's needs to Christ. If that sounds above your paygrade and you think there's no way you could ever do that, hang in there—I felt the same way, but little by little, God helped me take baby steps that eventually transformed our marriage and our family. Here are what I think are the five top objectives to get you started.

Five Spiritual Objectives

As with your financial responsibilities, your spiritual responsibilities come with five practical objectives:

1. Set the pace personally.

2. Know the spiritual condition of your wife and children.

3. Pray for and with your wife and children regularly.

4. Ensure that biblical instruction takes place at home and at church.

5. Make experiencing God and loving each other your top priority.

1. Set the pace personally.

Your family will follow your example. It's improbable that your children will grow up to love God's Word unless they see their father loving his Word. They are not likely to grow up praying with passion unless they see you praying that way. (This applies to many areas of life, not just the spiritual ones, like it or not. They drive the way you drive, talk the way you talk, and respond to setbacks the way you do. They watch, and they learn by example.) Jesus said it best: "The student is not above the teacher, but everyone who is fully trained will be like their teacher" (Luke 6:40).

That does not mean you have to be perfect. It means that when you mess up, they need to see a healthy response— admitting your flaws, apologizing for your mistakes, and learning from them. When I've blown it with Theresa, my kids need to see me apologize. When I

> *As husbands and fathers, we need to model following God's will and repenting for missing it.*

exaggerate something from the pulpit—it doesn't happen often, but sometimes a story takes on a life of its own—they need me to acknowledge that "it didn't actually happen like that."

As husbands and fathers, we need to model following God's will and repenting for missing it. We set the pace for our wives and children.

2. Know the spiritual condition of your wife and children.

One of the biggest mistakes I've made as a husband and father is assuming everything is okay because it seemed so by outward appearance. The old adage that "men are insensitive" really applied to me. I discovered the hard way that I needed to become a student of my wife to learn how she thinks, what her weaknesses are, and where she struggles so

141

I can relate to her with understanding and let the grace of God in me help her grow and develop. "Husbands, in the same way be considerate as you live with your wives, and treat them with respect as the weaker partner and as heirs with you of the gracious gift of life, so that nothing will hinder your prayers" (1 Pet. 3:7).

Sometimes we have to ask our wives, "How are you really doing?" and be prepared to really listen, not to try to fix whatever we hear.

The process works the same way with our children. Staying in tune with what they are struggling with is critical. One of my sons went through a period of struggling with pornography, even though he really had a heart for following God and had always been diligent about reading his Bible and talking to his friends about his faith.

As spiritual leader of my family, it was my job to walk with him through that difficult experience—first to know him well enough to notice the signs, then to ask him the right questions and talk honestly about the problem, and then to help him get free from it. It was a painful and uncomfortable situation, but avoiding issues like that sets the wrong spiritual tone. When my son later went to college, he was able to help many of his friends who were struggling with the same issue. Learning to step up as a spiritual leader sets the direction of your family and bears fruit in their lives for years to come.

Sometimes you will have to say no. When your daughter is dating a guy who acts nice but seems to have another side to his personality, when your child's friends are rubbing off on them in negative ways, when your kids develop unhealthy habits or pursue unwholesome activities . . . your job is to intervene.

Many parents are afraid of saying no because they don't want their kids to rebel. As a dad, you can't afford to focus on your own reputation with your kids, though doing the right thing will probably earn their respect in the long run. It is still your responsibility to do the right thing, even if they say they hate you in the moment. If your kids' hearts get attached to the wrong people or the wrong behaviors, you are going to lose them.

A spiritual leader is willing to confront, to risk favor in the short term in order to accomplish a long-term good. That's what love does.

3. Pray for and with your wife and children regularly.

Use meals, bedtimes, informal conversations in the car, and every other opportunity to center the lives of your family members on God. Lift them up constantly to God. Zealously guard the spiritual life of your family not only through your leadership but also in your prayers.

4. Ensure that biblical instruction takes place at home and at church.

Use those same meals, bedtimes, and informal conversations to bring biblical instruction to your family's hearts and minds. You don't have to do that alone; it should be a group experience, and your church is part of that equation.

143

But if your kids are not getting biblical instruction, it's your job to make sure they do. If your wife is struggling in her spiritual life, you are the one to walk her through it. When I stand before God one day, he is not going to ask me how well a church or Christian school guided my family. He is going to ask me how well *I* did. In reality, your wife and children will benefit from a variety of spiritual influences, and your church will be one of the biggest ones. But the primary responsibility for creating the right environment is yours.

5. Make experiencing God and loving each other your top priority.

Your aim is not morality. That's an outcome, not the main focus. Otherwise, you will end up being a legalistic (and probably very boring) husband and father who doesn't realize how easily the rest of the family tunes you out. Strict religious talk does not win hearts or change lives. A real relationship with God and genuine love between family members are a powerful combination. Superficial dos and don'ts are not. Your family needs life, love, joy, and authentic experience. When they see this in your life, it spills over into theirs.

> Your family needs life, love, joy, and authentic experience. When they see this in your life, it spills over into theirs.

Our family made it a habit to go out together after our Ssaturday night service and have a good time. They would "criticize" my messages—in a constructive way—and let me know which parts were boring and help me rewrite my notes for Sunday's services. I still remember how precious taking my daughter out for breakfast on Sunday mornings was for both of us. Even as a preteen, she would help me with my messages. She could point out all my failed attempts to talk about teenagers in their language and give me the right words. We would eat together, laugh, sing along with the radio on the way home, and have a great time.

I never wanted my family to experience a stuffy, religious home. I wanted them to know their opinions mattered, their views and experiences were important, and that part of following God is having a full and fun life.

Your Core Values as Protector

As in our discussion of financial responsibilities, behind each of these spiritual objectives are some critical core values. The details are far less important than the values you hold. In fulfilling your spiritual responsibilities toward your wife and children, you want to do more than check all the boxes. You want to live in dependency on God, evidenced by prayer and even fasting when necessary; to embody faith in God and his Word; to have a service and outreach orientation; to be outwardly focused; and to experience progressive growth in holiness.

> *In fulfilling your spiritual responsibilities toward your wife and children, you want to do more than check all the boxes.*

I think one of the best expressions of these values is in Philippians 4:8: "Whatever is true, whatever is noble, whatever is right, whatever is pure, whatever is lovely, whatever is admirable—if anything is excellent or praiseworthy—think about such things."

One of the most challenging obstacles to living out the core value of protection today is guarding what comes into your home in music, videos, and games. If you don't set limits, things can easily get out of control.

You will have to be consistent in deciding what is and is not allowed in your house in terms of violence, sex, and other questionable content. It gets even more difficult when you try to set limits on the heroes your son wants to emulate or on the immodest styles your teenage daughter wants to wear. You understand the message she is unintentionally sending better than she does and probably better than her mother does. She needs her father to have a gentle, sympathetic, but honest conversation with her about the ways a teenage boy's mind works. And she always needs to know from the man in the house that she is beautiful, so she won't have to seek that affirmation elsewhere.

There's a lot of ground in this practical chapter. Don't let time go by before intentionally thinking through what we've discussed to your life today. These questions and resources can help.

_____ **Questions for Reflection and Discussion** _____

1. What was most helpful in this chapter for you? Why?

2. Which of the five practices discussed in this chapter do you find come most naturally to you?

3. Which of the five practices do you sense needs some additional attention or focus from you? Why?

4. What's the biggest barrier or challenge you are facing in protecting your wife? Your family?

5. Who could help you take those next steps to protect your family the way you want and need to?

Recommended Resources

The Real God, by Chip Ingram

The Real God Family Devotional, by Living on the Edge (livingontheedge .org/marriagethatworksresources)

Sermon audio, book, and Bible study: "True Spirituality," by Chip Ingram (livingontheedge.org/marriagethatworksresources)

Sermon audio and Bible study: "Transformed—The Miracle of Life Change," by Chip Ingram (livingontheedge.org/marriagethatworks resources)

Sermon audio and Bible study: "Overcoming Emotions That Destroy," by Chip Ingram (livingontheedge.org/marriagethatworksresources)

Sermon audio, book, and Bible study: "Effective Parenting in a Defective World," by Chip Ingram (livingontheedge.org/marriagethatworks resources)

9

Stepping Up as a Man: *Nurture*

Husbands hold the primary responsibility for relational health, the welfare of their families. That means that in addition to being the CFO and the spiritual leader, you are also the coach.

Just as in the world of sports, the direction of your "team" depends to a large degree on the kind of coaching it gets. "If anyone does not know how to manage his own family, how can he take care of God's church?" (1 Tim. 3:5). This verse deals primarily with leaders in the church, but it assumes that men are meant to be household managers.

I am the head of the Ingram franchise; you are the head of your family franchise. Success is determined by how well the team functions with love, obedience, and respect toward God and one another. If the culture of the franchise isn't right, it's up to you to change it.

Five Relational Objectives

Again, your relational role comes with five practical objectives:

1. Verbalize and celebrate the marriage covenant.

2. Schedule time to develop marriage and family relationships.

3. Provide structure and boundaries to ensure that family relationships take priority over outside demands.

4. Build communication into the fabric and rhythm of the family schedule.

5. Implement consequences fairly, firmly, and lovingly among all family members.

1. Verbalize and celebrate the marriage covenant.

I have a friend who gathered his children together when they were all old enough to understand what divorce is and had friends whose parents had split up. He put a big dictionary on the table, pulled out a knife, opened to the word "divorce," read the definition out loud, and then cut the whole entry out of the dictionary. "In our home," he said, "we want you to know that this word is not in our vocabulary."

> Make it a goal to show outward signs of your commitment to your marriage.

Make it a goal to show outward signs of your commitment to your marriage. For example, be affectionate with your wife—even if your kids roll their eyes and tell you to get a room. Kids may think it's gross when you make it clear you still think their mom is hot. But something deep down inside them will find comfort in the fact that their relational world is stable. They need to know the honeymoon isn't over and that your life together is alive and full of love.

2. Schedule time to develop marriage and family relationships.

You know how to schedule appointments with colleagues, clients, doctors, and repairmen. Don't let your wife and children fall through the cracks of your schedule. Plan time together. Have a regular date with your wife. Determine to eat a certain number of meals together as a family each week. Work in a regular playtime or date time with your sons and daughters. Approach your task with the commitment of a Navy SEAL or Army Ranger, and find a way to fit it all in. This is one of the most important parts of your mission.

3. Provide structure and boundaries to ensure that family relationships take priority over outside demands.

You have to structure your life to make sure you allow enough room for your kids to be involved and well rounded without eating every meal on the fly. If you don't, your family life will be dictated by youth sports, music practices, academics, and all the important activities that kids will want to be involved in but may have a tendency to overdo.

Again, be the bad cop for the moment whom they will respect years down the road. Say no when they want to fit three sports into one season. You are not depriving your kids to limit their activities. You are providing a healthy home environment where relationships can strengthen and grow.

4. Build communication into the fabric and rhythm of the family schedule.

Have you ever been in the room with the rest of your family when every member is on some kind of device? Or when all your free time is taken up by TV programming rather than con-versation? Put the electronics away for meals

> Build a heart connection with every member of the family.

and set a time nightly when everyone (including you) signs off of email, texts, Slack, Instagram, and Facebook. Make sure you eat together regularly and make those times an occasion for regular communication. Take advantage of time in the car to talk instead of just listening to the radio or having everyone occupied with their earbuds. Build a heart connection with every member of the family.

5. Implement consequences fairly, firmly, and lovingly among all family members.

My kids didn't always like my efforts at discipline and setting boundaries, but I tried not to focus on how they would react in the moment. I wanted them to love me ten years down the road.

I know I made a lot of mistakes along the way, especially with one of my sons. But I recently had some father-son time with all three of them during a family vacation. We get away somewhere for a week every year with the children and grandchildren, and my three sons and I were on a porch, sitting in rocking chairs and talking. The son I had the most challenges with looked at me and said this: "Dad, there are no victims here. Even with all the things I really resented, I am who I am because of you. I chafed under some of those things, but even the ones you got wrong—and I appreciate your apologizing for them—turned out okay. God has sovereignly taken all of it, and I think about all of our lives, the women we married, the way we are raising our kids, and I know we are all in this together."

I don't know what you want to get out of life, but when you have sons and daughters who grow up still wanting to be your friend, who love God and live with integrity, it doesn't get any better than that.

I know I wasn't always a wonderful dad, but I was intent on being an authentic dad. And I think my kids recognized that their mother and I were doing our best to teach and train them, to be fair with them, and to set them up for a life of faithfulness and fruitfulness.

Your children are all unique, so you have to use different approaches with each of them. But they are all equally loved and valued, so you have to be fair. That's a hard balance, and sometimes you will get it wrong. But they will see your leadership and love for them, and they will grow up knowing their heavenly Father through their earthly one.

Your Core Values as Nurturer

The heart of all these objectives is, as always, your core values. The relational environment of your home needs to be filled with acceptance and affirmation given in the context of accountability.

You are called to be a man of God, spend time with your wife, play with your kids, and cultivate an atmosphere of love and affirmation. These things don't happen on their own. You decide to be that kind of man, you begin with specific steps (even if they are small), and you grow over time. It's a process.

> The relational environment of your home needs to be filled with acceptance and affirmation given in the context of accountability.

You will have to make some hard decisions along the way. You may have to make less money in order to give your family quality time. You may disappoint your kids by saying no right now in order to set them up for long-term success. But one of the greatest needs in our culture right now is for men to be men.

I didn't know how to do that at first. You may not either. But be encouraged by the fact that this is a journey. You are on it with other men, and you have the help of the God of the universe. In most cases, you will also have the enthusiastic support of your wife. With commitment, focus, and perseverance, you will be able to fulfill your financial, spiritual, and relational responsibilities—your roles as CFO, spiritual leader, and coach—with God's supernatural blessing and strength.

_____ Questions for Reflection and Discussion _____

1. How would you describe your ideal family environment? In what ways are you encouraged with your role in leading your wife and family?

2. If you are a man, which leadership role do you find most challenging: financial provider, spiritual leader, or relational guide? Why?

3. In what ways do your responsibilities as a man require commitment and perseverance? Who or what helps you strengthen your commitment?

4. In what ways has this chapter helped you understand the process of creating the family dynamics you want to experience? What specific steps can you take now to move toward your goals for your marriage and family?

5. Who could you invite to join you on this journey for encouragement, strength, and accountability?

Recommended Resources

Sermon audio: "Portrait of a Father," by Chip Ingram (livingontheedge .org/marriagethatworksresources)

Sermon audio and Bible study: "Experiencing God's Dream for Your Marriage," by Chip Ingram (livingontheedge.org/marriagethatworks resources)

10

What's a Woman to Do?

picked up a women's magazine while I was standing in line at the store recently. I had noticed the cover story of a famous actress, a single woman in her forties, who decided to have a baby. She is extremely wealthy, considered one of the most beautiful women in the world, and has dated, lived with, or been married to some of the world's most popular men. By most accounts, she has reached the pinnacle of success.

In spite of that success, I felt sad for her. The article explained how she had always wanted to have a baby and thought that she would be married at this point in her life. She felt that the one thing she was missing out on in life was being able to offer motherly love.

But, as she explained, women are realizing more and more that they don't need a man to have a child—that there are many more options than there used to be. So even though it would be ideal to become a mother with a man by her side, she was tired of waiting for the right guy. She was going to rearrange her life to make motherhood a priority, and she was confident she was strong enough to do it on her own.

This woman had accomplished everything our culture says will make a person happy, yet there was still a hole in her heart, an ache for something she had missed along the way. Situations like hers are a fruit of the sexual revolution in the '60s and '70s, when sex and marriage became disconnected. Men no longer feel compelled to commit to marriage in order to have sex, and women no longer feel compelled to give devotion and sex in order to build a relationship. When the components of a marriage relationship are separated and detached from marriage, you end up with many relationships that are not lasting or fulfilling.

By her own admission, this woman had been living in fear that she would never experience some of the things she was designed by God to experience. Yet she had followed the culture's prescription for fulfillment far more successfully than most people ever do. She was a role model who was missing out on one of her biggest roles.

Show Me *Which* Box Top

Women today are given a variety of roles to fulfill, and some of them are mutually exclusive. They can't fulfill them all. While the issue for men was finding the box top—discovering the model for manhood that most men have never seen up close—the issue for women is *which* box top to look at.

Are you supposed to be like the famous actress who has beauty, wealth, and lots of men who are uncommitted? Are you supposed to be like Mother Teresa and dedicate your life to a cause that may be far removed from the life you have always known? Should you pursue a career or get married and have a family? Or try to balance both? And if both, how long should you do one before you begin the other? In other words, what is your calling? What does God want you to be and do in life?

We have already discussed the basics of a wife's role—to step in and support her husband. That's the "what." In this chapter, we will look at the "how." I have to warn you, however, that it may come across as a little controversial. In fact, just as I offered the hypothetical warning label for women's studies programs I quoted in chapter 5, I offer a similar warning:

> The message you are about to hear may be hazardous to your emotional equilibrium. It may call into question assumptions and preconceived ideas you've had about womanhood, marriage, and motherhood. Though ancient in their origin and tested successfully for centuries, these concepts may sound strange, countercultural, and even bizarre to the ears of twenty-first-century men and women. The implications of this message for your life and family could be drastic, even disturbing. If applied en masse by those who claim allegiance to Jesus Christ, it could be revolutionary.

God's view of women is simultaneously liberating, countercultural, and counterintuitive—and it works.

Three Priorities

At first glance, God's prescription for your marriage and family relationships will look a lot like the husband's. As I've studied this, I've found that the wife has the same three priorities: to nurture, protect, and provide. That's because, as we have seen, the divine Designer gives us complementary roles that are neither superior nor inferior to each other. But as part of their complementary nature, the emphases are different.

The wife's three priorities are in exactly the opposite order of the husband's. The husband's first priority is to provide, then protect, then nurture. The wife's is first to nurture, then protect, then provide.

> The husband's first priority is to provide, then protect, then nurture. The wife's is first to nurture, then protect, then provide.

God has designed us to fit together in a way that creates unity and strength in our love and intimacy—that beautiful dance we have been talking about—and it creates a home instead of just a house. We see the same complementary nature whenever two parts fit together to work as one.

Much of my home is held together by nuts and bolts that I can't see. I see walls and floors and ceilings. But behind the visible appearance are pieces that hold everything together, and those pieces don't work by themselves. The bolt will not hold its place without the nut; the nut accomplishes nothing unless it fits around a bolt. Their threads look just alike, but they have to turn in opposite directions to fit together. It's the combination that provides the strength.

The "threads" of men and women look a lot alike, but we have to turn in opposite directions to fit together. The beauty is in the strength, and the strength comes from each person complementing or completing the other person's role.

So the divine Designer has given wives three priorities in opposite order of their husbands':

1. To *nurture* is to create a relational environment that promotes the spiritual, emotional, and physical welfare of those around you.

2. To *protect* means to minimize the harmful influences that affect the lives that have been entrusted to you.

3. To *provide* means to maximize all spiritual, emotional, physical, and financial resources to do good to those who are in your relational network.

Just as God has made husbands to step up with love and leadership to meet the needs wives cannot meet on their own, he has created wives to step in with honor and respect to meet their husbands' needs and do what they are not able to do alone. It's a role only a wife can fill, and when she does, she experiences the deepest levels of joy and fulfillment in her heart.

These priorities will shape a wife's approach to three specific roles: as champion for her husband, mother for her children, and mentor for younger women. As a woman, you know your responsibilities are more numerous than this, and the demands placed on you will reach far beyond these specific functions. You will be counselor, psychologist, medic, cook, cleaner, instructor, developer, discipler, traveler, chauffeur, and much, much more. But most of them fit into three main categories.

No one else can meet the needs of your husband, your children, and younger women in the ways you can. These are the main areas of responsibility God has gifted you to address.

Similar to our discussion of a man's responsibility, I've created three shorter chapters, each with questions and resources to help you digest and think through the implications of God's design for you in your marriage.

11

Stepping In as a Woman: *Nurture*

The three priorities God has given to wives may be expressed in different ways in the various seasons of life. Not all of them are at the forefront all the time. But they are all part of God's original design, and no one can do them like each individual wife can. The first is to be a nurturer to her husband.

At creation, God's intended role for the wife was to be a helper. "It is not good for the man to be alone," he said. "I will make a helper suitable for him" (Gen. 2:18). The word "helper," by the way, does not suggest a subordinate position. It is also used of God himself in several places in the Old Testament, such as when he was Israel's "helper" in battle. Take a look, for instance, at Exodus 18:4, Deuteronomy 33:7, and Psalm 33:20 which reads, "We wait in hope for the LORD; he is our help and our shield."

God is subordinate to no one. The term indicates a supportive role of offering strength at the right times in the right ways.

A wife's number one priority is to support, affirm, and empower her husband to fulfill the calling God has given him inside and outside the home. This is critical, and it explains why a good wife is so highly valued in Scripture.

"An excellent wife, who can find? For her worth is far above jewels. The heart of her husband trusts in her, and he will have no lack of gain. She does him good and not evil all the days of her life" (Prov. 31:10–12 NASB).

The "heart of her husband" feeds off the support of his wife. One of a man's biggest secrets is his insecurity. He wonders how things are going to play out when the pressure is on. One of his greatest needs is for respect or honor. Deep down, he wonders, *Am I really a man? Do I have what it takes?* A wife's yes—in her actions and her words—gives him strength. And it causes his heart to trust her.

The wife is to be her husband's champion—a supportive teammate and best friend. Organizations that thrive always have champions, people who are zealous for the cause, who embrace the values, and who dedicate themselves to the mission. They are the glue that keeps the organization together. The wife is the most powerful influence in the family, and when she is committed to the cause and says, "We can do this," she becomes the glue that holds everything together. She champions the things that matter most.

Five Relational Objectives

There are many ways a wife can champion her husband in different seasons, but there are at least five objectives:

1. Make time with God your number one priority.

2. Pray for your husband regularly.

3. Plan for him daily.

4. Prepare for him daily.

5. Protect your time with him.

1. Make time with God your number one priority.

You have the most demanding job in the world, spiritually, emotionally, and physically. You are constantly multitasking as you are pulled at by multiple people to meet multiple needs in and out of the home. You understand that running a home is more than making sure people have food and clothes. You realize that it is a transformational organization where love is created, received, and exported. The home shapes the direction of human lives.

> The only way you can run a home as a transformational, loving environment is with God's help.

Psychologists talk a lot about the dynamics of our family of origin. Everyone lives with the experiences of their early lives, carrying the strengths and weaknesses of what their parents did or did not provide. That early environment shapes who we are. Women understand that, and it can feel like an overwhelming responsibility. The only way you can run a home as a transformational, loving environment is with God's help. You need strength and wisdom.

Time for yourself and to be connected from the heart with other women is important too; that creates space for getting into the Bible, developing mentoring relationships, and allowing others to speak Jesus's truth into your life. But time alone with him is essential.

My wife has understood this for as long as I can remember. Even when we were young and did not always know what we were doing as parents—and when we went to marriage counseling early in our marriage to sort out a lot of the issues we were having—this was one constant for her. She made meeting with God her top priority. Sometimes that was only five or ten minutes before a baby awakened or twenty minutes before the kids got up, but I would often find her talking with God and reading God's Word at 5:30 in the morning. She understood how important that was.

2. Pray for your husband regularly.

Susanna Wesley had nineteen children, only ten of whom survived past infancy. The family often lived at the edge of poverty, and her husband was jailed twice for financial issues. Life was difficult, and Susanna was her children's primary source of education, so her hands were full.

According to one story told about her, she would often go outside and sit on a stump, with children running and playing all around her, and pull her apron over her head to pray for each one of them and for her husband. She knew she needed God, his wisdom, and his power to be a wife, mother, and godly influence in her home. She could not impart what she didn't possess; she had to give to her family from what God had given her. She made sure she received from him regularly. Two of her sons, John and Charles, grew up to change the world in some powerful ways.

One of the greatest promises a praying wife has among her spiritual resources is Proverbs 21:1: "The king's heart is like a stream of water directed by the LORD; he guides it wherever he pleases" (NLT). This is not just about kings' hearts; it applies to men, women, and children everywhere.

I've seen my wife rely on this promise again and again. She would have an issue with me, talk about it, make suggestions, and encourage me to read a book on that topic with her, and my heart still would not change. Then she would go to God.

> God longs to hear a wife and mother pray for her husband and children. He responds in very powerful ways.

"Lord, Chip isn't listening to me. Please take this into your own hands. Get under his skin. Show him what he needs to know in order to lead this family well."

And very often—not always, because this isn't about manipulation, and on occasion I might have actually been right—God would begin to work in my heart and mind to change me. Theresa learned that the greatest ally in accomplishing an impossible task, especially those related to the hearts and minds of her husband and children, is prayer: to ask God, seek God, and knock on the doors of heaven. God longs to hear a wife and mother pray for her husband and children. He responds in very powerful ways.

3. Plan for your husband daily.

There are two ways to go through life: letting it happen to you, or being proactive and managing it. Most people do at least a little of both, but with all the demands placed on you in your family life, and with all the juggling you will do, you need to be intentional. Somewhere in that mix of juggling and planning, you need to be purposeful about caring for your husband.

Sometimes that may be a simple act of kindness—putting a special note somewhere for him to find or lighting candles for your dinner together. Maybe you find a way to get the kids out of the house for a little while so you can have some time to be alone together. Whatever you choose to do, it is important to plan for your husband, just as it is important for him to carve time out of his schedule for you.

> You will find that whatever you invest in will grow, and whatever you neglect will eventually die.

You will find that whatever you invest in will grow, and whatever you neglect will eventually die. That's true in almost any area of life, especially in your relationships. We don't necessarily get what we hope for; we tend to get what we plan for. Intending something to happen rarely makes it happen. We have to structure our days for desired outcomes. Structure results in outcomes.

That's what wives and moms have to do—for every person in the family. Find ways to invest in your husband with tangible signs of honor, respect, and love—even if he does not seem to respond at first. Eventually, he will clue in and he will love it. As you begin to meet some needs in his life, he will start to lead a little better and love a little deeper.

4. Prepare for your husband daily.

Women do a lot to attract a man in the early days of their relationship. As time goes on, those efforts can be smothered by responsibilities with children and work. I understand that, and it would be completely unrealistic to expect the relationship to continue forever just as it was when you were dating. But think back to those times when you got excited about seeing him. How did you prepare then? Did you open the door wearing baggy sweatpants and no makeup? Probably not. You prepared to present your best self to him.

Over time and under pressure, we spouses get so familiar with each other that the desire to leave our best impression fades away. That's normal—to a degree. None of us will look like a twenty-year-old on a date for the rest of our lives. It would be unrealistic to spend our lives at a gym, invest in the most fashionable wardrobe, look and smell our best every day of every decade, and always get excited about seeing each other.

But there is a big difference between adjusting to the years and giving in to them, and being casual and being apathetic. Desire can get quenched under the demands of daily life. Couples need to keep the physical, emotional, and relational sparks alive, and part of that is preparing for each other.

God created men to be visually attracted to women. A husband typically is out in the world seeing other women who have determined to look and smell their best for everyone else. He does not need to come home to a perfect wife, but he does need to see a spark in her from time to time that reminds him she's still interested, which reignites his own interest.

A wife who prepares for her husband visually, emotionally, and relationally can make a big difference in the way he thinks about her and interacts with her.

Despite limited salary and four children, we had a personal conviction for Theresa to be a full-time homemaker during our children's formative years. It was a big assignment, yet I remember her setting aside time to put on fresh makeup, and she looked great when I walked in the door. Forty years later, she still takes the time to prepare for me, and it really matters.

This can be very difficult with all the demands placed on each of your lives, especially if both of you have an income-earning job. You often feel obligated to meet other people's needs above each other's. I remember how often I would answer the phone when cell phones first became commonplace. On one of my days off, Theresa once looked at me and said, "Do you want to be with me, or are you going to talk on the phone all the time?"

"Just taking a quick call," I assured her.

"You're always taking a quick call. I feel like taking that thing and throwing it away." (Those are my sweet wife's strong words.) I got the point. My attention was constantly being taken away from her. Many wives have a tendency to do the same thing—to fill the time with their husbands with quick conversations or mundane distractions. Be intentional about what occupies your attention. Plan to connect with your husband, and you'll be glad you did.

5. Protect your time with your husband.

Apart from your relationship with God, your marriage is the most important relationship you have. Your husband will feel empowered when he sees you saying no to the children or to other demands and interests that might make him feel like he's second place in your life. Don't neglect your other responsibilities, of course, but do always make him feel like he is your priority.

> *Apart from your relationship with God, your marriage is the most important relationship you have.*

You may feel that these five objectives are piling extra demands on you and stretching you beyond your capacity. In a sense, that's true; you will need supernatural help to be the woman God has called you to be. But in another sense, these objectives are less about adding responsibilities and more about removing *false* responsibilities so you can be the woman God designed you to be.

You do not need to take on extra burdens; you are being called to step into genuine, biblical femininity. You are fully equipped for that already, so be encouraged. You have everything you need—including the help of the Holy Spirit and plenty of grace as you grow—to do what you are called to do and, just as importantly, *not* do what you haven't been called to do.

Carve out the time to answer the following questions and look through the recommended resources below. Change doesn't happen unless something changes!

_____ Questions for Reflection and Discussion _____

1. What was most helpful in this chapter for you? Why?

2. Which of the five practices discussed in this chapter do you find come most naturally to you?

3. Which of the five practices do you sense needs some additional attention or focus from you? Why?

4. What's the biggest barrier or challenge you are facing in nurturing your husband? Your family?

5. Who could help you take those next steps to nurture and love your husband the way you want and need to?

Recommended Resources

The Read Scripture app, available on Google Play and the App Store (an amazing resource to help develop consistent routines of connecting with God through his Word)

The Power of a Praying Wife, by Stormie Omartian

Sermon audio: "Communication—How to Share Hearts Instead of Exchange Words"(livingontheedge.org/marriagethatworksresources)

Sermon audio and affirmation cards: "Precious in His Sight," by Theresa Ingram (livingontheedge.org/marriagethatworksresources)

12

Stepping In as a Woman: *Protect*

Your second priority as a woman is to create an environment in the home that nurtures and develops your children to fulfill God's will for their lives but also minimizes harmful influences. You are a shaper and protector of young hearts. The most influential people in the world are mothers. Period.

Great men of God like John and Charles Wesley first saw faith in their mothers, who gave them acceptance, confidence, an understanding of themselves and the world, and examples of devotion. When the camera turns to a football player who just made a great play, what does he say? "Hi, Mom!" Studies show that in every area other than moral development and sexual identity, in which fathers play a critical role, moms are by far the most powerful influence in their children's lives. Your priority as protector is vital not only to your family but also to the world your children will live in.

Scripture gives many examples of spiritual protection in the home, but one of the clearest statements is given in the context of young women in early church times whose husbands had died.

In the culture of the times, a young widow essentially had two options other than remarriage: to dedicate herself to the church and let the church support her financially or to become a prostitute. It was difficult for women to earn a living or live independently in Bible times. There were exceptions: women like Lydia in Acts 16 and some of the women who supported Jesus financially (Luke 8:1–3) were unusually self-sufficient. But often, single women were in a precarious position. So Paul wrote, "I counsel younger widows to marry, to have children, to manage their homes and to give the enemy no opportunity for slander" (1 Tim. 5:14).

The literal meaning of the words in this sentence imply that a married woman is to make things happen in the home—to be the chief operating officer, the COO, of her household. She sets direction and develops systems that enable her family to grow in love and have their needs met.

Somehow society has convinced many women that if motherhood is the only job they ever have, they are wasting their lives. This amazing, esteemed, God-given assignment has been dismissed as peripheral or unimportant to real life, and real fulfillment must therefore lie in accomplishing something else. Scripture says the opposite is true. Mothers have a unique opportunity to shape lives and empower the next generation to follow God faithfully. A mother is the key teacher, counselor, consoler, and refuge for her children, and her impact in their lives is unequaled.

Like the actress whose story opened chapter 10, many female celebrities have recently rediscovered their desire to be mothers. Many of them are single—it seems to be a trend in Hollywood now for unmarried women to adopt or get pregnant outside of a committed relationship—but it is happening more and more, especially to those who reach their forties and realize they have been missing something they were made to do. Even women who have had children earlier are adopting in greater numbers, as if they have suddenly realized that being a mother matters.

I realize not every woman will become a mother, and some who desperately want to bear a child may never get to have that experience. But those who do invest their lives in motherhood need to understand that even in a culture that marginalizes that identity, it is a high and holy calling.

Five Spiritual Objectives

Your priority as protector of your family involves these five objectives:

1. Model dependency on Christ.

2. Pray for your children fervently.

3. Create structures and scheduled times that make family life a priority.

4. Teach your children how to live.

5. Make time for your children.

1. Model dependency on Christ.

Contrary to what most parents believe, your children will not end up doing what you have told them. They will end up being like you. Your example matters much more than your words; behavior is generally caught, not taught. Jesus expressed the same principle: "Everyone who is fully trained will be like their teacher" (Luke 6:40).

How you think, how you drive, what you say when you're stressed, how you respond in a crisis, the ways you love God, the manner in which you treat your husband—all of these attitudes and behaviors are being passed on to your children. They will choose to modify some of those responses as they get older, of course. Most kids decide to do some things differently than their parents. But to do so, they will have to depart from what came to them naturally—your example. So the greatest gift you can give yourself as wife to your husband and mother to your children is a lifestyle that is dependent on Jesus.

One of my sons went through a season of rebellion that was really painful for us and for him as well. He has since become a godly husband, father, and prolific writer of Christian music, but it took a while. Shortly after that season ended, I asked him what made the difference for him. What was it that caused him to turn so powerfully back to his relationship with Christ? It wasn't one of my persuasive sermons but something even more gratifying.

"Dad," he said, "Jesus is so real to Mom and you, and your lives are so authentic. And when I rebelled, I didn't see you get uptight about what people at church would think. I saw tears come down your faces because I didn't embrace the Jesus that you love."

> *When you model dependency on Jesus, you are painting a picture day by day of what truly matters.*

What was he really saying? That children emulate what really matters to us. When you model dependency on Jesus, you are painting a picture day by day of what truly matters.

2. Pray for your children fervently.

If you're a mother, you know by now how little control you have over your children's choices, especially as they get older. When they eventually leave home, their decisions, values, and priorities are beyond your direct influence. The sense of control we have as parents is generally an illusion anyway, but that becomes painfully apparent as time goes on. You do the best you can and teach them what you know, but they will still have to make decisions in the heat of the moment, respond to peer pressure, and choose their own values.

You will not be there to enforce your will. So you talk to your heavenly Father a lot—specifically and earnestly. One of the most powerful things you can do for your kids is to pray for them fervently.

Make sure your prayers cover more than just the externals of their lives—like good grades, good health, and good friends. Pray that they would hunger and thirst for righteousness, that they would seek God with all their heart, that they would have a passion for God's holiness. Ask God to give them wisdom in choosing friends and the strength to resist temptation. Expect him to work in your children's lives.

Let me offer a word of caution here, however. Don't judge your prayers by how quickly God answers them. At times, he will dramatically intervene, but not always. Instead, see your prayers as seeds being planted in your children's lives that will one day bear fruit or as small investments that will grow over time into abundant returns. Sometimes the results of a mother's prayers are not seen until the child is grown. But be persistent, and don't give up. Your prayers *are* being answered, and you *are* making a difference.

3. Create structures and scheduled times that make family life a priority.

You are the COO of the home, and there will be times when you have to lay down the law. You will have to decide what structure or schedule you are going to have for mealtimes, bedtimes, days off, vacations, and any other time when family life needs to take priority over other activities. You may have to enforce dinnertime, at least on certain nights of the week, as a time when all phones and devices are off, no ball games are playing in the background, and everyone is together. Speed kills relationships—and if everyone is always running around doing their own thing, relationships will weaken and break down.

The mother is the glue that keeps binding those relationships. But if you only hope for family time, it won't happen. You have to schedule it. Structures, not intentions, result in outcomes.

4. Teach your children how to live.

I believe that the most powerful teacher in any person's life is his or her mother. You will have the deepest connection with your children. You have known your children longer than anyone else, by at least nine months. And for the first few months after birth, you are your child's dominant care-taker. The bonding that occurs during pregnancy and the early months of infancy has more impact on a child's early life than any other influence. That bond creates an extremely powerful connection and trust for teaching your children how to live.

Almost all mothers know how to train their children in be-havioral issues—using good manners, making polite con-versation, treating other people well, and that sort of thing. And most do not need suggestions for other things to try. But if you're looking for ideas beyond the basics, here are a few I've observed over the years:

- *Teach your children to read, even before they begin school.*

  Theresa did this with our children, and they learned to love reading early. That is an extremely valuable and influential activity that increases their intellectual ca-pacity and academic opportunities.

179

- *Teach them to pray.*

  Even when they are small, they can have meaningful conversations with God.

- *Teach them—girls and boys—to cook.*

  Boys (and girls) need to know how to take care of themselves.

- *Teach them to listen well.*

  Noticing what other people are feeling and thinking is a skill everyone needs.

- *Teach them to celebrate.*

  We live in a fast-paced world that is so focused on performance that many people don't know how to stop and enjoy the journey.

- *Teach them to be generous.*

  After all, our God is infinitely generous.

- *Teach them a craft, a musical instrument, a sport, or a skill that requires using their hands.*

  This develops not only their motor skills and discipline, it helps strengthen their creativity and imagination.

- *Teach them how to speak in public.*

  Verbal communication is a declining skill, and people who have it will have an advantage socially and in many career fields.

- *Teach them to resolve conflict.*

  Avoiding conflict leads to problems. Learning to dispassionately address issues with people will be an extremely useful skill throughout their professional and personal life.

- *Teach them how to relax and not feel guilty.*

  After all, the Lord rested on the Sabbath!

You won't cover all the possibilities, and none of them will happen overnight. But work some of these into your children's lives, even if it's just for ten or fifteen minutes a day in certain seasons. Your kids will learn some valuable skills that will serve them well the rest of their lives.

You and your husband are ultimately responsible—not as controllers, but as the main influencers—for how your kids think, relate, and value God and others. The school, the church, and other caretakers may play a role, but they are not primary. You are. You will give them the direction they need to learn and grow spiritually, emotionally, intellectually, relationally, and physically. Take the initiative and be intentional about teaching them what they need to know in life.

5. Make time for your children.

Be available. The best things in life rarely happen on your official schedule. The teachable moments and the memorable conversations come up between the items on the to-do list, so you have to leave some time between those tasks.

That isn't easy; you already juggle a lot of demands on your time. But think about what really matters. What is going on in your children's hearts? When is your daughter going to open up and talk about the huge fear she is facing or the relationship that is playing with her emotions? When is your son going to open up about the struggles he deals with or the insecurities that are eating at him? You can't schedule those conversations—they just happen—but you can create space for them. (Warning: this almost always involves setting some very strong limits on TV, phones, video games, and computer activities.)

> Create a world in which you are not always going somewhere, accomplishing something, or listening to something.

If you have developed a good relationship with your children and have quiet moments when they can open up, you may be amazed at what comes out of them sometimes. And you will be grateful that you were available to walk them through their challenges and concerns.

Don't let the typical North American lifestyle of being stressed, overworked, and overwhelmed deprive you of valuable moments with your children that you and they will never forget. Create a world in which you are not always going somewhere, accomplishing something, or listening to something. Boredom is the birthplace of spontaneity and creativity, and it's one of the most underappreciated gifts you can give your children. Make time just to hang out, and some pretty exciting things might happen.

Mentoring Younger Wives

Another area of a wife's protective priority mentioned in Scripture is toward younger women. The Bible says to train younger women in the art of becoming godly wives and mothers. In other words, if you have learned the art of family relationships, you need to pass that knowledge down to future generations. If you are learning that art now, you need to glean wisdom from those who have gone before you. This is one of the ways God has arranged for protecting and preserving a biblical culture among his people.

In the book of Titus, Paul is writing to the pastor of a church on the island of Crete, where women were known for being a little wilder than elsewhere, somewhat like today's celebrity bad girls. Paul even refers to the island's reputation for immorality and a lack of ethics.

In Titus 2:3–5, he instructs Christian women to impart something of their reverence and devotion to younger women who are still learning what God's Word teaches about family relationships. Why? So that the Word of God will not be dishonored.

> Likewise, teach the older women to be reverent in the way they live, not to be slanderers or addicted to much wine, but to teach what is good. Then they can urge the younger women to love their husbands and children, to be self-controlled and pure, to be busy at home, to be kind, and to be subject to their husbands, so that no one will malign the word of God.

183

In other words, people need to see homes where lives are transformed, where love, acceptance, affirmation, and intimacy in marriage are practiced and celebrated. Homes that do not function that way call into question what we believe. Homes that do function that way become a testimony of the transforming power of God's Word.

We used to live in a world where grandmothers and extended families lived close to each other and each generation would pass down its wisdom to the next. Husbands and wives learned how to resolve conflict and raise children from their parents and grandparents. Not many people experience that dynamic anymore. Many of us have families who live on the other side of the country or even on other continents.

It's left to a young woman to sort out the right box top from all the other options the culture gives her. She is taught to be well educated, to be pretty, to find the right man, to have a great career, to make a lot of money, and to be upwardly mobile, and then to consider whether or not she ought to have kids. And if she does, should she stay home with them or send them to a daycare or create some hybrid options to fit her unique needs? How should she raise them in today's world? She needs the advice of an older, godly woman to sort out all her options and navigate her challenges, and she may not find one in her extended family.

Some more mature women may not be convinced they have anything to offer. I've heard the humility: "Oh, I just raised three kids. By God's grace, they turned out better than we deserve. We may not have the most exciting marriage, but we've somehow managed to keep it together and love each other deeply for forty years. I guess it works."

If that sounds like you, there is more wisdom in those forty years than you realize. With a little bit of encouragement and training, you could actually be one of the greatest difference makers in the lives of younger wives. And if you are a young wife, find a more experienced one who is willing to mentor you. Times may have changed, but human nature and family dynamics are a lot like they always have been. You may have a wider range of choices than many women of the past, but a lot of women who have made some of those choices can tell you how fulfilling (or not) some of them are.

The church is full of women of every age who have found success as our culture defines it and are now trying to figure out how to be really fulfilled, and they need cross-generational relationships. They need to know how God's plan has worked in the lives of women who have lived it. They need someone to talk through the important questions of work and children and marriage with them. There is no "one size fits all." Different women have different gifts and challenges. God will show you how to navigate your specific situation as you commit to fully follow his design.

> *Don't be overwhelmed by the role God has given you as a wife.*

So don't be overwhelmed by the role God has given you as a wife. It is extremely significant, but it is also a perfect match for the gifts he has placed within you. If no one recognizes that you are shaping history by influencing your husband and children—God sees. You may have a more prominent role outside your home at certain stages of life, but even when you feel like you aren't doing anything significant, you can rest assured that you are. You are a vital part of God's plan, and he will empower you in every way you serve those around you. Even more, you will eventually see the fruit of your labor in the lives of those you love.

Answer the following questions and then pray about steps you can take to strengthen areas of your life as a wife and mother. Consider using the listed resources too.

———— Questions for Reflection and Discussion ————

1. What was most helpful in this chapter for you? Why?

2. Which of the five practices discussed in this chapter do you find come most naturally to you?

3. Which of the five practices do you sense needs some additional attention or focus from you? Why?

4. What's the biggest barrier or challenge you are facing in protecting your husband? Your family?

5. Who could help you take those next steps to protect your husband and family the way you want and need to?

Recommended Resources

The Power of a Praying Mom, by Stormie Omartian

Sermon series: "Precious in His Sight," by Theresa Ingram (this series covers what Theresa taught our daughter about her identity and self-image) (livingontheedge.org/marriagethatworksresources)

Sermon audio: "How to Fight Fair in Marriage" (conflict resolution is critical in marriage and family; this message will teach you how to attack the issues rather than the person) (livingontheedge.org/marriagethat worksresources)

13

Stepping In as a Woman: *Provide*

Y ou will find that you provide for your husband and children in a variety of ways, many of them having little to do with finances. You may be much more hands-on in managing the budget than your husband is, but as the one who often takes care of the necessities and details of daily life, your provision also includes matters of diet, health, clothing, instruction, and much more. The financial aspect of your role is not your highest priority.

But one of the questions that always comes up in discussing a woman's role in the home is her potential role outside of it. Should she have an income-earning job? And the short answer I always give to that question is, "It depends."

That question should be asked only after other priorities are well established and covered. If your marriage is your highest priority and you are fulfilling your responsibilities as a champion for your husband and a mother for your children, if you have them, then it is reasonable to consider whether, when, how, and why you should work outside the home.

Many factors come into play: the ages and stages of your kids, your energy level, your personality and gifts, and your capacity. But it is always important to remember what research tells us about how children develop and mature.

For the first six to eight years of a child's life, his or her personality will be formed through the parent-child bond, and specifically through the mother-child bond. Children's personalities are like wet cement at that age. They are forming their values, morals, sense of security, and understanding of what life is all about. Whatever it takes, you want to be around for that.

So how much is a second job, a second car, or a nice home worth? That's a really important question to ask before you take on a mortgage payment, get that extra job to pay for it, and put your hopes in the character of the person spending those precious hours each day with your child.

I taught this a number of years ago, and a young Christian came up to me afterward to ask if we could talk. He had been a believer for only a few years, so he had not built up all the justifications and excuses a lot of us come up with to sound spiritual and still do what we want.

"I have a decent job and my wife is a teacher. With both of our incomes, we can afford to live in Santa Cruz," he said. At the time, our area of California was the second-most expensive place to live in the US. "But we can't live here on one income. We believe after hearing your talk about God's design for the family that we need to move so she can stay at home with our two kids."

"That's a big step for you all; are you sure?" I asked.

"Yeah. We really enjoy living here, but if we stay, twenty years from now we will wish we had spent our time, energy, and money on the things that matter most. We're moving to Oregon."

All I could tell him was, "I'll miss you all, but I think you are making a wise decision."

Three years later, I got a letter from him. "Chip, it's the greatest decision we ever made," he wrote. "Maybe we can move back one day when our kids get older, but for now, this was the right thing to do. Our marriage and family are thriving."

It's great to live where you want to live and have the kind of cars and home you want to have, but these are not priorities. God may move you somewhere else so you can reprioritize your family life. There is no law that says you have to own a home, build up equity, or work outside the house to achieve some kind of financial security. I don't mean to sound negative, but during thirty-five years pastoring and counseling God's people, I've watched countless couples end up with a nice house and plenty of money but with kids who don't know them very well, don't walk with God, and don't spend time with their parents. It's tragic. Sometimes the right choices are the hardest ones.

> *Sometimes the right choices are the hardest ones.*

God will honor the right choices. I know that from experience, and I also know how hard those choices can be.

Our third child came along when I was going to seminary full-time and working a full-time job. I made $1,000 a month, but Theresa and I were committed to her being home to nurture and protect our children. So I got up at 4 a.m. every day, did my schoolwork, and went to classes until dinner. Then I ate dinner, spent some time with the family, and went to work until 11 p.m. or midnight. I slept four or five hours on weeknights and then made up for it a little on weekends. We lived in government-subsidized housing and had one car without air-conditioning—in Texas. We would go to a doughnut shop for our dates because they gave free refills on coffee. We'd buy one doughnut and split it. It was an incredibly difficult time of life. God provided at just the right times, like someone giving us a bag of groceries or an unexpected check coming in the mail. Our kids lived on peanut butter and honey sandwiches with bread Theresa made from scratch almost every day for nearly five years.

At one point when we were having trouble paying our bills, we had a neighbor with a five-year-old and an infant who had been abandoned by her husband. We felt led to pay her rent for her, and it was kind of terrifying—we paid the $236 in government-subsidized housing, but it left us with only about $15 in our checking account, and our rent was going to be due in a couple weeks.

The due date came, and we just didn't have any money. I felt stupid. Of course, Theresa was convinced God would provide. We had a three-day grace period to submit our rent check, and on day one I was pointing out Philippians 4:19 to God with more than a hint of accusation in my attitude, reminding him that he was supposed to provide. But nothing came.

Then on the third day, I got a letter with a football insignia on it and a Lombardi Avenue return address. It had come from the home of the Green Bay Packers.

It was from a guy I had met seven or eight years earlier, when he played basketball for one of my friends who was a coach. He later went to college in California to play quarterback and was eventually drafted and played professional ball. All these years later, he contacted my friend the coach and said, "Remember that guy who led the Bible study back when you were coaching me? I can't get him off my mind. I think I'm supposed to send him some money. Do you know how I could get in touch with him?"

So out of the blue, an NFL quarterback was praying, without having any idea about our needs, and he sent a check for $1,000 that arrived at exactly the right time to pay our rent. I could tell at least another dozen stories like that.

I'm not saying it's wrong for moms to work; we make different decisions at different times, depending on our situations and changing priorities. But for us, it was a step of faith and obedience for Theresa to stay home with the kids, and even though that was a hard time, I don't even see it as a sacrifice today. We decided we would rather be poor in finances and rich in family relationships. It was a short season and I wouldn't trade it for anything.

I realize many families would make different decisions in those circumstances. All I can tell you is that your role as a champion, a mother, and a mentor will pay more dividends than the extra money you can bring in during your children's critical early years.

> *One study suggested that the average couple's income increases by only about 15 percent when they both work.*

Sometimes that extra money doesn't amount to very much additional income after you account for all the issues that come with a second job—the work wardrobe, gas in the second car, childcare expenses, taxes, and the amount of time and money you spend eating out because neither spouse has time to cook. One study suggested that the average couple's income increases by only about 15 percent when they both work.

Again, I'm not saying it's wrong for a woman to work. Proverbs 31 commends a wife for being industrious and earning income. But there are a lot of things to consider, especially when your children are young.

Supporting Single Mothers

The question that always comes up at this point is, What about single mothers? Sometimes a woman has very little choice about whether to earn an income or not. I wish I had an easy answer and unlimited financial resources to help single parents. It is one of the most demanding and difficult assignments for a parent. I believe the church can play a vital role in relational and even financial support in times of crisis, and I have watched God sustain single moms who have to work to support their families. I believe the grace of God is sufficient to cover your children and care for your needs, but the cost is high and we, the body of Christ, need to support each other to make up for what you cannot do on your own.

Working single moms tend to feel guilty and exhausted. God does not require of you what you cannot accomplish. If you do not have a husband around, you are carrying more weight than most women have to carry. Seek out a Bible-teaching church to be a part of your kids' lives and don't be ashamed to ask for help. Ask God for the miraculous provision of friendship, role models for your children, and finances in times of need.

That's good advice in any situation. Life is full of challenges and hard decisions, and the bottom line is you'll have to ask the Holy Spirit for guidance and follow him as he directs your steps. As uncertain as that can feel sometimes, you can be confident that God has a lot of grace for those who seek him. His own promises keep him zealously seeking your welfare. He is committed to taking care of you; you can rest confidently in him.

Finally, as you read the paragraphs above, who is a single mom that could really use your help, support, friendship, and financial support? If we really care about women, this is an opportunity for us to practice what we believe. God's grace usually comes through ordinary people like you and me who decide to proactively help those in need.

Husbands Need to Help

Finally, just as wives help their husbands fulfill their priorities, husbands need to help their wives fulfill theirs. Your job, men, is helping your wife be the best COO she can be.

In most homes, women do the lion's share of the organizational and maintenance tasks—washing, cleaning, shopping, cooking, balancing the checkbook, waking the kids up and getting them dressed, and so on. I recommend that the husband list all the jobs that need to happen for the home to function and identify who currently owns each responsibility, then figure out some significant ways to lighten his wife's load.

Refuse to let your wife bear all the burden. I'm not much of a cook, unlike all my sons and daughter, but I do the dishes, vacuum, and share the errands, and I have honestly learned to enjoy doing it. It's our responsibility as men to make sure our wives have some time to spend with other women. I met a man recently who brought his daughters to the gym with their coloring books so his wife could go to a Bible study with her friends. Be creative. Find ways to create some margin in her life. With your actions, tell her that you are in this with her and want to help her out.

That attitude makes a great picture of mutual submission, which takes us back to where we started. It is the foundation of all relationships in the home, and it feeds the marriage relationship in ways that allow each person to grow individually and in deeper intimacy with each other. It cultivates the kind of intimacy we see in the Trinity, where the Father, Son, and Spirit overflow with divine love one for another. A good marriage is a beautiful dance that reflects the nature of God, is deeply fulfilling to each partner, and is a blessing to everyone who sees it.

_____ **Questions for Reflection and Discussion** _____

1. Why does a man need a champion on his side? In what ways can a wife fulfill this role to nurture her husband?

2. Why are mothers so important in the lives of their children? What do they provide for their children that no other person can provide?

3. Why do you think Scripture singles out the mentoring role for women in matters of marriage and family? In what ways do you think this is needed in modern times?

4. If you are a woman, which of your three roles—nurturer, protector, or provider—do you find to be most challenging? What do you need to do to overcome those challenges?

5. In what ways has this chapter helped you understand the process of creating the family dynamics you want to experience? What specific steps can you take now to move toward your family goals?

14

How to Make It through the Hard Times

W e've seen a lot of natural disasters over the last
few years—devastating hurricanes and flooding
in places like New Orleans, Houston, and the Ca-
ribbean; mudslides and fires in California; earthquakes and
violent storms in many regions of the world. In some cases,
these events do not come with any warnings. But when they
do, we can be sure of one thing: those who are prepared and
responsive to the warnings have a much better chance of
surviving than those who are not.

As we come near to the end of this journey, I think it's important to warn you about the possibility of storms coming your
way. If you are unprepared, these storms could devastate your
marriage. But if you are prepared and know how to respond,
you can come through them unscathed—even stronger. It all

depends on your expectations, your understanding of the situation, and your willingness to make preparations.

Some storms in marriage are very predictable. In this chapter, I want to share some of them with you. I didn't see them coming in my marriage, and Theresa and I experienced a lot of difficult challenges and stress as a result. After more than four decades of my own experiences as a husband, pastor, and counselor of married couples, I can now look back and see how a little bit of preparation would have helped us— and how an underlying belief and commitment that many couples have not yet grasped can make *all* the difference.

Weathering the Storms

Not every storm in marriage will fit into a specific category, but there are some predictable kinds of challenges we all face. Some of the most common ones look like this.

Storm #1: "I Can't Believe They Did That"

When you first get married, the euphoria and the infatuation can run pretty high for a while. We call this the honeymoon period. It's a wonderful season of marriage and a beautiful part of God's design. But eventually that first fight comes. I remember the first major fight Theresa and I had, and it was over something that, looking back now, seems ridiculous. But what we fought about wasn't nearly as disturbing to me as the fact that someone I loved so much could make me feel so angry and disillusioned—and only a few weeks into our life together as husband and wife.

I didn't know how to resolve anger at the time. I was caught completely off guard. I found myself slamming the door, getting in my car, driving around for two hours, and actually telling God that I may have made the biggest mistake of my life. I can look back on it and laugh now, but I certainly wasn't laughing then. And if you don't recognize the wounds that can come from an experience like that and view them as somewhat normal, you end up sowing seeds of distrust and resentment in your heart and your marriage.

> *Whatever it takes, find a safe place to share your frustrations, both individually and as a couple.*

I have always believed in the importance of premarital counseling, but I have also found that postmarital counseling in the first few months of marriage can be vital. Sometimes that may come from a professional counselor or a pastor, but even getting advice from an older couple can help you prepare for and weather the early storms. Just taking that step will help you learn some basic communication skills, begin to understand how your mate works, and recognize that what you are going through is normal. Whatever it takes, find a safe place to share your frustrations, both individually and as a couple.

Storm #2: The New Baby

One of the greatest joys you can ever have is bringing a new life into the world with the person you love. But that great joy can also be the occasion for one of the greatest storms in your marriage. Pregnancy is not an easy time for many couples. The wife doesn't always feel good and may not be very affectionate, and the husband may be surprised at how the dynamics of the relationship change during pregnancy and shortly after the baby's birth. Men tend not to understand how vulnerable their wives feel and do not realize that they will need to be far more sensitive than ever before. And women tend to assume that their husbands will naturally understand fatigue, mood swings, and negative remarks and attitudes. Many of these tendencies and assumptions are not verbalized; communication becomes absolutely critical.

Sexual intimacy can be a sensitive subject in this season of marriage. It is possible nearly throughout the entire pregnancy, but it is often a casualty of the process, and the impact on the man is usually more traumatic than it is on the woman. She is dealing with all kinds of emotions and changes in her body, and the way she deals with them can feel to the man like subtle forms of rejection. That is not her intent, of course—far from it. But he is not getting the physical and emotional validation he craves, and even though he knows he needs to be more sensitive to her needs than ever before, the lack of intimacy begins to do strange work in his brain and emotions. Some men find that their greatest times of temptation are during the season of their wife's pregnancy. Just knowing that ahead of time can be helpful in weathering that storm.

The storm doesn't end as soon as the baby is born. I will never forget the joy and excitement of the first few weeks after our first child together was born. We were euphoric parents with this wonderful bundle of a miracle God had given us. But after about six weeks of being as patient and sensitive as I knew how to be, I began to notice the fact that my wife's full attention, all her emotions and affection, were on a seven-pound bundle of joy and not on me. Intellectually, I understood why. But by the third month, I was developing quite a bit of resentment. She didn't want to go out. She couldn't leave the baby even for an hour to go get a cup of coffee. Even after six months, Theresa still didn't trust anyone to take care of our child without one of us being there. We never had any time alone.

One of the worst feelings I can remember was being jealous of a little baby whom I loved with all my heart. This miraculous event was changing our relationship in some really difficult ways. It isn't easy for a man to tell his wife that he is jealous of their child. It seems selfish and insensitive. But as important as this season is, marriage always takes priority. A woman will find it very stretching to recognize that as wonderful as this new baby is, she still needs to direct some of her emotional energy to her husband. He needs to see and feel that the marriage is still top priority. It wasn't easy for Theresa to take the big step of getting away from time to time, but eventually she did, and we made it through this wonderful but challenging time of our lives.

Storm #3: Growing Families and Workloads

Families tend to grow in the same seasons that careers get more demanding. All the diapers and demands of the preschool years added to the financial strain of a new family can stress you out. Older people will tell you again and again that it doesn't last forever, but it feels like it does. Husbands and wives will find themselves stretched in ways they have never been stretched before, and attitudes—toward each other and life in general—can deteriorate quickly.

A wife needs more help during this time than ever before and in many cases will have a young husband who doesn't quite understand everything she is going through. I often came home to a thoroughly exhausted wife, and I wasn't nearly as sensitive as I needed to be. I tried to be patient, but I felt the stresses too—demands at home and at work, with a domestic life I had never experienced and a career that was beginning to ramp up. For many couples, the overwhelming challenges of everyone in your life needing more energy and attention than you can give them creates a perfect storm that may cause a lot of relational friction and a tendency to drift apart. When marriage and family seem to be more of a sacrifice than a joy, endurance is critical.

> *When marriage and family seem to be more of a sacrifice than a joy, endurance is critical.*

Getting through this time was not easy for us. We had to learn some different communication skills. We found ways to get some breaks—time together and alone. We didn't have extended family nearby, but we shared our kids with other couples for time away, rearranged how we would get everything done at home and at work, and learned to partner together. We also believed what we had been told—that this time would not last forever—and kept going back to the commitment we had made to each other. It took everything we had. If you aren't prepared for storms, they can cause you to question your commitments. But the commitments last longer. Storms do pass.

Storm #4: The Teen Years

When your children hit the teen years, they are going through some pretty stressful challenges and changes of their own, which in turn creates stressful challenges and changes for you as a couple. The teen years are particularly taxing not only because your children are learning to spread their wings but also because their schedules can pull a family in fifty directions. The wife balances being counselor, chauffeur, cook, friend, and her husband's lover, often while trying to hold down full-time or part-time work. The husband is often at the prime of his career, with even greater demands being placed on him at work. Life can feel like it is nothing more than a never-ending act of spinning plates or putting out fires. Cultivating the marriage relationship is easily pushed to the margins or even completely out of the picture.

The most significant thing you can do in this season of life is to remind yourself of what is really important and consider whose voices and values you are going to listen to. As important as your family's work, school, and extracurricular activities may be, putting your marriage relationship first and foremost is the greatest influence you can have on your children. Eating together; blocking off time for you and your spouse to date; determining when, where, and how you are going to discipline the children; and keeping communication open on all issues will help you get through this storm. It may not be easy, and sometimes you may feel like you aren't succeeding. But if you keep your focus on your values and priorities, you will get through.

I don't believe the teenage years have to be as traumatic as people make them out to be. In many ways, they can be very exciting and fulfilling times. Some children navigate those years without much stress; others seem to create crises in their own lives and in your relationship with each other. We had a range of those experiences. But when you and your mate have different approaches to those experiences, the storm gets a bit more intense.

For whatever reason, people often marry someone who has the opposite view of how to discipline children. You may find that in the balance between truth and mercy, one of you leans toward truth and the other toward mercy. That tension can lead to incredible conflict. Our differences over disciplining our kids and keeping commitments resulted in a lot of late-night talks as we sat in bed to figure out what we were going to do and why, knowing we had to present a united front to our children. It takes a lot of time to get on the same page, but the process can make you stronger and keep you balanced as a person. The conflict isn't fun, but it can be very productive.

Just remember that counseling isn't only for people in trouble. Sometimes the best thing you can do is get outside help at the earliest sign of friction, whether that is formally through a counselor or pastor or informally by asking an older, wiser couple for advice.

Theresa and I found ourselves gravitating toward people who were ten or fifteen years older than we were and who had raised their kids well. Just gleaning some wisdom and insight from them was very helpful, and it reminded us that what we were going through was normal. Knowing that we were vulnerable in our relationship, we also found ourselves reading a lot of books on marriage, scheduling one or two weekends away each year, and making our weekly dates a priority. By "dates," I don't necessarily mean the romantic, "isn't life wonderful" kinds of experiences—though they are great if you have them. I mean we planned times to go out, be alone, and not talk about work or the kids and just have some fun.

Maintaining the relationship beyond work and parenting issues helps create trust and unity for dealing with those issues and having difficult conversations when you need to. Your marriage becomes the context for everything else rather than everything else taking priority over your marriage.

Storm #5: The Empty Nest

You may have noticed that most of the storms we have discussed so far come with a major change in your marriage or family, whether that change is an event or a new age and stage. Major changes shift the dynamics, and shifting dynamics create uncertainty and stress. That is true whether the change is adding a new child to the family, beginning a new job, moving to another place, or any other significant transition you face. You can navigate change when you have an unswerving commitment to— and good tools for—resolving conflict. Whether some of these transitions qualify as storms or just windows of vulnerability in the relationship may vary from couple to couple, but any of them can present a challenge.

> You can navigate change when you have an unswerving commitment to— and good tools for—resolving conflict.

One of those vulnerable times is the empty-nest season. After working so hard at our marriage, I assumed this would not be a tough time for us. We would have more time together, and it would be an exciting new experience. I could not have been more wrong. I greatly underestimated what it's like when a woman's God-given nurturing role goes through a radical shift. When kids leave the home, and especially if they are doing well, husbands often feel like it's a sign of a job well done and that a season of reward is beginning. For a wife, this can be a period of grief and loss.

We had some really challenging times, and I developed some resentment when Theresa was still feeling blue a few months after our last child left home. We went through that a little bit every time we dropped one of our children off at college, but when the last one left, it was one of the most difficult experiences I have seen my wife go through. It's one thing to understand that; it's another to live through it. As in the early stages of marriage and parenting, men have to develop an extra level of sensitivity.

That isn't easy, as we men are often going through changes during this time too. A man's energy and desires tend to diminish rapidly in midlife. Sometimes he begins to question whether he still "has it," if he's still attractive, if he can still be the man he longs to be. When those questions are paired with a woman's empty-nest vulnerability, the temptations can skyrocket. In the first five years, 20 percent of marriages end in divorce. On the other end, the divorce rate among adults ages 50 and older doubled between 1990 and 2010. Roughly 1 in 4 divorces in 2010 occurred to persons ages 50 and older, the typical period of empty-nesting.[1] You have to be prepared for that storm.

Obstacles Become Building Blocks

There are plenty of other marital storms. Infertility or miscarriages, trouble with in-laws, work disappointments, serious illnesses, or the death of a child. But I think the preceding five storms are predictable and touch almost every marriage. And preparation is the key to weathering them. If you know what is happening, prepare yourself, and have an unswerving commitment to each other, you'll be fine. In fact, you'll be more than fine; you'll come through the storms stronger and wiser. Instead of tearing you apart, the conflicts, difficulties, and differences will bond your hearts and minds together and build the kind of relationship that lasts.

The things that looked like obstacles to the kind of marriage you always dreamed of actually become the building blocks for that kind of marriage. The storms actually serve as catalysts to achieving your ultimate goal in marriage— oneness. But don't underestimate the cost, the struggle, or the temptations that will come with those storms.

If you are going through a hard time in your marriage, you may find it hard to believe that it will work out for your good, or even that you will be able to endure it. But it really is possible to have a marriage that is fulfilling spiritually, emotionally, and physically, even in the most trying times. The key is your and your spouse's comprehension of the very definition of marriage, which we'll discuss next.

_____ Questions for Reflection and Discussion _____

1. What are a few of the characteristics of a "storm" in marriage? Do any of these hard times resonate with you? Why?

2. As I mentioned in this chapter, Theresa and I found ourselves gravitating toward people who were ten to fifteen years older than we were and who had raised their kids well. Who are the people in your life you can glean wisdom and insight from? Ask to meet up with them over coffee. What questions would you want to ask them?

3. Is there a couple you know going through a hard time in their marriage? How can you come alongside and help them through it?

4. What "predictable" storm could be coming your way, and what preparations can you make to help your marriage come out stronger in the end?

5. In the business of life, how are you making your marriage relationship a priority? Make a list of date ideas that give you time to be alone, talk, and have fun together.

15

Marriage: *Contract or Covenant?*

If you were to ask your coworkers or friends, you might find couples who, if they're honest, wish they could trade in their spouse for a new model. Yet God has given us the means to rekindle the fires and keep them burning for life. But it involves letting go of our perceptions and embracing his definition of what a marriage really is. At a fundamental level, we have to understand the nature of marriage, what it is based on, and how God sees it. If we're missing that, we will not have the wisdom or endurance to follow the design to the end.

From outward appearances and many people's experiences, it often looks like the costs of marriage outweigh the benefits. Many people give up before they get to the payoff. From God's perspective—and ours, if we will trust him and align ourselves with his truth—the benefits far outweigh the costs, and we will enjoy those benefits if we embrace the true nature of the marriage covenant.

This issue of perspective is the reason some people lose their way in the storms and others come through them stronger. It all depends on their view of marriage. I believe one of the greatest determiners of marital fulfillment—and one of the greatest predictors of whether you make it through the storms—is the understanding you have going into marriage. Our perspective on marriage is profoundly shaped by our upbringing, our society, and our own expectations—and it is rarely spoken or acknowledged. But that unspoken assumption will determine whether a marriage endures and fulfills or ends in brokenness and disappointment. It is huge.

That perspective or assumption is this: Do you see marriage as a contract or a covenant? Today, even among Christians, marriage is viewed primarily as a contract, a purely social construct, an agreement we enter into with another person for mutual benefit. We may write our own vows, pledge our undying love, or express whatever terms of the contract we want to express. But contracts have conditions, and they can be very pragmatic.

Committed No Matter What, Until . . .

The typical marriage contract today, even when the terms are not spelled out (and they usually are not), says something like this: "I am absolutely committed to you, no matter what, until I am no longer fulfilled or the relationship just gets too hard for us to continue with. You meet my needs, and I'll meet yours. I will stay in love with you as long as you are responding in ways that make sense to me and make me feel loved. When you cease to fulfill me or meet the needs that

I perceive you ought to, then I have the right to tell you we have grown apart, we are falling out of love, and I can't bear to think of being this unhappy the rest of my life." That's an agreement, but it's a very conditional one.

So with multiple excuses, reinforced by a culture and a media that see marriage as disposable, many couples quit the marriage contract in one way or another. Many Christians quit not by divorcing but by living silent, parallel lives that miss the joy and intimacy God intends and, even more tragically, the beauty he wants to represent in our relationships.

A Binding Agreement

By contrast, Scripture defines marriage not as a contract but as a holy covenant. Those words may come across as strange or a little archaic; people don't think much about covenants or about anything being holy today. But if this concept becomes the bedrock of your marriage, you will weather the storms. This is what kept Theresa and me together in spite of all our baggage, all our struggles, our blended-family issues, and more. We saw marriage as a holy covenant.

> *A covenant is different from a contract because it is not just an agreement; it is a sacred promise.*

A covenant is different from a contract because it is not just an agreement; it is a sacred promise. There may be some conditions written into it—there was a lot of "if you remain faithful" language in God's covenant with Israel—but if the terms are met, it is unbreakable. It is a solemn agreement with binding force.

213

This idea of marriage as a covenant comes from the earliest pages of Genesis and is the foundation of the triangle we looked at in chapter 1. God created man and woman to be united (Gen. 2:24), and the entire relationship—one spirit, one soul, and one body—grows from that foundational truth. Male and female, joined together in a marriage covenant, grow toward God in unity with each other and with him, representing the larger picture of Christ's love for the church. As we saw in Ephesians 5, marriage is not just for the benefit of a man and woman who love each other; it reflects the direction of all of creation, God's ultimate purposes for his people.

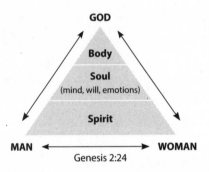

Malachi 2:14 addresses people who had strayed from God's purposes, and one of the areas of their unfaithfulness was in marriage: "The LORD is the witness between you and the wife of your youth. You have been unfaithful to her, though she is your partner, the wife of your marriage covenant." The prophet was speaking to those who were not living up to their promises, and because of their unfaithfulness, their fields were not producing crops and their enemies had the upper hand. People were wondering why God wasn't making

life work for them. The prophet's answer was that they had forsaken life's design by forsaking the marriage covenant.

A covenant is a guarantee—a binding vow. "When you make a vow to God, do not delay to fulfill it," wrote the wisest man in the world. "He has no pleasure in fools; fulfill your vow. It is better not to make a vow than to make one and not fulfill it" (Eccles. 5:4–5). When a couple stands before a minister and a congregation—"before God and these witnesses"—to make a vow about sticking with each other for better or for worse, for richer or for poorer, in sickness and in health, "until death do us part," that is very serious business to God. We may try to redefine it later. We might attribute it to the emotions we felt in that season of life before times changed. We might have a vision for how life would be better for both parties if we just went our separate ways. But none of those things were in the vow. The vow is what keeps people in the relationship when times are tough, so they can work through the difficulties and fulfill God's design for their lives.

A Promise Sealed with Blood

God established several covenants with his people throughout biblical history. The Hebrew word for covenant literally means "to cut," because it was sealed by blood—you didn't make a covenant, you cut one. The parties to an Old Testament covenant sealed their promises with a sacrifice because there is life in the blood (Lev. 17:11). It was an all-or-nothing commitment—no matter what happened, no matter who came against it, no matter how the circumstances changed, the agreement would not be violated. That is a holy covenant as Scripture presents it.

The first time we see this kind of covenant explicitly spelled out in Scripture is with Noah (Gen. 9:1–17). God judged the earth for its violence and sin, but he spared a remnant by telling Noah he would make a covenant with him. God promised never to destroy the earth with a flood again, and he gave the rainbow as a sign. There were conditions that Noah had to follow, which included worship and sacrifice.

God "cut" a covenant with Abram (whose name was later changed to Abraham) in Genesis 15 in order to establish a special relationship with him. He promised to give Abraham the land of Canaan and create a great nation from his descendants, who would be as numerous as the stars of the sky or the sand of the sea. This was unique as a unilateral covenant, a promise given by God for Abraham simply to believe. To establish the covenant, Abraham cut the prescribed sacrificial animals and waited until sunset. Normally, both parties to a covenant would pass between the halves of the sacrifices as if to say, "Breaking this covenant would be like severing our own selves." It was a symbol of how thoroughly the covenant became part of the person's identity. But in this case, God actually put Abraham to sleep and sealed the covenant himself (Gen. 15:10–17). He solemnly bound himself to his word.

A couple chapters later, the sign of remembrance was given: Abraham's descendants were to circumcise every male as a symbol of faithfulness (Gen. 17:9–14). In Exodus 34, God made another covenant with Moses and Israel, to be added to the one he had already made with Abraham. He would do wonderful, miraculous things among this nation of Abraham's descendants and establish them in the Promised Land, and they would serve God and keep his Law. The outward sign of remembrance was keeping the Sabbath.

Then in the New Testament—"testament" is another word for "covenant"—God sent his only Son, fully man and fully God, to live a perfect life among us, authenticate his ministry with powerful teachings, healings, and resurrections (above all, his own), and reveal the nature of the Father in grace and truth. And in his death on the cross—the blood of the covenant—and in his resurrection, he would save all those who believe in him so that we would not perish but have eternal life.

That's the vow. It's summarized in John 3:16, ratified in Mark 14:24, and affirmed in Hebrews 7:22, but it's really the theme of the entire New Testament. It is literally a "new covenant." And the condition that human beings must fulfill is to receive it by faith—to turn from sin and receive Christ as Savior. Jesus sealed it with his blood, we signify it by our baptism and faith, and the Holy Spirit is given as a down payment. That's the guarantee of the covenant, and God takes it very seriously.

You will find that all of these biblical covenants have four key characteristics:

- Covenants are initiated by a vow.

- Covenants include conditions.

- Covenants are ratified by blood.

- Covenants are sealed by a sign.

God's covenants nearly always include conditions. In Leviticus 26, God followed up the covenant with the consequences that would happen for those who were faithful to it and those who were not. "If you follow my decrees and are careful to obey my commands," he told them, "I will send you rain in its season, and the ground will yield its crops and the trees their fruit" (vv. 3–4). He promised to give them plenty to eat, protect them in the land, give them peace, lead them to victories over their enemies, make them fruitful, and dwell among them. "I will walk among you and be your God, and you will be my people" (v. 12). These wonderful promises were preceded by a very significant "if."

Wherever there's an "if," however, there is also the possibility of an "if not." The passage continues: "If you will not listen to me and carry out all these commands, and if you reject my decrees and abhor my laws and fail to carry out all my commands and so violate my covenant, then I will . . . bring on you sudden terror. . . . I will set my face against you so that you will be defeated by your enemies. . . . You will flee even when no one is pursuing you. . . . I will punish you for your sins seven times over" (vv. 14–18). Those are strong words, but that's the nature of a covenant. It is serious business.

Life-or-Death Consequences

God is emphatic about his purposes. He has a plan, a design for his people. He is the engineer of creation and redemption. His plan comes from a heart of love. He tells his people that he loves them, has delivered them, and wants to be with them. He wants to do life together. Now because of his love, there are some restrictions that go along with the relationship in order for it to function as it should and be as fulfilling as possible. And to discipline his people to stay within those restrictions, there are some serious consequences that come from violating them. These are not to be taken lightly. They are life-or-death kinds of consequences. Life will be really hard if his plan is not followed. But the point is that God offers his best, and we receive the best he has to offer—when we are faithful to his design. We follow his purposes, and he fulfills his promises.

> But the point is that God offers his best, and we receive the best he has to offer—when we are faithful to his design.

That was his word to Israel in the Old Testament, and it's his word to us today. Our sins are covered if we believe in Jesus and enter into his covenant of salvation, but life works only when we align ourselves with God's design. Those who remain hostile to him—whether actively in rebellion or passively by ignoring his instructions—will experience undesirable consequences. Those who embrace the grand design of the Master Engineer will find that life works as it was meant to. That doesn't mean it will be easy. It does, however, mean it will be more fulfilling.

Many Christians are wondering what went wrong with their lives. They are thinking, *But I'm a Christian! I believe in God. I have faith. I'm a follower of Jesus. Why isn't life working? Why isn't my job fulfilling? Why aren't my kids growing up right? Why is my marriage so unrewarding?* And the answer may be that they have violated God's covenant.

219

I am not suggesting that if you are faithful to God's covenant, then everything will work out for you. You might struggle with a job or a mate or a serious illness. We live in a fallen world, and some of God's most faithful servants have gone through extremely difficult times. What I am suggesting, though, is that if you see a pattern of all your fruitfulness being eaten up before you get to enjoy it—finances draining away, relationships stuck and stagnant, the joys and pleasures of life being overwhelmed by the constant stress of trying to make things work—you might want to consider that one possible cause is being out of line with the way God has designed you to live. If you can't figure out why you're having a lot of problems, at least consider the possibility of Malachi's message: that neglecting the covenant with your spouse can cause a sense of futility and lead to those kinds of questions.

Marriage vows— all covenants, actually—are a big deal to God.

I have had several conversations with disillusioned spouses after giving this message. I remember one in particular; a woman came up to share her story about how unsatisfied she had been in her marriage. She and her husband had been married a long time, and she eventually filed for divorce. As she listened to the message, she realized she didn't have any biblical grounds for a divorce. But as she talked, I realized she was hoping for some kind of permission to go ahead with it anyway—that it probably wouldn't matter to God because he understood how difficult things had been. And as much as I would have loved to tell her that it would be okay, I couldn't. It isn't true. Marriage vows—all covenants, actually—are a big deal to God.

I don't mean to imply that if you are divorced, you are irrevocably out of line with God's will for your life. He is a restorer by nature, and he restores broken lives. The entire story of redemption is about God taking the initiative to repair us and replace the broken covenant with a new one that is entirely on him to fulfill. He is loving and forgiving, and whatever your experience with a broken marriage happens to be, you can experience that love and forgiveness completely. But God is also holy and just, and violating a covenant comes with consequences. You can be forgiven, without a doubt, but you are probably already aware that restoration is a painful process. My desire is for people to come to an awareness of the sacredness of marriage and the beauty of living according to God's blueprint. It will save you a lot of heartache.

An Irrevocable Commitment

There is hope for every marriage and for society's perceptions of marriage, but it doesn't come from presuming on God's grace, denying that there is an original design, blowing off God's standards, and imbibing the feel-good philosophies of our day. It comes from getting back to the original blueprint and honoring the One who created it. An engineer does not change his most critical specs in order to accommodate the whims of the consumer. The consumer adapts to the design. We aren't "consumers" of God, of course, but we are called to be his followers, and we cannot expect him to adapt to our changing culture. We have to conform to him.

That means embracing the true nature of the marriage relationship as a holy covenant initiated by a vow and ratified

221

by blood. When a virgin woman has sexual intercourse for the first time, the thin membrane called the hymen is penetrated and bleeds. That's serious stuff. It's the biblical picture of making a covenant and why it is described as consummating the marriage covenant. It leads to a different definition of marriage than most of us have grown up believing. While most of society treats it as a contract, God sees it as a covenant.

Marriage is an irrevocable commitment of unconditional love toward an imperfect person. It is holy, and it is permanent.

Why is this so important? Because this is an impossible task without a permanent commitment. If you go through marriage with an escape clause—knowing in the back of your mind that you can get out if it becomes too difficult—you may not press through to the end. You may get stuck in the wilderness and never make it to the promised land. The covenant functions as a glue that keeps you together through the hard times. It creates safe boundaries for each partner to be himself or herself while trying to make things work without fear of losing it all.

> The covenant functions as a glue that keeps you together through the hard times.

Without it, you and your mate will act not out of commitment but out of fear and insecurity, which often distort perceptions and decisions in unhealthy ways. The covenant becomes a gift, an act of grace that protects you and gives you the freedom and security to cultivate a healthy relationship. You need the certainty of the covenant to bind you together when nothing else does.

———— Questions for Reflection and Discussion ————

1. What is the difference between a contract and a covenant? Do you think marriage is mainly viewed as a contract or a covenant today? How have your upbringing, society, and personal expectations played a role in your view of marriage?

2. Read Malachi 2:13–16. What stands out the most to you in this passage? Why?

3. Review the four key characteristics of biblical covenants described in this chapter. How are these characteristics seen in a marriage covenant? How do you respond to the idea that the marriage covenant is serious business?

4. Why is permanent commitment vital to a marriage? How have you seen this in your marriage?

5. We know that God answers prayer (Phil. 4:6–7). Will you commit to pray for your spouse and with your spouse?

16

Building a Bright Future Together

Following a common custom in Indonesia, young women who are about to get married sometimes gather together all their childhood toys and dolls and invite their girlfriends to a party to look at them one last time. Then they burn everything in a bonfire. It is a highly symbolic event that recognizes the bride's new reality: she is leaving her family and joining another one. Her old life is gone, and she is entering a new life with her husband.

Leaving, Cleaving, and Becoming One

The biblical covenant of marriage has three distinct aspects to it: leaving, cleaving, and becoming one flesh. These are based on Genesis 2:24, which spells them out: "That is why a man leaves his father and mother and is united to his wife, and they become one flesh." As the Indonesian custom illustrates, marriage involves a separation from the old and an embracing of the new. That doesn't have to involve burning old possessions or cutting off family ties, and it doesn't require you to leave town or even your old neighborhood. In biblical times, "leaving" often meant moving into another room that had been prepared for the new couple in the family home. But however far you end up from your families of origin, leaving does mean recognizing the reality of a new relationship. Old family relationships don't have to be ignored, but they do have to change. The primary relationship in a husband and wife's life is with each other.

The "leaving" implies separation. When you get married, you leave behind your dependence on former relationships, including financial and emotional strings. When you have a problem, you don't go running to Mom or Dad anymore, and you don't gossip with your friends like you might have done in high school. There's nothing wrong with getting advice from older married couples, including your parents; in fact, that's highly recommended. But they are peripheral now. They are outside counsel, not insiders. They are not your focus in sorting things out. You say to yourself and to your spouse, "This is really difficult, but I'm going to leave my attachments to them behind, and my new focus is you." That's leaving.

Then you "cleave," a word that comes from the King James translation. The best picture of cleaving is an epoxy adhesive: you are bound together. You don't just live together with your mate. You actually become one. You are no longer "you and I"; you are "us." Sometimes spouses take advantage of that reality to deny that the other person has any real individuality or personal needs, but that isn't what this means. You don't cease to be a unique individual. But you do cease to be an independent individual. Your decisions are no longer only yours. You live and move in tandem with someone else as though you are integrally connected or irrevocably joined. That is, in fact, what has happened in spiritual terms.

> You don't cease to be a unique individual. But you do cease to be an independent individual.

The result of cleaving is being "one flesh." If you were to mix up a pint of my blood and a pint of my wife's, it would be really hard to tell whose is whose, right? You would not be able to separate them again. That's what it means to become one flesh, and it plays out in a beautiful way when you have children, who embody the DNA each of you brought into the relationship.

In a sense, "one flesh" is an instant reality for a married couple, but living life as one flesh is a process. I had to go through counseling and read books to learn how to be one flesh with Theresa. Sometimes I've gotten stuck and have needed mentoring. When you bring all your dysfunction and baggage into a relationship with someone else who has brought all of his or hers, it isn't easy to become one flesh. It may be the biggest challenge of your life. But it comes with one of the biggest rewards you'll ever experience.

Leaving, cleaving, and becoming one are not automatic. The covenant of marriage declares some things to be true of you and your spouse; you are bound to each other as one. But experiencing oneness is another matter. A husband and wife need to be able to say to each other, "I know we have responsibilities to carry out, children to care for, money to earn, food to prepare, and bills to pay, but *regardless of whatever else is going on in life, I'm going to figure out how to get close to you.* I'm going to learn how to resolve anger, to communicate effectively, and to find some common interests and activities we can do together. Whatever we need to deal with in the meantime, we'll deal with. But whatever we need to do to make this happen, we're going to make it happen." I can almost guarantee that in eighteen months, that marriage would be radically different. And radically rewarding.

Instead, most of us want a shortcut—a quick fix. And when it doesn't happen, many people give up and either turn off on the inside or literally walk away. But quick fixes rarely have any long-term effect. Shortcuts in marriage don't work. The rewards come to those who are willing to make an effort and persevere.

The Implications of a Covenant

Because marriage is a covenant and not a contract, as we saw in the last chapter, it comes with at least four implications that fly in the face of our culture today.

1. Divorce is not an option.

We read Malachi 2:14 earlier. As we read on to verse 16, we see in the NASB and the NLT that God says he hates divorce. The verse goes on to say that the man who divorces his wife does violence to her by leaving her with no protection, no provision, and no prospects, which was especially true in ancient times. The covenant of marriage is meant to be inviolable.

I understand the nuances here. I realize there are times when divorce is unavoidable or grounded in Scripture. From the evidence in Jesus's teaching and other biblical passages, I believe there are two circumstances in which the Bible clearly allows for divorce: when a mate is unfaithful (because in that case, the covenant has already been broken) and when an unbelieving mate abandons the relationship. In fact, I married someone who had experienced that kind of abandonment. In neither case am I suggesting that reconciliation is impossible or undesirable; I've seen couples reconcile after one partner abandoned the other or had an affair, and it is a beautiful testimony to God's grace and restoration. But divorce is permitted in those cases. I would also suggest that in cases of physical or extreme emotional abuse, times of separation may be necessary.

I also understand that many people reading this book have already gotten a divorce when none of those exceptions applied. If you're one of them, you may be thinking, *I messed up, but there's nothing I can do to go back and fix things.* As I mentioned earlier, I want to be clear that even when you divorce without biblical grounds, it is not the unpardonable sin. Yes, there are consequences. But God forgives that sin just like he forgives theft, deception, and murder.

I've known plenty of men and women who have done unwise, unhealthy things and been used by God in powerful ways. The Bible itself is a book full of those kinds of people. If you read about the patriarchs' family situations, you begin to wonder how God could ever have made something good out of such a dysfunctional mess. But he did. I believe he still does that today, again and again. But if you're in a marriage now, you need to see it as a covenant in which divorce is not an option. If you leave divorce open as a possibility, you may not be able to withstand the trials, do the hard work, and eventually experience the greatest rewards of intimate union.

A covenant creates a safe arena for the kind of intimacy God wants to give you. Every human being longs for someone who can look into their eyes, see all their faults and flaws, and still love them. But because every human being is desperately insecure, we all pose and posture ourselves to hide the flaws and settle for superficial love. We act like we know more than we know and accomplish more than we can accomplish.

> Every human being longs for someone who can look into their eyes, see all their faults and flaws, and still love them.

But superficial relationships don't feed the soul. What we really need is to be loved in spite of ourselves.

If someone can see your baggage, your blind spots, your arrogance, your bad attitudes, and all your other imperfections and *still* accept and affirm the whole you, that's powerful. It does something for you. It is the closest experience you can have to seeing God's love in the flesh. And God designed that kind of love for marriage. But it cannot happen without openness and transparency, and no one gets that open and transparent in a relationship that isn't absolutely secure. Divorce needs to be off the table for that kind of love to flourish.

As I've said, the first five years of marriage and after the nest is empty are the two most vulnerable times in a marriage. In between, couples tend to focus on the kids—schedules, activities, schools, parenting strategies, and goals for the future. When those preoccupations are removed, many couples no longer remember how to relate to each other. They realize they have been living parallel lives all those years. It doesn't take much at that point to think about the limited time you have left and to redirect your attention somewhere else.

I remember my first really difficult and painful moment in marriage—not the first argument or problem, but the first big conflict when I questioned whether our marriage was going to succeed. We had a huge blowup, and I was hurt and angry. I slammed the door to the house, got in my car, and drove off. I thought, *Man, I can't believe how she's acting. What's wrong with her? I've married the wrong person!* At that moment, I just wanted out of the relationship. But the minute you start thinking that way, other options start coming to mind. Other people look better. You stop working at your marriage and let it fall apart.

As I was still stewing about my blowup with Theresa, God gave me a word picture. Theresa's family lived in the mountains of West Virginia, and when you walked out of their house, you'd see a rock face and hillside with a cave-like area cut out of it. There was a spring underneath this area where they had built storage for canned goods. It had a water supply and remained cool enough to store food in it.

I imagined my friend Dave, a bricklayer I had helped out some summers when I needed work, leading Theresa and me to that room. It was about 10 x 10 feet and had food, water, and (in my mind) even an exercise bike for working out. In

231

my word picture, Dave began to fill up the doorway with blocks three feet thick. At the end, he waved, filled in the last block, and walked away. Theresa and I could eat and drink and get some exercise, but there were no TVs or books. We could go to the corner and sulk or refuse to talk for a while. But eventually in a 10 x 10 room, you have to talk. There's no way out. You can't leave until you figure some things out. So it wouldn't do me any good to spend time thinking about how insensitive she is to my needs and unaffectionate she is being, or to complain about how I don't know what to do. And it wouldn't do her any good to think the same things about me and complain about how I'm only interested in sports, my work, or anything else I get self-absorbed about.

> Quitting simply is not an option. It's a life commitment; so figure it out.

If you're stuck in the room, at some point you realize it isn't any fun, and whatever needs to happen, it had better happen. Your only resort is really to sit down and talk and resolve some things. Quitting simply is not an option. It's a life commitment; so figure it out.

That word picture became my understanding of covenant. I know I can share anything with my wife, and she can share anything with me, because neither of us is going anywhere. The relationship is not in question. The health of the relationship may go up and down over the years, but the fact of it is not going to change. We no longer look at our relationship as win-lose because if one of us loses, we both lose. It has to be win-win. And that's the context in which intimacy can really flourish because the relationship is safe.

That is why living together before marriage doesn't work. If you think there's always an escape clause, you are never really free to be yourself without worrying if it's going to offend the other person to the point of breaking the relationship. There's never complete security. So in a covenant marriage, divorce is not an option. In fact, eliminating that possibility is the key to intimacy.

2. Adultery is a serious, covenant-breaking offense.

Proverbs 2:16–19 tells us that adultery puts people on a pathway toward death. No one wins. It is a physical expression of "one flesh" with someone you have not made a one-flesh commitment with and are not involved in a one-flesh growth process with. It is a violation of what God has intended.

3. Sex before marriage is a violation of this holy covenant.

We have come across Hebrews 13:4 before, but here is the full verse: "Marriage should be honored by all, and the marriage bed kept pure, for God will judge the adulterer and all the sexually immoral." If you are sleeping with someone you are not married to, or if you are logging on to websites that encourage you to envision sexual acts with someone you are not married to, stop.

That applies long before you are married because God looks at your life as a whole, not as a sequence. If you are searching for his will for your life, this is step one. That kind of sex is not about love—it's about selfishly satisfying your own lusts. I understand why it's so compelling; it comes from a broken place inside you. And God has compassion on you and wants to heal the wounds you are trying to heal with false remedies. But that is not the way. It will not lead to healing. God will judge the adulterer and the sexually immoral.

I understand that whether this is an actual relationship or a mental habit, ending it can be really, really hard. It will play on all your insecurities and magnify your greatest weaknesses. If you are involved with someone physically and emotionally, it may cause him or her, as well as you, emotional pain. But breaking it off and changing course will be good for everyone involved. The question you have to ask yourself is what kind of marriage, now or in the future, you really want to have. If it is to look anything like God's blueprint, all the counterfeits have to end.

> The question you have to ask yourself is what kind of marriage, now or in the future, you really want to have.

4. Same-sex relationships are forbidden as a violation of God's design.

Holding to God's Word on same-sex relationships is a really unpopular thing in today's culture. But regardless of what apologists for alternative lifestyles would say, the Bible speaks clearly on this. "Do not be deceived: Neither the sexually immoral nor idolaters nor adulterers nor men who have sex with men nor thieves nor the greedy nor drunkards nor slanderers nor swindlers will inherit the kingdom of God" (1 Cor. 6:9–10).

Notice that God distributes his judgment fairly among heterosexual and homosexual sins—as well as among other sins that have nothing to do with sex. This is a sobering verse for everyone, not just the sexually sinful. (Whether you've ever stolen or reviled anyone, you have certainly coveted and had idols in your heart.) But it does address sexuality, and illicit sex will not only bring God's judgment but it will also undermine your own desires for intimacy. It doesn't deliver what it promises. These guardrails are given by God because he loves us. To any type of sexual activity that prevents us from experiencing the best according to the blueprint, God says, "Don't."

If you have violated these terms of the covenant or any others, the first step to restoration is always to repent. Don't let the word intimidate you; it often comes with a lot of baggage, but it simply means to turn away from the old and turn toward the new. "God, I need help" is a beautiful and effective starting point. And it's necessary because you won't be able to follow the blueprint on your own. It doesn't matter how far away you think you are from God's best; his goal is to get you there, and he will help you do it. He always gets excited about putting his people on a new path.

> *Whatever mistakes you have made in the past, the way forward is open before you, and God will walk it with you.*

Wherever you are in your journey with him, make a commitment to the path that he has laid out for you in his Word. You will never go wrong by adhering to the design. If you are in a marriage that needs some change, or even if you consider yourself to be happily married right now, make a commitment to embrace these terms of the covenant. If you are single and hoping to experience the best marriage possible, make a commitment to begin with an understanding of what the covenant means and how to live it out. Whatever mistakes you have made in the past, the way forward is open before you, and God will walk it with you.

———— **Questions for Reflection and Discussion** ————

1. If God will forgive us for a broken covenant anyway, why is it important to treat the marriage covenant as a sacred, unbreakable vow?

2. For those who are married, which of the three aspects of marriage—leaving, cleaving, and becoming one flesh—has been most complete in your experience? Which needs the most work?

3. In what respects is the biblical view of marriage a countercultural statement? Why do you think there is such conflict over this issue in our culture today?

4. Are there any steps you need to take or commitments you need to make to align yourself more completely with God's design for marriage?

Conclusion

Throughout this book, we've talked a lot about biblical models and God's original design. That means, of course, that we have been looking at ideals—not unrealistic ideals, but still a template to aim for. God doesn't give us mediocre goals to match our human standards; he gives us divine goals to bring us up to his. So by nature, we have been considering things that many of us—all of us, at some point in our lives—will fall short of.

If you have read the pages of this book with a sense of frustration, a feeling that God's ideals will forever be out of reach, don't despair. I know from my own experience, my conversations and counseling sessions with numerous other men and women, and the pages of Scripture that there is plenty of grace for the journey.

God is on your side, walking with you to empower and encourage you every step of the way. I've seen him come through again and again because this life of intimate union between two people is a reflection of who he is and is always on his heart. In your efforts to align yourself with God's design for marriage, you can be confident that you are walking in his will. This is not an easy process, but it is a rewarding one. You *will* experience his blessing and favor.

In this book, we have also emphasized the "what" and the "why" about God's design for marriage and explored a lot of the "how." But no discussion of "how" can be comprehensive. I know how much of a challenge it can be to live out God's purposes in today's culture, and I know there will always be questions. Scripture is clear on God's nature, his character, and his intentions for marriage and family.

> Scripture is clear on God's nature, his character, and his intentions for marriage and family.

It is not exactly clear on every point of how to apply his truth to your life. But by prayer, his Word, and wise counsel, he will give you the wisdom that will lead you in applying it to your situations.

Again, know that there is grace in this process. God is not waiting for you to take a wrong step so he can harshly correct you. He gives you and your family the latitude to make decisions, even wrong ones, with every intention of getting you back on course if you have misunderstood or misapplied some aspect of his guidance. Rebellion and negligence will lead you away from him, but he will always honor honest attempts to seek his will and follow it. Keep your heart focused on him, and even your mistakes will work out for your good. He has promised to make all things work together "for the good of those who love him, who have been called according to his purpose" (Rom. 8:28). "All things" include your imperfect attempts to become the husband, wife, father, or mother he has called you to be.

If you have picked up this book on the back end of your marriage and parenting years, or somewhere later in the process than you would have preferred, you may have the tendency to think, *Wow, I should have done a lot of this, but I missed it. My kids are grown. My marriage is past its prime. It's too late.* Resist that thought. God has a way of redeeming lost and broken years for those who turn to him after the fact. I'm not sure how he does that, but he does. I've seen many people make decisions they should have made long ago and still reap the benefits of them. He is a redeemer and a restorer. He knows how to turn past mistakes into present blessings. Don't ever make the mistake of assuming it's too late for him to do that.

Finally, I would encourage you again to see this entire endeavor as a journey—not as a dichotomy of right and wrong ways to do things but as a spectrum between less biblical and more biblical, less effective and more effective, further from God's purposes and closer to them. Ultimately, we want to reach the goal of aligning as closely as possible with God's perfect design. But an either-or approach almost always ends in frustration and futility, at least at many points along the way. Your daily goal should be incremental progress.

> *Ultimately, we want to reach the goal of aligning as closely as possible with God's perfect design.*

You will probably never feel as if you have arrived, but that's okay. You may never feel as if you started early enough, but that's okay too. It's always a process, and God will bless any effort you make to move toward the destination. He will meet you at any point along the way and guide you with loving encouragement, correction, and strength. You can do this not because you are highly capable or smarter than the average person but because he says you can. Bring your willing heart to him, receive the guidance and power he gives you, and I am confident you will experience the satisfaction and fulfillment he designed you to enjoy.

Appendix

A Wife's Choice:
To Build or to Tear Down

BY DR. JULI SLATTERY

God's Word is filled with paradoxes. The weak are strong, to find your life you must lose it, the wise are foolish, and the greatest are the servants. Here's a paradox that no one seems to talk about: *a wife's greatest power is found in submission.*

I've spent the last twenty-four years striving to live out this paradox in my marriage to Mike. As a young bride, I wanted to trust God's call for me to submit to my husband's leadership. But I was also very skeptical. With a doctorate degree in psychology, why would I trust my husband's leadership in marriage and parenting? Didn't I know more than he did?

As a clinical psychologist, I also witnessed marriages in which women were minimized and even harmed because they believed they should be "submissive." I asked the Lord, "Help me make sense of your design for marriage!"

He answered with Proverbs 14:1: "The wise woman builds her house, but with her own hands the foolish one tears hers down."

Here is the revolutionary truth: every wife has power. Wives or wives-to-be, I'm speaking to you. Whether you are building or tearing down, you have power. Submission isn't about being passive but about using your power to build your home.

A Failure or a Hero

Your husband is very sensitive to failure. He secretly fears being exposed as a fraud or as incompetent. As much as he longs to be your hero, he is terrified of letting you down. Some men respond to this fear by taking a back seat. They don't make decisions or take leadership so that they don't have to risk failure. Other husbands handle their fear with bravado. They present a controlling, perhaps arrogant façade.

You, dear wife, have been given the power to frame your husband as either a failure or a hero. You are a mirror that reflects back to him either his strengths or his weaknesses— you are a reminder of his successes or of his failures. By wisely using your power can you encourage your husband to grow into the leader God designed him to be.

I have seen women develop two destructive patterns in relation to their power. Some women employ their power (even unintentionally) to gain the upper hand by dominating, manipulating, or treating him like he's another one of the kids. Often wives do this because they fear losing control or they want to avoid the vulnerability of trusting an imperfect husband. As a result, a wife's words, actions, and attitude consistently tear down her husband's confidence.

The second destructive pattern is for a woman to ignore her power in marriage—to be silent when she should speak.

Abigail or Sapphira

Submission is not weakness. It is power under control, directed toward a greater goal. Unhealthy teaching about submission in marriage has resulted in abusive, controlling, and dominating relationships. Tragically, this has contributed to the exploitation of women in our Christian culture and beyond.

Jesus was a defender of women and children. God's Word should never be used to justify or cover up abusive behavior of any kind. In a culture in which women are often viewed as sexual objects for a man's pleasure, the Christian home and church should be places in which women are highly valued, empowered, and fiercely protected.

Godly women are those who wisely use their power for great good in their homes, communities, churches, and places of work. I deeply appreciate the biblical account of a woman named Abigail recorded for us in 1 Samuel 25. She lived in a patriarchal culture, yet she was wise and judicious with her power as a woman.

243

Abigail had the misfortune of marrying a man named Nabal, who is described as harsh and evil. His name actually means "fool." Nabal insulted the future king, David, so greatly that David was ready to destroy Nabal and his family. Abigail wisely intervened, persuading David to show restraint. In this story, we see Abigail using her power to go against her husband's destructive and evil actions. She also uses her power to convince David to be merciful and trust in the Lord for revenge.

In contrast, in Acts 5:1–11, we witness the terrible result of a woman who did not confront her husband's evil actions but joined him in sin. Ananias and Sapphira sold a piece of property and lied to the church about what they did with the proceeds. Peter (their pastor) confronted both of them separately. When they lied, they were each struck dead by the power of God, a sobering demonstration of God's holiness.

Here's the point: God did not excuse Sapphira as a "submissive" wife following her husband into evil. We are each held accountable and called to stand up for what is right, good, and true.

Tearing Down or Building Up

Remember what Proverbs 14:1 says, "The wise woman *builds* her house" (emphasis added). This is an active role that requires discernment, wisdom, patience, and power. A weak woman isn't building anything. Due to passivity, her house may simply crumble around her. If you find yourself in an abusive marriage or church community, I urge you to reach out for help. God's design for marriage reflects Christ's relationship with the church. A Christian marriage that involves abusive behavior of any kind is a grave distortion of the Lord's will for husband and wife.

Submitting to your husband isn't ultimately about who is smarter, who has the better idea, or who was right last time. It also doesn't mean meekly obeying like a child. Submission is a conscious choice to use your power to equip and build your husband's leadership. Sometimes it means expressing your opinion or even putting your foot down. Other times it means biting your tongue or speaking words of encouragement.

God's design for marriage reflects Christ's relationship with the church. A Christian marriage that involves abusive behavior of any kind is a grave distortion of the Lord's will for husband and wife. If you find yourself in an abusive marriage or church community, I urge you to reach out for help.

Submission is a wife's conscious choice to use power to equip and build her husband's leadership. You have been given the power to frame your husband as a failure or as a hero. You have been given the power to tear down or build your home. Choose wisely!

For more information, visit authenticintimacy.com and read Dr. Juli Slattery's book *Finding the Hero in Your Husband* (Deerfield Beach, FL: Faith Communications, 2010).

Acknowledgments

Thank you, Marty and Ralph, better known as Mom and Dad, for keeping your commitment to one another when alcoholism threatened to end your marriage and fracture our family. Thank you, Dave and Polly, for showing me what a Christian marriage looks like. Thank you, Prof and Jeanne, for teaching us what God says about marriage and how to put it into practice. Thank you, Drs. Paul and Richard Meier, for the timely counseling that showed us how to repair what was broken.

Thank you, Chris and Anita, for the much needed help in turning messages into chapters; and a special thanks to Jerry for superintending the entire process and providing wise counsel as we added the final polish to the manuscript. Thank you, Charlotte, for your personal support and assistance with all the logistics.

Thank you, Chad, Mark, Erin, and Barb of the Baker Books team for helping me see the need for this book and for your excellent support all along the way.

Finally, this is a book about marriage, and the one person who I am most indebted to apart from the supernatural grace of the Lord Jesus Christ is my wife, Theresa.

Thank you, Theresa, for loving me, forgiving me, persevering with me, learning with me, and becoming my very best friend, my passionate lover, and my spiritual soul mate.

Notes

Chapter 1: God's Design for Marriage

1. Marist Poll, "'It's Destiny!': Most Americans Believe in Soul Mates," Marist Poll, February 10, 2011, http://maristpoll.marist.edu/210-its-destiny-most-americans-believe-in-soul-mates, accessed March 22, 2018.

2. Robert T. Michael et al., *Sex in America: A Definitive Survey* (Boston: Little, Brown, 1994).

3. Zack Carter, "Internet Infidelity: Today's Blind-Spot Threat to Marriage," PsychologyToday.com, posted June 1, 2017, accessed July 23, 2018, https://www.psychologytoday.com/us/blog/clear-communication/201706/internet-infidelity-todays-blind-spot-threat-marriage. See also Samantha Yule, "Facebook Now Crops Up in a Third of Divorce Cases over Cheating and Old Flames," Mirror.com, posted January 20, 2015, https://www.mirror.co.uk/news/technology-science/technology/facebook-now-crops-up-third-5011205, accessed July 23, 2018.

Chapter 3: The Evolution of the American Man

1. U.S. Census Bureau, "The Majority of Children Live with Two Parents, Census Bureau Reports," news release, November 17, 2016, https://census.gov/newsroom/press-releases/2016/cb16-192.html, accessed July 23, 2018.

2. The National Institute of Justice and the Executive Office for Weed and Seed, *What Can the Federal Government Do to Decrease Crime and Revitalize Communities?* (Washington, DC: U.S. Department of Justice, 1998), 11.

3. U.S. Department of Health and Human Services, ASEP Issue Brief: Information on Poverty and Income Statistics, September 12, 2012, http://aspe.hhs.gov/hsp/12/PovertyAndIncomeEst/ib.shtml, accessed July 21, 2018.

4. Warren E. Leary, "Gloomy Report on the Health of Teen-Agers," *New York Times*, June 9, 1990.

5. James C. Dobson, *Bringing Up Boys* (Carol Stream, IL: Tyndale, 2001), 54.

6. U.S. Department of Health and Human Services, *Morehouse Report*, National Center for Children in Poverty, Bureau of the Census (Washington, D.C.). Quoted in Dobson, *Bringing Up Boys*, 55.

7. Dobson, *Bringing Up Boys*, 56. See William Pollack, *Real Boys: Rescuing Our Sons from the Myths of Boyhood* (New York: Henry Holt, 1998).

8. Dobson, *Bringing Up Boys*, 56. See Hannah Cleaverin Berlin, "Lads Night Out Can Save Your Marriage," *London Daily Express*, April 25, 2000.

9. Pierre Mornell, *Passive Men, Wild Women* (New York: Simon & Schuster, 1979), 52.

Chapter 5: The Evolution of the American Woman

1. Encyclopedia on Early Childhood Development, "Importance of Early Childhood Development," http://www.child-encyclopedia.com/importance-early-childhood-development, referencing R.E. Tremblay, M. Boivin, RDe.V Peters, eds., http://www.child-encyclopedia.com/sites/default/files/dossiers-complets/en/importance-of-early-childhood-development.pdf, updated March 2011. See also Centers for Disease Control and Prevention, "Early Brain Development and Health," https://www.cdc.gov/ncbddd/childdevelopment/early-brain-development.html; and Laurie Sue Brockway, "When Does Your Child's Personality Develop? Experts Weigh In," P&G Everyday, https://www.pgeveryday.com/family/activities/article/when-does-your-childs-personality-develop-experts-weigh-in. All accessed July 25, 2018.

2. Apollodorus, quoted in Demosthenes' *Against Neaera*, Dem. 59. Included in *Demosthenes: Selected Speeches* (Oxford: Oxford University, 2014) 11, but likely written and presented by Apollodorus during a legal dispute in fifth-century BC. See https://tinyurl.com/ycfgwfg9.

3. Gene A. Getz, *The Measure of a Man* (Grand Rapids: Revell, 2004), 35.

4. See William Barclay, *The Daily Bible Study Series: Letters to the Galatians and Ephesians* (Philadelphia, PA: The Westminster Press, 1976), 171.

5. Association of American Medical Colleges, "More Women Than Men Enrolled in U.S. Medical Schools in 2017," December 18, 2017, news release, https://news.aamc.org/press-releases/article/applicant-enrollment-2017, accessed July 24, 2018.

6. *Profane Existence* (May/June 1992): 1, quoted in Robert H. Bork, *Slouching Towards Gomorrah: Modern Liberalism and American Decline* (New York: Regan Books, 1997), 212.

7. Christina Hoff Sommers, *Who Stole Feminism? How Women Have Betrayed Women* (New York: Simon & Schuster, 1994), 91.

8. Patricia Edmonds, "Now the word is BALANCE," *USA Today*, October 23–25, 1998, n.p.

9. "Porn in the Digital Age: New Research Reveals 10 Trends," Culture and Media, Barna Group, April 6, 2016, https://www.barna.com/research/porn-in-the-digital-age-new-research-reveals-10-trends/.

Chapter 7: Stepping Up as a Man: Provide

1. "Project on Student Debt: State by State Data 2015," The Institute for College Access & Success, ticas.org/posd/state-state-data-2015#, accessed July 24, 2018.

2. Financial Samurai, "The Average Savings Rates by Income (Wealth Class)," https://www.financialsamurai.com/the-average-savings-rates-by-income-wealth-class, accessed July 23, 2018.

Chapter 14: How to Make It through the Hard Times

1. Susan L. Brown and I-Fen Lin, "The Gray Divorce Revolution: Rising Divorce among Middle-Aged and Older Adults, 1990–2010," *Journals of Gerontology Series B: Psychological Sciences and Social Sciences*, 67(6), 731–41, doi:10.1093/geronb/gbs089, https://scholar.harvard.edu/files/goldin/files/graydivorce_0.pdf, accessed July 24, 2018.

Chip Ingram is the teaching pastor and CEO of Living on the Edge, an international teaching and discipleship ministry. A pastor for over thirty years, Chip is the author of many books, including *Culture Shock*, *The Real Heaven*, *The Real God*, *The Invisible War*, and *Love, Sex, and Lasting Relationships*. Chip and his wife, Theresa, have four grown children and twelve grandchildren and live in California.

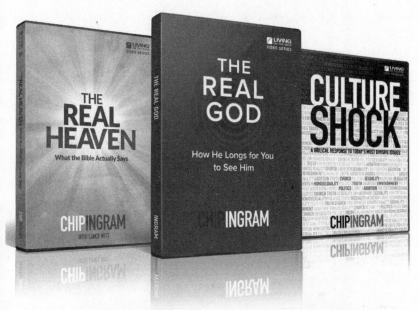

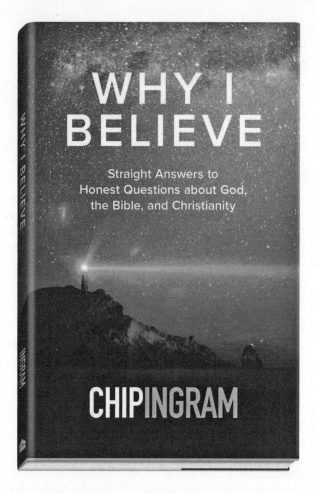

WHAT DOES THE BIBLE ACTUALLY SAY ABOUT HEAVEN?

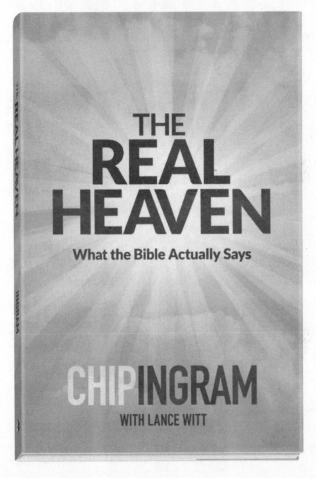

Chip Ingram sets aside the hype and myths and digs into the Scriptures to discover what God actually wants us to know about the afterlife. Most importantly, he shows why our understanding of Heaven matters now, in this life. Because what we believe about Heaven actually affects us today in ways we may not have imagined.

Also Available from
CHIP INGRAM

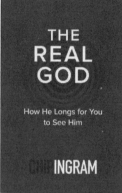
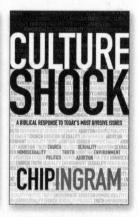
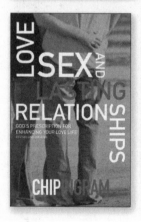
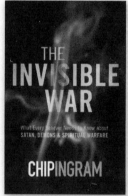

THE MILESTONES OF
ROCK & ROLL
THE EVENTS THAT CHANGED THE HISTORY OF MUSIC

WHITE STAR PUBLISHERS

1-4-23

WS White Star Publishers® is a registered trademark
property of White Star s.r.l.

© 2016 White Star s.r.l.
Piazzale Luigi Cadorna 6
20123 Milano, Italy
www.whitestar.it

Historical notes: Renata Moro
Translation: Katherine Kirby
Editing: Norman Gilligan

ISBN 978-88-544-1062-6
1 2 3 4 5 6 20 19 18 17 16

Printed in Malta

THE MILESTONES OF
ROCK & ROLL
THE EVENTS THAT CHANGED THE HISTORY OF MUSIC

TEXT BY
ERNESTO ASSANTE

Introduction

History is made up of events, dates and places and of people who create events in specific places at specific times. The history of rock is no exception to this rule, and thus, in addition to albums, it too is made up of concerts, festivals, special days and special places. And, it is to these very events, which have shaped, revolutionized and changed the history of rock and popular music, that this book is dedicated. These were events that contributed just as much to the making of today's world as those political and social events we studied at school. The musicians you will find in this book do not form an exhaustive list, and the moments that we have remembered here are, for obvious reasons of space, some of the most important moments of one story, that of rock, which, for just over sixty years, has been a symbol of culture, customs and contemporary society. These are moments that include fundamental figures such as Elvis, the Beatles, Jimi Hendrix, and Nirvana, but also James Brown, Bob Geldof and Johnny Cash because all of them, for one reason or another, have been a part of that great flow of popular musical culture that began in 1954 and which we know today as "rock."

The history of rock, from time to time, has also taken sudden and unexpected turns. What would modern music be like if, for some reason, that morning, Paul McCartney hadn't gone to meet John Lennon? What would global culture be like if, that day, Elvis hadn't gotten on stage for that first time? What would the history of the United States have been like if, on that evening, James Brown hadn't calmed those souls inflamed over the death of Dr. Martin Luther King, Jr.? It's obvious that everything would have been different, but, given that history isn't concerned with "what if," we'll never know the answers to these questions. But, we like to believe in the inevitability of rock; that it would have been born regardless, that electric guitars would have conquered the scene in any case, hair would still have grown long and the songs that told new stories and imagined a new world would have been written anyway. If it is true that rock isn't a genre or style but rather a "way of doing things," then the arrival of that way of dressing, of playing, of seeing the world and social and personal relationships, the dreams and hopes of different generations would have happened anyway. Without a doubt.

It would have happened anyway because, in addition to albums, radio and, today, the internet, there are concerts: those moments when a musician, a singer, "must" step in front of an audience and perform. Rock has radically transformed the performances of singers and musicians, who, up until the 1950s had "entertained" the audience with entirely different shows, that had within them a ritual component, a sexual and physical component, an intellectual component, and, at the same time, were based on a substantial transfer of energy between stage and audience. Rock concerts have nothing to do with the performances of jazz musicians in clubs, or with musical performances in theaters; rock has its own unwritten rules that are regularly torn down and rebuilt. It has its own visual and expressive force that does not accept compromises; it has its own particular appeal (which doesn't exist in any other kind of performance) that comes from the involvement of an audience that is never a group of simple "spectators" but, on the contrary, key players in a show's success. It is a show that is almost never closed into itself, but that refers to, or tries to refer to, something else, be it mystical, political, sexual or fantastic.

Moreover, the musician or group that takes the stage at any concert takes that stage thanks to a mandate from the audience to represent them. The rock public may never dress like Ziggy

Stardust, or be able to write a song like Bob Dylan, or scream about their burning desires like Jim Morrison, or devastate the stage like the Who, or mix art and life to the extreme like Janis Joplin, or find poetry in electricity like Nirvana, so they entrust this work to the musicians who represent them, who put the truth that the audience wants to affirm on center stage, doing so with the strength and the immediacy that the fans need in order to recognize themselves in the band or the artist on stage. It's a completely different artistic pact than that linking other musicians – jazz, pop, classical or opera – to their public, and it is what transforms rock concerts into collective rituals that, when the connection is alive and working, are unrepeatable.

This book, however, is not a history book. There is no linear path, no story that has a beginning and an end. Instead, it is a collection of snapshots, of legendary moments that have helped make us what we are today. Moments in which music has taken precedence over everything else – life, feelings, emotions, and history – and changed them. Instants, hours, and days that have served to awaken consciousness, spark reaction, light a fire in an abandoned heart or in a lost spirit, warm the body and soul, and push someone to run, to seek and to dream. These are concerts, songs and events that have taken music beyond itself, mixing it singularly and permanently with life, and doing so in a way that the confusion between art and existence is complete, total and essential. And that is precisely why we want to remember them. Like a puzzle, we have tried to take the various pieces – the moments between them seemingly unrelated and distant, with different characters, diverse music, sounds and rhythms from blues to soul, from folk to rap – and combine them in order to compose the most complete, true, suggestive and clear painting of the power and force of rock.

Within these pages are events that, undoubtedly, have helped construct rock's history, from its origins, from Elvis' first movements on stage, to the present day. Events that, for the most part, have had an audience, witnesses. Because, it's good to remember that rock doesn't just live in the creativity of the artists that have written its most beautiful and passionate pages, but also, especially, in the audiences that transform the songs, the events and the concerts into something more, something else, something different that has an incredible impact on life.

These are events that have given birth to other events, that have given rise to other works of art, more music, more life, moments that have contributed substantially to the development of popular culture in our time and to culture in general, because they have intercepted, interpreted and represented emotions, dreams, passions and collective needs as only rock has been able to do and done so extraordinarily.

Contents

The Genesis of Rock 'n' Roll: Elvis' First Concert

[July 30, 1954]

As the story goes, Elvis' first recording was a gift for his mother Gladys: two songs, "My Happiness" and "That's When Your Heartaches Begin," recorded on July 18, 1953 at Sam Phillips' Memphis Recording Service that was part of Sun Records studios. It would take another two self-produced songs six months later, in January, 1954, and a further six months before Phillips, constantly on the lookout for potential new stars, contacted Elvis at the urging of his secretary, Marion Keiser. On July 5, 1954, with Scotty Moore and Bill Black, Elvis recorded his first real disc with the songs "That's All Right (Mama)" and "Blue Moon of Kentucky."

The most important local DJ, Dewey Phillips, began playing the tracks on his show and their success in the city of Memphis was immediate. It was Phillips who brought Elvis to the stage for the first time at the Bon Air Club on July 17, as a guest singer for the Starlite Wrangler, a group that also included Scotty Moore and Bill Black. When Elvis took the spotlight to sing his two songs, the other members of the group left the stage, leaving the trio – Presley, Moore and Black – to play on their own. The performance that night wasn't particularly successful, but it

HISTORICAL NOTES

1953 – Presley begins to play the guitar at the age of 11. After graduating from high school he cuts his first single at his own expense.

1954 – When he is 19 he records his first 45 with Sun Records. He takes a job as a truck driver but leaves it after his successful performance at the Overton Park Shell.

1955 – He signs a contract with RCA and debuts with the local TV stations in the *Louisiana Hayride* show.

1956 – His debut album *Elvis Presley* is released. He makes his first national TV appearance on the CBS *Stage Show*.

Elvis Presley performing among his adoring fans.

spurred Moore and Black to leave the Wranglers and stick with Elvis, justifying Phillips' own choice as well.

Phillips then called another famous DJ from WMPS in Memphis, Bob Neal, asking him to let the brand new trio play an evening at the Overton Park Shell, a large outdoor amphitheater, when Slim Whitman and Billy Walker were headlining. Neal accepted and Elvis officially became part of the line-up planned for July 30, 1954, along with "Sugarfoot" Collins, Sonny Harvelle, Tinker Fry and Curly Harris. Elvis, who couldn't have been more excited, wrote to his fiancé, Dixie Locke, telling her to come back from her vacation right away so she wouldn't miss the event. He then started practicing with Scotty and Bill to fine-tune their little show. A few announcements were published to promote the evening, some of which featured misspellings, such as "Ellis Presley," but a small article in the Memphis Press Scimitar got it right. The anticipation in Memphis grew, as the single had been played more and more frequently on local radio stations. In addition, for the first time, different audiences – listeners to pop, country and African-American radio stations – were all listening to the same songs, Elvis' songs, causing increased sales and forcing Sun Records to quickly press new copies.

On the evening of June 30, it seemed as if all of Memphis was at the Overton Park Shell. Elvis arrived with his fiancé Dixie and his parents, Gladys and Vernon, nervous and excited. Backstage, all the musicians waited for their chance to take the stage, "He was uneasy," remembered Phillips afterwards, "he didn't know how it would go and it truly was his first time in the spotlight as a star, as Elvis Presley. I told him it would all be ok, that the audience would love him."

But Phillips' words didn't calm him down and it didn't help that Elvis couldn't find his guitar, forcing him to borrow one from another musician. Scotty Moore would later say that when it was his turn to get on stage, Elvis was shaking so much that you could hear his knees knocking together. There were four thousand people in the audience to see these three young men who only had two songs in their repertoire and only a few weeks experience behind them. But as soon as they were in the spotlight it all changed, and Elvis' instinct told him just what to do, how to move, how to let himself go, putting his body to work for the music. He was "possessed" and free at the same time; he moved, shaking his leg, tossing his arms in the air like no one had ever moved on stage before. His voice was beautiful, deep, and clear, with extraordinary pitch, and the audience greeted the first notes of "That's All Right (Mama)" with a roar. Elvis didn't immediately realize he was a success, initially thinking they were laughing at him and his mannerisms; instead, they were enjoying – loving – what Elvis was doing. Bill Black followed suit by twirling his bass, straddling it as if he were riding a horse, and the crowd went wild.

Once their two songs were finished, Elvis and his musicians left the scene, but the audience demanded an encore and Elvis returned the stage to sing "That's All Right (Mama)" and "Blue Moon of Kentucky" again, as well as a third song they were trying out, this time shaking his leg on purpose while he looked out onto the crowd that was yelling with enthusiasm at his gesture.

From backstage, Bob Neal couldn't believe his eyes. In just a few minutes, Elvis had changed completely: he was no longer the shy and terrified young man about to step into the spotlight, but had, instead, become confident on the stage, jumping, singing, twirling his arms, shaking his legs and inciting the audience with incredible confidence. It was a triumph; it was undeniable that the young man from Tupelo had something more, something better, than other stars. He was different, handsome, sexy, intense, believable, strong and original.

In a few minutes, Elvis Presley was born, the king of rock 'n' roll. In a few minutes, Elvis Presley's first official live show was over. However, it was all just about to begin.

An amateur photographer, Robert Dye, snapped a few pictures of this extraordinary moment, when the history of rock began, as well as a great photograph of Elvis with a child, Charlie Torian Jr., the son of Memphis' lieutenant fire-fighter, who was backstage to meet the star that night. When Elvis died on August 16, 1977, that child (who had, by then, become a Memphis police sergeant) was assigned to guard Elvis' body at Graceland.

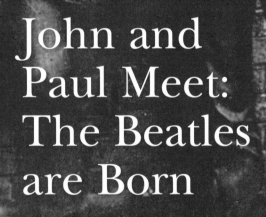

John and Paul Meet: The Beatles are Born

[July 6, 1957]

S kiffle was an early form of popular rock 'n' roll, revived in England during the mid-1950s, which was combined with traditional music and folk, and was often played with instruments improvised from objects of daily use, such as washboards or boxes turned into a rudimentary bass (a tea chest bass) by the addition of a brush handle and a tight piece of string. It was the music of youths in England who were searching for something with the right rhythm and spirit after the Second World War.

John Lennon loved rock 'n' roll, he attended Quarry Bank High School in Liverpool and he wanted to have a band. Thus began the Quarrymen, a teenage skiffle band that played whenever and wherever they could. On July 6, 1957, the Parish Church of Woolton, the neighborhood where Lennon lived with his Aunt Mimi, decided to organize a garden fête – a dance – with live music. What better occasion for the Quarrymen to perform? John and his friends, Eric Griffiths, Colin Hanton, Pete Shotton, Rod Davis and Len Garry, boarded a pickup truck and, playing on the move, arrived at the church with the pro-

HISTORICAL NOTES

1956 – John Lennon forms the Quarrymen band.

1957 – John (16 years old) and Paul (15) meet at a parish church party.

1958 – George Harrison joins the band, which offers a mixture of skiffle and rock and roll.

1960 – The band plays in Hamburg, where they change their name to The Beatles and meet Ringo Starr.

1962 – "Love Me Do," the Beatles' first major international success, is released.

1970 – Let It Be is their last disc. On April 10 McCartney publicly announces that the band has decided to break up.

George, John and Paul in front of McCartney's house.

cession. Ivan Vaughan, John's close friend and "fan" of the Quarrymen, decided it was the right occasion to introduce him to another friend of his. This friend was Paul McCartney, who could play the guitar well, who had a nice voice and who would be a perfect addition to the band. So, he called Paul and introduced them to each other at the fête.

At the end of the concert, they went into the church's oratory, where Ivan introduced Paul to John. To tell the truth, the two didn't like each other at first. But, when Paul began to play the guitar and sing an Eddie Cochran song, "Twenty Flight Rock," John immediately realized that Paul was the perfect person for his band, that his addition would be a good thing, and he invited Paul to join the Quarrymen. It would be a few months (during which time the two became inseparable) before the Quarrymen had their first performance with Paul, on October 18, 1957 at the Conservative Club. But the start of the greatest legend, or fable, or better yet, revolution, in the history of modern popular music, was a garden fête at a church where a certain Eleanor Rigby was buried.

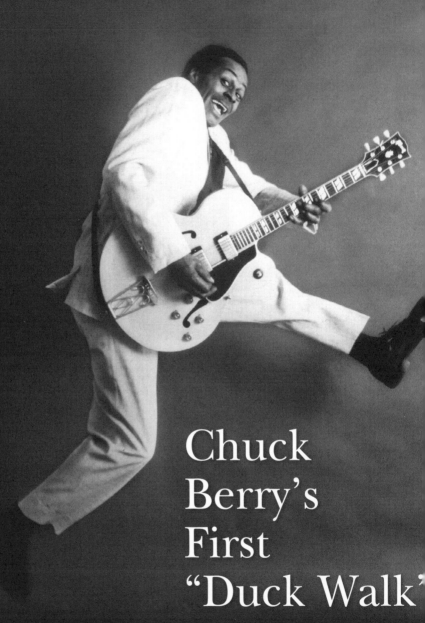

Chuck Berry's First "Duck Walk"

[July 9, 1957]

The history of rock is, obviously, made up of great songs, important lyrics, and original and innovative sounds. But it is also made up of gestures that, without a doubt, have contributed, in their own way, to the creation of rock 'n' roll myth. Gestures that in their immediacy, their simplicity and their strength were able to speak to the public along with music and lyrics. Moreover, rock isn't so much a musical genre as a way of doing things, meaning that the essence of rock isn't necessarily or only a sound. The way one acts on stage, for example, has always been crucial to determining rock's existential boundaries, as Elvis Presley quickly made clear by shaking his hips. We can then legitimately ask ourselves: would rock have been the same if Chuck Berry, on the night of July 9, 1957, hadn't invented his famous "duck walk" on the stage of Radio City Music Hall?

First, we'll try to define what exactly the "duck walk" is. The dancer squats down slightly, putting his weight on his right leg and raising his left leg in the air, which, hopping, allows him to move forward as he kicks his raised left leg back and forth, clutching the guitar to the right side

HISTORICAL NOTES

1926 – Chuck Berry is born in Saint Louis, Missouri.

1941 – His first public performance takes place at Sumner High School.

1955 – After playing a few years in various St. Louis clubs on the side, he records the single "Maybellene" for Chess Records of Chicago; almost a millions copies are sold.

1956 – "Roll Over Beethoven" is released. Berry becomes a star.

1979 – President Jimmy Carter asks Berry to perform at the White House.

1984 – He receives the Grammy Lifetime Achievement Award.

Chuck Berry with his inseparable Gibson Hollow Body.

of his body. Chuck Berry was a master of the "duck walk," which he had been doing since he was a child to entertain family and friends at home. But it was that night in 1957, at the height of his success at Radio City Music Hall in New York, that, with a stroke of sudden genius, Berry decided to transform a guitar solo into a complete, physical gesture and change rock history. In a single blow, that gesture derided a goose's walk, military marches, the rules of good manners and those of show business. With his nonsensical, spectacular and explosive "duck walk," Berry spoke to young people more clearly than he did with his songs or his guitar, saying, "it's possible to do strange, fun things; you're free, you can do it too," and opening the gates to an infinite series of equally nonsensical, spectacular and explosive gestures that rock has offered throughout its history. In one night, Chuck Berry brought rock to a new dimension; he announced loud and clear that it wasn't just about music, but a way of life, of transforming it into art. Ten years passed between Berry's duck walk and Jimi Hendrix's guitar being set on fire; and yet another forty years between the latter and Lady Gaga's stage shows. But the meaning of a rock gesture, made not just to amaze or entertain the audience but to carry the real sense of the music itself, has not changed.

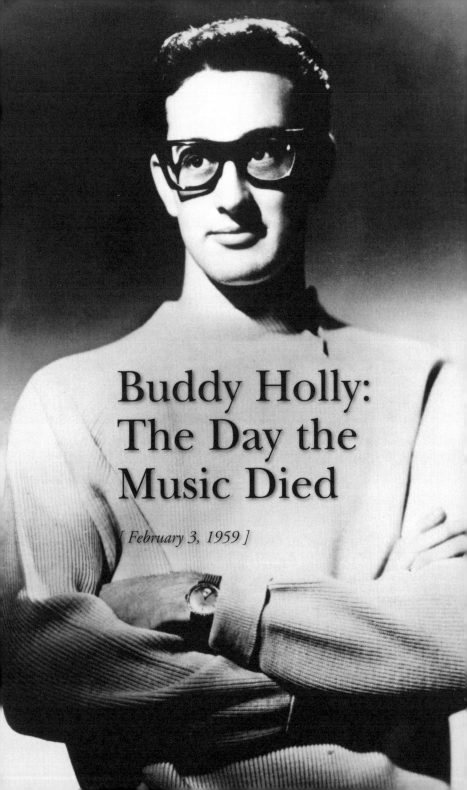

Buddy Holly: The Day the Music Died

[February 3, 1959]

B uddy Holly wasn't a star like all the others. The heroes of early rock 'n' roll were excessive, spectacular, rebellious: Little Richard, Chuck Berry, Elvis Presley, or "The Killer" Jerry Lee Lewis weren't exactly the types you'd want your sister to go out with. You would want her with Buddy Holly, however. He had the looks and manners of a calm type and, as was the fashion, he wore a pair of over-sized spectacles like a classic school nerd. His songs, still steeped in country and rockabilly, were perfectly written to win over anyone's heart.

Yet in just two years, between 1957 and 1959, Buddy Holly and his Crickets had swept the world of rock 'n' roll. They were the first band with the now-classic format (two guitars, one bass and drums); they were able to break the mold and the fences of the rigid American market, becoming the first white band to appear on a tour made up of African-American stars and lineups. Holly, in addition to having had a string of very successful hits, was quickly becoming one of the songwriters most requested by singers of the era.

Everything was going well in February of 1959, and everything was sup-

HISTORICAL NOTES

1957 – Holly forms The Crickets band. The debut album *The 'Chirping' Crickets* is released by Coral Records and becomes a hit.

1958 – *Buddy Holly*, his debut solo album, is released. He and his band make a tour in Australia and, two months later, in the UK. His third and last album, *That'll Be The Day*, is released.

1959 – The Winter Dance Party Tour debuts on January 23 at the Million Dollar Ballroom in Milwaukee. Holly dies in a plane crash on February 3. Less than a month later Coral releases *The Buddy Holly Story* album.

Buddy Holly is one of the musicians who made rock'n'roll great.

posed to get even better. First and foremost, there was love: young Buddy was set to be married within five months to Maria Elena Santiago, who was two months pregnant. Having ended his adventure with the Crickets, Holly had a brand new band with Waylon Jennings, Tommy Allsup and Carl Bunch, and he had already started a new tour with them. The 24-date Midwestern "Winter Dance Party" tour was also to star Ritchie Valens, fresh from the success of "La Bamba;" Dion DiMucci, star of Dion and the Belmonts; J.P. Richardson, a.k.a. the Big Bopper; and many others. The tour was poorly organized, however, with too much distance to cover between one venue and the next, and too tight a schedule, in a run-down tour bus without heating that caused many of its passengers to get sick, which was the reason that Carl Bunch ended up in hospital with frostbite. Once Holly arrived in Clear Lake, Iowa, tired from the difficult journey, he decided that he and his band wouldn't continue on the bus, but instead would rent an airplane from Dwyer Flying Service, that would have taken them all the way to Fargo, North Dakota. The Big Bopper, who was also sick, asked Waylon Jennings to give him his spot on the plane; Ritchie Valens asked Allsup if he wanted his seat, but Allsup refused the offer. At Valens' insistence, the matter was to be decided by fate, flipping a coin that landed in Valens' favor and he boarded the plane. Dion DiMucci, however, declined Holly's invitation, saying the cost of 36 dollars per ticket was excessive.

The flight didn't last long; Roger Peterson, the plane's young pilot, lost control of the aircraft and it fell from the sky. Peterson, Valens and Richardson lost their lives in the impact.

In 1971, Don McLean wrote a wonderful song, "American Pie," that refers to the plane crash, defining February 3, 1959 as "The Day the Music Died." The tragedy was a forceful blow to the collective imagination, partially because of how it happened, but much more so for the fact that three young rock 'n' roll stars, three members of a generation that was just starting, slowly, to get moving, were unexpectedly and tragically killed.

Shortly afterwards, rock 'n' roll itself would meet its own end, with Jerry Lee Lewis' and Chuck Berry's legal problems, and with Elvis' departure for the military. There was an eventual restoration, a return, of pop: the era of the teen idol. But the gauntlet thrown down by Buddy Holly was quickly picked up on the other side of the ocean; in Liverpool, the Beatles would pick it up and transform it into beat, bringing music back to life.

Music in Black and White: Ray Charles

[*May 28, 1959*]

There are some concerts that have marked historic turning points in music history. One of these was Ray Charles' concert at the Heddon Stadium in Atlanta, Georgia, on May 28, 1959.

Charles was already a star, having started his long musical adventure when he was still a teen in the mid-1940s, and having had some success from 1949 onwards, especially in the early 1950s when he signed a contract with Atlantic Records. He had already gained "stardom" in 1955 with "I Got a Woman," which had launched him into the upper echelons of black music.

But the African-American audience wasn't enough for Ray Charles. His musical roots were in gospel and blues, but he loved pop and country, the music from the South, where he had had a difficult childhood.

Charles had many successful songs in the world of black music, a few of which would become legendary, such as "It Should Have Been Me," "Lonely Avenue," "This Little Girl of Mine," and "Hallelujah, I Love Her So," but for some time his creative efforts had been centered

HISTORICAL NOTES

1948 – Charles forms the Mc-Son Trio.

1949 – His first record, "Confession Blues," is released by Down Beat Records (also known as Swing Time).

1951 – "Baby, Let Me Hold Your Hand" is his first hit to reach the charts.

1953 – "The Things I Used to Do" becomes a best-seller.

1960 – *In Person*, a live recording of his May 28 1959 concert in Atlanta, is released.

1986 – He establishes the Ray Charles Foundation for the blind.

2004 – Charles dies two months before the release of his last album, *Genius Loves Company*, which sells more than 5 million copies.

Ray Charles in 1959 with his beloved piano.

on a song that was different from the rest. This song essentially arose from an improvisation that Charles and his band had played at the end of a concert in December 1958. The legend goes that Charles still had a few minutes of stage time available and that, to fill them, he asked the band and The Raelettes to follow him as he went along, starting with some riffs and then arriving at the classic "call and response" of gospel, with both the backup singers and the band. The effect was explosive and Charles began to experiment with improvisation at the end of his concerts for a number of consecutive nights. Finally, in February 1959, at the Atlantic Records Studios, Charles and his group recorded "What'd I Say." At first listen, the song may have seemed just like all the others. Charles had already recorded other hits, but that song was to become a turning point not only in the career of "The Genius," but also in the history of popular music.

The turning point came in Atlanta, on the evening of May 28, 1959 at the Heddon Stadium, when Ray Charles first officially played not the improvised jam from before, but the actual song itself, which had arrived in stores shortly before. It wasn't just African-Americans (who were in the majority at the stadium) who went wild for the song's rhythm, but many white people as well, who had come precisely to hear that song, just as it had begun to be played on the radio. "What'd I Say" was a bomb launched against the habits of the American music market, which was rigidly divided racially. African-American music was for blacks, and pop was for whites, but this song offered a new category, "soul music," founded on undeniably black roots, but created to be enjoyed by a much wider and indistinct audience. It was music that met the tastes, the emotions and the lives of people in a direct, unequivocal way, breaking down the wall of "race music" once and for all. "What'd I Say," sung in a chorus at the stadium in Atlanta, signaled the start of a new era, that of soul music. Together with rock, it soon changed the characteristics of popular music the world over as it rose in the charts – not just the African-American charts, but pop as well. It was the first time that that had happened so clearly and explosively. The world was changing.

Eddie Cochran: Rock 'n' Roll Arrives in the U.K.

[*January 24, 1960*]

If it is true that beat and the revolution of the 1960s started in England in 1962 when the Beatles released *Please Me*, it is also true that without the tour at the start of the 1960s that brought a rock 'n' roll "package" of the caliber of Eddie Cochran and Gene Vincent to English stages for the first time, music in Great Britain probably would have taken a very different course.

Rock 'n' roll had already arrived in England, first in the movies with "Blackboard Jungle," and with the explosive performance by Bill Haley and his Comets in 1956, then in 1957 with Haley's solo tour. In 1958, Buddy Holly warmed the hearts of young Brits, but nothing else really significant happened in the following two years. However, for British youth everything was changing: their lifestyle, fashion, dreams and, obviously, the music they listened to. Larry Parnes, an active impresario who had already brought about the success of some British stars such as Tommy Steele and Billy Fury, realized that life was changing for young people and that he could organize a successful "package tour" by putting young English stars such as Billy Fury, Joe Brown and Tony Sheridan

HISTORICAL NOTES

1955 – He drops out of school to concentrate on music. With Hank Cochran (no relation) he forms the Cochran Brothers band and records country-rockabilly albums.

1956 – Influenced by Elvis Presley, Cochran abandons country music for rock'n'roll, a decision that leads to the break-up of the Cochran Brothers.

1958 – "Summertime Blues" and "C'mon Everybody" become hits.

1960 – He leaves for a tour of the United Kingdom, playing to full houses every night, beginning with the gig at the Gaumont in Ipswich.

Eddie Cochran on the stage of the Wembley Empire Pool, 20 February 1960.

together with stars from the United States. So, he organized a series of concerts from January 24 to April 16 that had Eddie Cochran and Gene Vincent as the headliners. Cochran was fresh from the clamorous success of two songs, "C'mon Everybody" and "Summertime Blues." After the triumph of "Be-Bop-A-Lula," Gene Vincent had gone through a difficult period, but he was in top form, with his excessiveness and lack of moderation, to conquer England.

The first night at Ipswich was a triumph; the hall was full, the crowd was enthusiastic, the fans (at least those in the front row) were going wild and screaming. In just one night the history of English music switched gears: it was no longer the time of elegant, well-behaved stars that up until then had risen in the charts. A new generation was ready for something stronger, gutsier, and different. They were ready for the explosive Eddie Cochran and his bottles of whisky and Gene Vincent's leather jacket as he shook his metal leg on stage. They were ready for an electric shock that soon would take over the UK and the world. They were ready to leap out of the 1950s, away from conformity, from dullness, from a future that was already written by their parents. And anyone who was at that concert, just as at the following tour dates until mid-April, left convinced that his life had been changed forever, that the old rules were on their way out and that the world could be seen through new eyes. This was especially true for anyone who played an instrument and who went back home, back to their bands, ready to set the UK alight. The fire of the new teenage music craze had been lit and no one, truly no one, could put it out.

The Cavern from Which the Beatles Took Flight

[February 9, 1961]

1 961 had started only a few weeks earlier, and the future for John Lennon, Paul McCartney, George Harrison and Ringo Starr seemed bright. Their band, which after a few name changes had become the Beatles once and for all, had just returned from Hamburg, Germany, from some sort of hellish round of amphetamines, sex, freedom and pleasure where they had honed their abilities as entertainers and musicians, playing in smoky clubs full of sailors as many as three times a day. They were back in Liverpool and they felt bigger, ready to try to take on a leap of quality and conquer a bigger slice of success. To do so, they had to get to Matthew Street, the street known for its clubs in the center of Liverpool. That's where the Cavern Club was, in a basement, a large cellar with various rooms, which was beginning to align itself with the new musical styles in vogue with young people (such as skiffle, blues and rock 'n' roll) after many years of booking only jazz bands. Lennon had already had the satisfaction of playing at the Cavern in 1957 with the Quarrymen, but the show back then was little more than a game. Now, for the

HISTORICAL NOTES

1960 – The Beatles play at the Indra Club in Hamburg. When they return to the UK they make a hit at the Casbah in Liverpool and sign a contract for 37 concerts.

1961 – They have their first concert at the Cavern Club. In June they work in a recording studio for the first time as a backup band for the vocalist Tony Sheridan. Brian Epstein becomes their manager.

1962 – Parlophone releases their first single, "Love Me Do/ P.S. I Love You," which peaks on the charts.

1965 – Queen Elizabeth appoints them Members of the Order of the British Empire.

The Fab Four at the beginning of their career.

41

Beatles, a debut at the Cavern meant so much more, because if the band was able to convince the club's owner, they would have the chance to be heard by a significantly larger audience than at the Casbah Club where they began.

The band had returned from Hamburg in a scattered formation: first was George, forcibly sent home because he was still a minor; then came Pete Best and Paul McCartney, arrested for trying to start a fire (according to the theater's owner) on November 29, 1960 while they were preparing their suitcases to leave the Bambi Kino (the movie theater above which they were sleeping), causing them to be subsequently deported. John Lennon and Stuart Sutcliffe had stayed on in Hamburg for a while longer, the latter returning to Liverpool at the end of January, leaving his heart in Germany, in the hands of Astrid Kirchherr.

Other bands from the new Liverpudlian music scene had already played at the Cavern, from the Remo Four to Rory Storm and The Hurricanes, whom Ringo Starr played with in the afternoon and evening shows. But the Cavern had chosen the Beatles to open a new lunchtime concert series, guaranteeing the band a payment of 5 pounds sterling. When they arrived at Matthew Street for their first Cavern gig, things immediately took a turn for the worse, since the stewards at the door didn't want to let Harrison in. The reason? He was wearing jeans, clothing that was banned from the club. The owner, Ray McFall, thought that a more refined dress code would bring a less quarrelsome and chaotic crowd, perhaps even one that was more likely to buy something at the bar. George had to convince him that he was a musician in the band in order to be let in.

The Beatles were anything but a band of novices. The experience in Hamburg had allowed the band to grow musically, but it had also taught each of them how to behave on stage, how to react to the audience's demands and how to entertain. They worked as a team, as a band: each one of them assumed leadership for a song or two, or they threw in some gags or jokes. This division of labor and responsibility was one of the secrets of their success. No one was ever completely alone; no one was the front man with the others at his back. They were a band, a group, united and compact, and they projected this democratically collective image to the audience in front of them. Lennon's job was to warm hearts, McCartney's was that of singing the most passionate songs, Harrison was to enrich everything with his talents as a guitar player, and behind them were the solid Pete Best and the dark and mysterious Stu Sutcliffe.

The set was simple: rock 'n' roll classics, songs with easy impact. They knew what they were doing; they played every day in various clubs in the city – at the Casbah (their "home"), managed by Pete Best's mother, but also at the Aintree Institute, Litherland Town Hall, the Casanova Club and Lathom Hall, where they were followed by a small squad of fans. But the audience at the Cavern was what they wanted, and that's what they would get. The trick worked. The public looked with favor on that first show and in the following years the Beatles would play at the Cavern nearly three hundred times, until August 1963, when they would say goodbye to the cavern of their beginnings to conquer the world and change it forever.

The Birth of
a Legend:
Bob Dylan
Arrives in
New York

[April 11, 1961]

He had arrived in the city just a few weeks prior. A pilgrim to a saint he had worshiped for years. He had to see him, talk to him, and make him listen to his first songs. For young Robert Zimmerman, Woody Guthrie wasn't just the greatest folk singer alive: he was the idol, the road to follow – his role model. And New York was the Promised Land. That meeting in a hospital, still shrouded in the mists of legend, would give Bob Dylan the strength and courage to leave everything behind, to start *his* journey without a destination, without any set goal. His first show, in what was soon to become his city, would take place a few days later.

Bob Dylan arrived in New York after having wandered about with his guitar for a while. Leaving Minneapolis, where he had quit college in 1960, he started to play on the folk club circuit, singing traditional songs. He went to Denver, to Chicago and to Madison, but he knew that if he really wanted to sing and play he had to go to the "center of the world" – New York. And he did. In early 1961, he seized the opportunity to

HISTORICAL NOTES

1959 – He begins to perform in Minneapolis clubs. At the Ten O'Clock Scholar café he uses the name Bob Dylan for the first time.

1961 – In New York City he plays in Greenwich Village. The show at Gerde's Folk City earns him an enthusiastic review in *The New York Times*.

1962 – Columbia Records releases his debut album, *Bob Dylan*.

1963 – His second LP, *The Freewheelin' Bob Dylan*, influenced by the prevailing social tension in the US, is released. He gives his first concert at Town Hall in New York.

Bob Dylan performing at Gerde's Folk City in New York.

pay a visit to the grandfather of folk, Woody Guthrie, who was recovering in hospital. The meeting was essential for Bob Dylan, who had devoured the pages of *Bound for Glory*, Guthrie's youthful autobiography. Bob Dylan had begun to imitate his tone, his attitude; he learned his songs, and his small "obsession" was what allowed him to find his own path, to see the light – it gave him a new identity.

In New York, Bob Dylan began a new life. "I was there to find singers, the ones I'd heard on record," as he described in his autobiography, *Chronicles*, "Dave Van Ronk, Peggy Seeger, Ed McCurdy, Brownie McGhee and Sonny Terry, John White, The New Lost City Ramblers, Reverend Gary Davis, and a bunch of others – most of all to find Woody Guthrie. New York City, the city that would come to shape my destiny."

And, his destiny would change, permanently, on April 11, 1961. Gerdes Folk City, in the heart of Greenwich Village, was nothing less than the altar where the rites of the Folk Revival were celebrated night after night. A small stage, a smoky room, and Mike Porco, the manager who oversaw the performances. That night, Mike decided to give a novice a chance since he needed someone to open for John Lee Hooker, who already was a blues legend. The unknown kid from Minnesota took his acoustic guitar and, stooped over the microphone, began to sing.

Those present couldn't have numbered more than fifty. Fifty chosen ones who attended the first appearance that night of the greatest mystery in the history of rock, hearing for themselves that graceless voice that would become nothing less than the vehicle of grace itself. Robert Zimmerman was no longer; Bob had already decided to change his name to become Dylan in honor of Dylan Thomas, the great Welsh poet. Among the audience members was the avant-garde of folk: Pete Seeger, Cisco Houston, and Ramblin' Jack Elliott. They had already heard of the "boy," having read his stuff, and they were impressed. But where did this prodigy come from, capable of presiding over the structures of folk songs with absolute authority while also fully submerging them in contemporary life? Capable of moving, without constricting rules, between tradition and innovation? They were there to listen, to see if Bob could maintain his impact on stage, to see if he was able to display his talents in public. And like everyone present, they instantly realized how much that boy was able to stimulate the mind of the listener. Dylan sang his songs in front of an unreal silence. It seemed as if the entire city was holding its breath. "The House of the Rising Sun" and "Song to Woody," dedicated to his idol, his teacher, were hypnotic. Dylan landed on earth to fulfill his mission: inject a mutation into the heart of popular music. The song closes its eyes to entertainment, abandoning all compromises and begins to dream its own dream: to become art, pure and simple in Bob Dylan's hands. This dream began in the smoke-filled rooms at Gerdes Folk City.

"Stones" Roll on to the Stage at the Marquee in London

[July 12, 1962]

Mick Jagger and Keith Richards met in October of 1961 while they were waiting for the train from Dartford to London. Jagger was going to the London School of Economics and he had a few of his best-loved blues albums under his arm. Richards was headed to Sidcup Art College and he was carrying his electric guitar. While waiting for the train, the two former neighbors found each other by chance and started talking about music and their dream of starting a great blues band. That's exactly what they would do, along with a mutual friend of theirs, Dick Taylor. In the meantime, Brian Jones, who was also deeply passionate about the blues, had been frequenting the Ealing Jazz Club where he had seen Alexis Korner's Blues Incorporated play, a group that included Charlie Watts, and which Brian Jones soon joined.

Less than a year after that meeting in the Dartford train station, Jagger and Richards' dream came true and their band — with Elmo Lewis (aka Brian Jones), Dick Taylor (who would later play bass with the Pretty Things), Ian Stewart (who would become a legendary personality of English

HISTORICAL NOTES

1961 – Jagger forms the Little Boy Blue & the Blue Boys band in London.

1962 – They give their first concert as the Rolling Stones at the Marquee Club. The name comes from Muddy Waters' song "Rollin' Stone".

1963 – The band plays in various London clubs. Decca Records produce their first 45.

1964 – Their first LP, *The Rolling Stones*, is released and makes them famous in England. Two months later the band makes its first American tour.

1966 – Decca produces *Aftermath*, their first album with only their own original songs.

The first Rolling Stones band photographed in 1962. From left to right, Charlie Watts, Bill Wyman, Mick Jagger, Brian Jones, Keith Richards.

rock, with many other bands besides the Rolling Stones) and Mick Avory (who would join the Kinks) – walked on the stage of the legendary Marquee Club on Oxford Street for their first concert. Fate was on their side that night, and Blues Incorporated, which was to play that night at the club, was invited to the BBC to play live on a radio broadcast. Harold Pendleton, the famous owner of the club, decided to give the young bluesmen, who had settled on calling themselves the Rolling Stones, a chance. Jimmy Reed, Bo Diddley, Chuck Berry, classic blues – the band's repertoire was made up of solidly groovy songs by the big names – Muddy Waters, Billy Boy Arnold, Elmore James…songs that the guys knew by heart, that they had consumed by listening to jealously guarded discs. Blues and nothing else, the band's musical universe was just that, and would remain so for a long time. It was the beginning, the start of a journey that would last another fifty years. Charlie Watts left Korner's band shortly after to join the Rolling Stones full time, and Bill Wyman took on the role of bassist to fill out the band definitively in 1964. Two years later, they released their first album, immediately winning the hearts of fans in England and, shortly after, in the USA.

James Brown Captures the Heart of Harlem

[October 24, 1962]

J ames Brown started on his road to success towards the end of the 1950s, riding the wave of rock 'n' roll, which had opened new opportunities for musicians of color. But it still wasn't easy to climb over the fence, to crossover, to leave the "black music" market, and entering the universe of white American pop music was incredibly complicated. Brown, however, knew he had it in him to do it; he knew that his mix of R&B, soul and gospel had what it took to please a crowd of young people, the youth that was coming into existence and that needed to hear his rhythm. Brown knew how to win the audience over because through the years he had perfected an absolutely explosive, unbeatable show, created with meticulous attention, night after night, in an endless series of concerts in every corner of America. It was no coincidence that he had earned the nickname of the "the hardest working man in show business."

On October 24, 1962, however, Brown got on the stage of the Apollo Theater, in the heart of Harlem, to change the fate of his career as well as that of popular music, with an overwhelming performance that would push him to heights that

HISTORICAL NOTES

1933 – Brown is born in Barnwell, South Carolina.

1955 – He moves to Macon, Georgia with The Flames band and they perform in local clubs.

1956 – Over one million copies of his first single, "Please, Please, Please" are sold.

1958 – He moves to New York, where he performs with different musicians and cuts "Try Me," which is number one on the R&B chart.

1962 – *Live at the Apollo*, the double LP recorded during the historic concert at the Apollo Theater, becomes a hit.

2006 – Brown dies in Atlanta on Christmas day.

James Brown on the stage of the Apollo Theater in New York.

no other black artist had reached. He was already famous in the world of R&B; he was incredibly popular, loved and praised by the audiences of his concerts. He had climbed the "black" charts with "Please, Please, Please," but this fame hadn't corresponded to success in the white music market, which he still hadn't managed to conquer. This was because none of his albums had, in any way, managed to capture the force, energy and overwhelming enthusiasm of his live shows. But Brown had decided that things had to change, and he would do so that night by recording an incredible live album. To prepare, he had incessantly stressed to his band, the Famous Flames, who were ready for anything, perfectly structured, that they had to be capable of playing without committing even the smallest of errors (Brown had instituted a strict system of fines within the band to "punish" any mistakes by docking their pay). He reminded them that on this occasion his tolerance would be absolutely zero, since the show that night was one of "win or lose" in no uncertain terms, and the possibility of being second best couldn't even be considered. Risking everything, even financially, was James Brown himself, as he was unable to convince the record label he worked for, King Records, of the merit of his plan, and he had decided to finance the recording himself, certain that his plan would be successful.

James Brown was right, the show was perfect and the album that was pressed and released in 1963, *Live at the Apollo*, is still seen as one of the most important albums in popular music of the Twentieth century – an essential album for anyone who loves music, especially soul and rock. Yes, rock, because none of the artists who would soon revolutionize the world of music with new electronic sounds would be able to overlook that album, that stage presence, that way of involving the audience and transforming a concert into an event. The album basked in the beauty of sixty six consecutive weeks on the charts, selling more than one million copies to a market that was no longer limited to "race music," but a black and white public that would crown James Brown as the king of R&B and soul.

"I Have a Dream": Dylan and Baez in Washington, D.C.

[August 28, 1963]

The speech made by Martin Luther King, Jr. in Washington, D.C. on August 28, 1963 has, rightly, gone down in history. "I have a dream. It is a dream deeply rooted in the American dream. I have a dream that one day this nation will rise up and live out the true meaning of its creed: 'We hold these truths to be self-evident, that all men are created equal.' I have a dream that one day on the red hills of Georgia, the sons of former slaves and the sons of former slave-owners will be able to sit down together at the table of brotherhood. I have a dream that one day even the state of Mississippi, a state sweltering with the heat of injustice, sweltering with the heat of oppression, will be transformed into an oasis of freedom and justice. I have a dream that my four little children will one day live in a nation where they will not be judged by the color of their skin but by the content of their character."

Bob Dylan also shared this dream. He had arrived to New York from the small town of Hibbing, Minnesota after having spent time in Minneapolis and attending university. He had decided to become a folk singer, like Woody Guthrie and Pete Seeger, like Odetta whose singing had brought him down the

HISTORICAL NOTES

1962 – During a concert of the Congress of Racial Equality, Dylan presents his first protest song, "The Death of Emmett Till". The same year he performs with the Student Nonviolent Coordinating Committee, two of whose members are Joan Baez and Pete Seeger.

1963 – At the Newport Festival he sings "Only a Pawn in Their Game", and sings it again during the march on Washington to around 250,000 persons.

1972 – Joan Baez releases "To Bobby," in which she asks Dylan to resume his politically oriented activity.

Joan Baez and Bob Dylan singing together in 1963.

road of folk. And in New York, that's what he became. He knew Ramblin' Jack Elliott, Dave Van Ronk, Joan Baez; he played in the folk clubs of Greenwich Village; he slowly became aware of the reality that surrounded him; he wrote increasingly cutting, serious songs. If his first album, in 1962, was already full of traditional songs, his second work, *The Freewheelin' Bob Dylan* from 1963 saw his transformation into a modern singer of reality, into a militant artist that tried to make it so that every one of his songs could, in some way, communicate a message, speak out. "Blowin' in the Wind," "Masters of War," and "A Hard Rain's A-Gonna Fall," are songs in which he speaks about war and changes in society. They are songs of protest, directed at a new audience, at the youth movement that was starting to grow in universities and schools, at the civil rights movement that was marching in the streets and the folk revival movement that brought its songs to the struggle in every corner of America. Because, like he sang that same year with disarming, poetic clarity, "The times they are a-changin'." And by his side was Joan Baez, young and beautiful, extraordinarily talented and, even more militant and involved, ready to fight not just with music, but also for a change in the status quo.

In 1963, Martin Luther King, Jr. organized the largest protest for civil rights ever in the USA, on August 28, 1963 in Washington, D.C. – "the march on Washington for jobs and freedom" at the end of which he gave his famous speech. African-Americans are there, the movement is there, students are there – anyone who thought that the time for change had arrived was there. And there they were, ready to sing for that human tide: Odetta, Mahalia Jackson and Marian Anderson, but also two white musicians, Bob Dylan and Joan Baez.

They're small compared to the crowd, but they have courage and strength when they reach the small podium from which they are to sing in front of hundreds of thousands of people. Joan Baez is bold and confident when she starts to sing "Oh Freedom" and then "We Shall Overcome," the extraordinary anthem of the civil rights movement that was played at every protest, every march and every sit-in. And then Bob Dylan sings "When the Ship Comes In," written at night in a hotel room that they had a hard time getting, as Joan Baez recalled in the documentary by Martin Scorsese, *No Direction Home*, because everyone would have happily offered a room to the queen of folk, but no one wanted to let that scruffy, shabby youngster in. Bob Dylan then sang "Only a Pawn in Their Game," a fierce protest song written some weeks prior to remember the assassination of the young black activist Medgar Evers. And then, when the most successful folk trio in America, Peter, Paul and Mary, arrived on the small podium, it was Dylan's triumph, because the three began to sing "Blowin' In The Wind" to the applause of the crowd. The music of change and the change of music – rock injected its own DNA with the genes of protest, politics and rebellion, but also pacifism, non-violence and freedom through Bob Dylan and Martin Luther King, Jr. on that day in August.

For Bob Dylan, it would be the most important political protest of his life. And it was also the last, because shortly thereafter, the image of the clear, shining protest singer-songwriter would be substituted by that of a dark, mysterious rock poet. BobDylan would forget the dedication, folk ballads and popular songs and transform into something else many times over. Something that he's still doing today, with great commitment.

The Night the Beatles Conquered America

[February 9, 1964]

Did you know that England in the 1960s invaded the United States? Yes, and the start of the invasion also has a date, February 9, 1964, when the Beatles appeared for the first time on television on the show hosted by Ed Sullivan. Seventy three million people tuned in for the broadcast, and event that deeply marked television history but also, even more so, helped changed the path of popular culture in the United States.

The Beatles had set the stage for that historic performance in the weeks prior. Their singles had already gotten airplay on all the major radio stations in the country, young people awaited the show eagerly, and even their parents were curious to see these "phenomenal" musicians in action. They had already swept England and Europe and they were about to conquer the USA, as was the plan of Brian Epstein, the band's manager, who wanted, at all costs, to bring the Fab Four to the top of the American charts. Sullivan was already aware of the growing "Beatlemania;" he had been to England with his wife and he had seen with his own eyes not just the success, but the collective hysteria around the band, and he had decided

HISTORICAL NOTES

1963 – Their TV performance on *Val Parnell's Sunday Night* show at the London Palladium triggers Beatlemania in Great Britain.

1964 – After appearing on the *Ed Sullivan Show* they make their live US debut at the Washington Coliseum, Washington D.C. to an audience of 8,000 persons. The following day they perform at Carnegie Hall, New York and in August begin their first American tour.

1966 – The Beatles give their last public concert in Candlestick Park, San Francisco. The band concentrates on studio recording until their break-up.

The Beatles rehearsing for their appearance on the Ed Sullivan Show.

that he must be the first to present the group live on American television. Contact between him and Epstein went on for some months before they came to an agreement, signed at the Hotel Delmonico in New York, for three performances as the "main act" and $10,000 in compensation. Their record's conquest, however, had started with "I Want to Hold Your Hand," given to radio stations before the release of the album. It became the song that DJs all over the USA rewarded with blanket coverage, causing the record label to release the single earlier than expected, on December 26, 1963, selling 250 thousand copies in just three days, reaching number one in the charts by the end of January. The song with its chorus of "I want to hold your hand," the boys in the group with their clean faces, their happy, positive air, their fresh, immediate, electric and promising, was exactly what the American people needed two months after the assassination of John F. Kennedy in Dallas. "Beatlemania" exploded in no time, the newspapers raced to publish stories on the group, stores began to sell Beatles posters and knick-knacks and Ed Sullivan began to warn his audience: "The Beatles are coming."

And the Beatles really did arrive. They landed in New York on February 7, 1964, awaited by a few thousand fans, held a press conference at the airport and then went to settle in to the Hotel Plaza. The show was planned for 9 o'clock, at CBS's TV Studio 50; fifty thousand people had asked to participate, but only seven hundred were so lucky. Sullivan joked in the episode before the performance, saying "Coincidentally, if anyone has a ticket for The Beatles on our show next Sunday, could I please borrow it? We need it very badly."

At 8 o'clock in the evening on February 9, 1964 America

turned on its televisions and began to listen. 60% of television sets were tuned in to CBS; Ed Sullivan brought the Beatles to more than twenty-three million homes.

"Now yesterday and today our theater's been jammed with newspapermen and hundreds of photographers from all over the nation, and these veterans agreed with me that this city never has witnessed the excitement stirred by these youngsters from Liverpool who call themselves The Beatles. Now tonight, you're gonna twice be entertained by them. Right now, and again in the second half of our show. Ladies and gentlemen, The Beatles! Let's bring them on."

With these quick words came the music of the Fab Four and the continuous screams of their young fans: "All My Loving," "Till There Was You," with the cameras covering every member of the group, writing each one's name on the screen. When it was John's turn, after his name appeared the words "sorry girls, he's married!" The four came back on to the stage at the end of the broadcast to play another two songs, "I Saw Her Standing There" and "I Want to Hold Your Hand." Their success was clamorous, not so much among adults (*Newsweek* reviewed the performance, writing that the fame of the four would fade quickly), as it was among young people, who huddled around their television sets for their two following appearances on February 16 and 23 (the last of which was, in reality, the first to be recorded). The impact on American youth was incalculable. The following day nothing was the same: boys started to grow their hair and dress like the Beatles, it was as if a door had immediately been flung open and an entire generation had suddenly rushed out. American music was overwhelmed by a colossal invasion by

English groups: the Rolling Stones, the Who, the Animals, the Dave Clark Five, the entire squad of bands managed by Brian Epstein, Gerry and the Pacemakers, Lulu, and on to Them, Herman's Hermits, the Hollies, the Searchers, Peter and Gordon and many others. Everyone, suddenly, had to face the beat that arrived from Merseyside, the blues that the English brought back to its source, with pop that changed heart and soul. Nothing was the same ever again in music, culture and fashion, just as was happening in all of Europe. The Beatles had conquered America and the world was about to change.

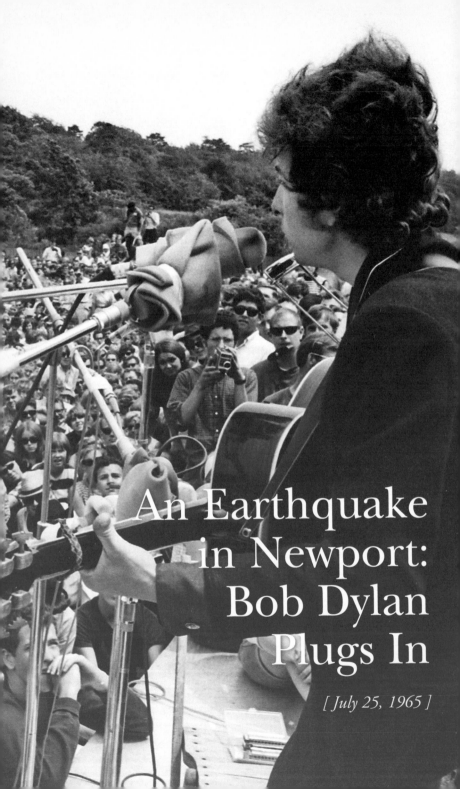

An Earthquake
in Newport:
Bob Dylan
Plugs In

[July 25, 1965]

We left him hunched over his guitar, to disseminate hypnosis during his first concert at Gerdes Folk City. Three and a half years later, Bob Dylan was simply a divinity. A prophet. The man who was not only able to sing history, but who had the power to change it, to create it. And everyone was saying so, every second, in every situation: fans, critics and record executives venerated him and stood in awe of him, as if the truth itself flowed from his lips. And, everyone in the world equipped with average intelligence and a normal dose of common sense would have done whatever it took to escape from the cage he had been put in, let alone Bob Dylan.

It was July 25, 1965 in Newport, Rhode Island. There were thousands in attendance at the folk festival par excellence. A crescendo of performances in the place where they celebrated the marriage of music and political engagement: Vietnam, civil rights, the still-present shadow of Kennedy. It was a sacred atmosphere. Bob Dylan drew around fifty thousand fans, each one of them there, once again, to listen to the Word, to learn the secrets of existence from Bob Dylan. 1963 was met with enthusiasm and 1964 had

HISTORICAL NOTES

1963 – *The Freewheelin' Bob Dylan*, the first album consisting almost entirely of Dylan's songs, marks his relationship with the civil rights movement.

1964 – With *The Times They Are A-Changin'* he establishes himself as a protest folk singer, but *Another Side of Bob Dylan*, released a few months later, reveals a more personal and introspective approach.

1965 – *Bringing It All Back Home*, the first album of the 'electric trilogy' (with *Highway 61 Revisited* and *Blonde on Blonde*), is released.

Bob Dylan during a performance at Newport.

won the public over with songs like "Mr. Tambourine Man." But now, in 1965, it was the star from Newport; it was "the spokesman of a generation" as the press called him. But the singer that folk fans knew, was no longer there. It had been months since Bob had been sowing the seeds of his heresy. He recorded *Highway 61 Revisited*: that hit of a snare drum, "Like a Rolling Stone," the formalization of what we still define as rock today. He had met the Beatles, he had smoked a joint with Lennon, he had re-tuned to the times. He saw his "Mr. Tambourine Man" fly to the top of the charts in the version sung by the Byrds. In short, he was tired of folk, tired of being penned in, tired of seeing a label on his art: he needed to drop that duty, to plug in his electric guitar, and give a new shape to his poetry as well as a shock to those who were listening.

Saturday, July 24, 1965, Dylan took the stage of an afternoon workshop with his acoustic guitar and sang three songs: "All I Really Want To Do," "If You Gotta Go, Go Now," and "Love Minus Zero/No Limit." But it wasn't enough; he wasn't satisfied. And more than anything else, according to a few witnesses, he was irritated by the words pronounced shortly before by Alan Lomax to the Paul Butterfield Blues Band, which was considered too electric for Newport, too "rock 'n' roll" for the guardians of folk orthodoxy. So, just to deny the "folkies" any satisfaction, Dylan decided to put on a completely electric show. He called two musicians who had recorded the "Like a Rolling Stone" single with him, Mike Bloomfield and Al Kooper, and some other musicians that made up the Paul Butterfield Blues Band with Bloomfield, Jerome Arnold and Sam Lay, to which he also added Barry Goldberg, and at night held a few tests at a house made available to him by George Wein, one of the festival's organizers. At sunset on the following day, Dylan took to the stage and the difference was all in his perception: instead of his acoustic guitar, he hugged a Fender Stratocaster. He didn't look at the audience, and he started right away with the riff to "Maggie's Farm." Simply put, all hell broke loose.

Dylan plugged in, his music charged with electricity, and he first played "Maggie's Farm" followed by "Like a Rolling Stone," in front of a flabbergasted audience, stunned and ready to protest, loudly, with prolonged hisses and boos, that became even louder after the execution of "Phantom Engineer." The rift had arrived, and the old world of folk watched, astonished, as its young champion abandoned the thread of orthodoxy and threw himself, body and soul, into the "noise" of rock – rock that, in 1965, was taking on its shape and substance, with "Help" by the Beatles, "Satisfaction" by the Rolling Stones, and "My Generation" by the Who. Rock that Dylan had helped create, offering his lyrics, and that now he had to follow, adding electricity to his music, searching for a new audience that was ready to change, to take risks, to look for new paths and tensions along with him. After just three songs, Bob Dylan left the stage. Peter Yarrow found him behind the curtains and convinced him to get back on stage with his acoustic guitar. Two more songs it was, the classic "Mr. Tambourine Man" and the official farewell to the world of folk, "It's All Over Now, Baby Blue," and everything ended there and then, after three songs that caused the history of music to change course.

There are many versions of what happened with the audience and backstage. Many, including Bob Dylan, were convinced that the audience's protests were aimed at him and the band due to the music, which was too electric and too far from folk. Others, including Mike Bloomfield, thought that their reaction was instead solely linked to the excessive brevity of the set and not the rock feel of the performance. But the most interesting "case" is that involving Pete Seeger, the "pontiff" of the American folk scene, the uncontested father, moral authority, and monument to the liberal culture of the United States. Seeger, during Bob Dylan's performance, told the audio technicians: "Cut the distortion from his voice, it's terrible. If I had an axe, I'd cut the cable right now." Seeger then said that the only thing he wanted to do was cut the cables so that the audience could hear the songs better, since the audio quality was awful. In *No Direction Home*, the wonderful documentary about Bob Dylan by Martin Scorsese, the testimony of John Cohen of the New Lost City Ramblers confirms that Seeger wanted to cut the cables because the excessive volume was bothering his father Charlie, who had a hearing aid. It is certain that in the afternoon, Bob Dylan's band's sound checks had been interrupted by Mack McCormick's unplugging the cords, forcing Bob Dylan and his band to free the stage so other artists could carry out their sound checks as well.

Twenty-five minutes (fifteen electric, ten newly acoustic) was all Bob Dylan needed to change skin, to transform, to enter with his head down in his new electric life. With strength, with rage, with pain, the passage to electricity would be the cutting of the umbilical cord with the world of folk that had welcomed and coddled him. Pete Seeger's negative reaction, as Bob Dylan would say later, was like a "stab in the heart." He would be called a Judas, but in the following year he would simply become the Picasso of rock, someone who wasn't able to follow conventions. He was someone who nine months later would press that precious gem that goes under the name *Blonde on Blonde*. Someone who, tired, would leave everything to retire for a few years at his farmhouse near Woodstock. Someone who, for his entire career, would always keep the aura of Newport: because when Bob Dylan has a guitar under his arm, anything can happen.

Ken Kesey and the Acid Tests: The Start of Psychedelia

[November 27, 1965]

If the use of drugs for preceding generations was little more than a decadent pastime, something to allow them to try the "thrill" of losing themselves in a way that was decidedly more fashionable than alcohol, for the kids of the new generation in the 1960s, the consumption of drugs was a sign of declared diversity, of the need to see reality with new eyes, the desire for something "astounding" that would be able to expand the horizons of their consciousness, allowing them to reach a higher level of understanding about the world, but at the same time letting themselves go, rejecting society's race for wealth and possessions, deliberately slowing their mental traffic, distancing themselves from the oppressive world of their parents, school, university, work and family. Marijuana unleashed a series of chain reactions, it was the start of a voyage that promised to take them elsewhere, a collective, not individual, voyage, a fantastic voyage that had no limits and had the advantage of combining fun, surprise and abandon with a life that these kids didn't want to live in the same way their parents did. The diffusion of marijuana among young people was, at the dawn of the 1960s, viral, unstoppable and complete. "Smoking" was a

HISTORICAL NOTES

1959 – Ken Kesey volunteers to take part in a Stanford University study of the effects of psychoactive drugs.

1963 – Timothy Leary and Richard Alpert are fired from Harvard University because of their mass experimentation with LSD.

1964 – The Merry Pranksters, the group headed by Kesey since 1962, make a cross-country trip in a school bus that is described in Tom Wolfe's *The Electric Kool-Aid Acid Test*.

1965 – After this trip, the group organizes the first Acid Test at Soquel, California.

During the Acid Tests, live music, lighting and special effects created a psychedelic experience.

collective act through which these youths entered into an entirely new psychological and personal condition, trying to establish new rules of coexistence. It was an act of simple, immediate and direct rebellion that placed whoever did it immediately outside of the conventions of adult society. The consumption of drugs in the 1960s began to spread like wildfire and, slowly, the consumption spread to other substances, the properly psychedelic ones, most notably LSD.

LSD was created in 1938 in the Sandoz laboratories in Switzerland, where Dr. Albert Hofmann synthesized it, when researching alkaloids present in rye, to try to extract pharmaceutical substances. But it was in 1943, when the professor accidentally came into contact with a drop of lysergic acid, that he discovered its hallucinogenic capacities. Before long, LSD was out of the pharmaceutical industry's laboratory and into medical studies, universities and the world of culture. Among the first proponents for use of psychedelics was Aldous Huxley, Harvard professor Timothy Leary, and a young writer who had enormous success with *One Flew Over the Cuckoo's Nest*, Ken Kesey. Kesey had come into contact with LSD when participating in medical experiments financed by the CIA to verify the drug's effects, and he was intrigued. In LSD, he saw the key to open an inner world that was no less real than the external one, and he believed that this change, if practiced on a mass level, would have been able to improve the human race, bringing it to a higher level of consciousness than ever before. He thus decided to use the money earned from his book to take up residence in La Honda, San Mateo County, 45 miles south of San Francisco. He bought an old school bus, painted it dayglo and decided to set off with his comrades and friends (including Neal Cassady) for an uproarious psychedelic trip all the way to New York.

Not satisfied, he and his friends, the Merry Pranksters, thought that the next step was to spread the psychedelic experience, the lysergic acid "trip," to the largest number of people possible. To do so, with the help of the first hippie communes in San Francisco and people such as Allen Ginsberg, they organized the first "Acid Tests," parties with live music and special effects lighting, creating the first platform for the launch of the psychedelic experience. The first one was held at the house of Ken Babbs, one of the Merry Pranksters. The test was open to everyone – anyone who bought a symbolic $1 ticket could enter and drink a "magic potion" laced with LSD made by the main chemist in the area, Augustus Owsley Stanley III. The goal was to allow all present to have a transcendental experience that, in Kesey and company's opinion, would bring them to a higher state of consciousness. There was a slide show by Stewart Brand, mantras sung by Allen Ginsberg, strobe lights and music provided by the Warlocks, who within a week would change their name and become Jerry Garcia's Grateful Dead, the quintessential Californian psychedelic band. It was only the first of a series of Acid Tests that Kesey organized up until 1966, when LSD became illegal. The psychedelic era officially started with that Warlocks concert, and shortly after, by way of flower power, hippies, Haight Ashbury and the summer of love in 1967, the world of rock would radically change.

Exploding Plastic Inevitable: Warhol and the Velvet

[April 1, 1966]

Without really exaggerating, you could say that the era of multimedia shows was inaugurated on April 1, 1966 by the Exploding Plastic Inevitable Show that Andy Warhol organized at the Dom in New York , the first in a series that the American artist and his colleagues held for over a year. First and foremost, there was music, that of the explosive and unpredictable Velvet Underground and Nico. There were also films directed by Warhol, dance performances by Gerard Malanga, Edie Sedgwick, Mary Woronov, performances by other artists, lighting effects by Danny Williams, projections by Jonas Mekas and much more. Warhol had imagined the show as a sort of live artistic experience, in which each participant would have both the role of spectator of the events presented by the artists involved, but also that of a protagonist, because every show was designed to involve (even if not directly) the audience in a sort of large-scale happening in which only a few things were planned and the majority of the evening was unpredictable. It is no accident that the Velvet Underground's set was almost entirely improvised: just one song, "I'll

HISTORICAL NOTES

1962 – Andy Warhol opens The Factory at 231 East 47th Street, New York City.

1966 – Warhol creates the first multimedia spectacle, *Andy Warhol UpTight*, for the Expanded Cinema Festival at the Filmmakers Cinematheque of New York. This event marks the official debut of the Velvet Underground with vocalist/actress Nico. After the performances in Los Angeles, the show, now called *Exploding Plastic Inevitable*, returns to New York.

1967 – Warhol's last performance with The Velvet Underground at The Scene in New York.

1966: Andy Warhol and the Velvet Underground in New York.

Be Your Mirror," sung by Nico, after which Lou Reed, John Cale, Sterling Morrison and Maureen Tucker threw themselves into a long jam session. It was perfectly in line with Warhol's desire to create a happening, in which little was planned, nothing was predictable, in which the artist's role was the act of creating, then and there with the collaboration of other artists on the stage, interpreting the moment in the freest and most creative way possible.

The relationship between the Velvet Underground and Warhol began a few months earlier, when Warhol, Malanga, Barbara Rubin and Paul Morrissey went to Café Bizarre, in the heart of Greenwich Village, to see the band play. They were so impressed by the group's mixture of rock, provocation and avant-garde that they called them to collaborate at the Factory and then to be key players in the Exploding Plastic Inevitable Show. The performance was the exact opposite of the Californian happenings organized by Kesey: there was no trace of flower power, love and optimism. Instead, there was the hard representation of extremes and excess, symbolism of death, extreme sex, solitude and alienation. And as one final difference, in this case the public, though involved, was much less of an integral part of the show, completely in the hands of the artists that created, with lights, videos, photos, music, dance, painting; it was a multimedia experience that was intellectually more complex, less direct, immediate and personal than that of the "Acid Tests." These shows would launch the work of many artists that would develop Warhol and the Velvet Underground's discourse in the 1970s, until it became an integral part of rock.

The First Time for Hendrix in Swinging London

[November 25, 1966]

The Bag O'Nails was a club in the center of London, on the edges of Soho, on a street parallel to Carnaby Street. It was one of the quintessential rock clubs of the Swinging London of the 1960s, and the club, for one thing, was where Paul McCartney met Linda, and where the royal family of English rock frequently – very frequently – met at night after concerts or recording sessions in the various studios around the capital city. What better place, then, in 1966, to present to the crème de la crème of British rock, a young American guitarist that hailed from Seattle, where he had cut his teeth playing with various bands, and ending up as the guitarist for the Isley Brothers and Little Richard's band as well. But that young disheveled guitarist had other things in mind – other sounds, other possibilities – and he started down his path as a solo artist. It was during a concert in New York that he met Linda Keith, Keith Richards' girlfriend, who introduced him to Chas Chandler of the Animals. In turn, Chandler, impressed by the American musician's extraordinary abilities, decided to bring him to England.

Hendrix's debut in Swinging London hap-

HISTORICAL NOTES

1964 – He wins first prize in an amateur contest at the Apollo Theater and begins to perform in the Harlem club circuit.

1966 – Hendrix plays with the Cream at Regent Polytechnic College in London. In December he releases his first single, "Hey Joe/Stone Free," which enjoys great success.

1967 – His US debut is at the Monterey International Pop Festival. The albums *Are You Experienced* and *Axis: Bold as Love* are released.

1969 – The last concert with The Jimi Hendrix Experience is held at Denver Pop Festival.

Jimi Hendrix at the Bag O'Nails club, which brings him into the limelight on the London rock scene.

pened on the night of November 25, 1966 at the Bag O'Nails. That night seemed just like all the others, but instead it was to mark a radical change in the history of rock. That young guitarist, unknown up to that moment, caused an explosion in the world of British rock. From then on, all guitar players had to face his explosive, innovative style, his way of acting on the stage – spectacular and provocative. Jimi was in London for two months, and Chandler (after having him play in a few concerts in Europe and having signed a record deal for him with Track Records, run by Kit Lambert and Chris Stamp, the manager of the Who), had decided that Hendrix's "official" moment of presentation to the heart of London had arrived. That night at the Bag O'Nails, Jeff Beck, Pete Townshend, Brian Jones, Mick Jagger, and many others were in attendance, all of whom were left speechless in front of Hendrix's innovative, surprising and visionary style and his unheard of way of playing the guitar. After that concert, English rock was no longer the same and Hendrix became a star.

The first Pink Floyd concert at the UFO Club

[December 23, 1966]

I f we wanted to pinpoint an exact date for the start of the psychedelic era in England, we could easily use this one. On December 23, 1966, Pink Floyd played at the UFO Club, a venue opened by John Hopkins and Joe Boyd a few weeks earlier and that would soon become the center of the British psychedelic movement. The first night of live music saw the appearance of Soft Machine and Pink Floyd on the stage, then solidly in the hands of Syd Barrett, who guided the band towards entirely surprising sonic improvisations in which the instruments of Nick Mason, Roger Waters and Rick Wright interlaced rhythmic and sonic weaves over which Barrett's slippery guitar and voice soared. The band had already played in a few other venues in London: they had been seen on a few nights at the Marquee and participated at a big night at the Roundhouse. But it was with their debut at the UFO Club that things for Barrett and his band changed drastically. The UFO Club wasn't just a music club, but a cultural hub, a place where writers, filmmakers, designers, photographers, models, poets and everyone else in search of a new vision of the world came to meet up. And with this new

HISTORICAL NOTES

1963 – Sigma 6, the first nucleus of the band, is formed.

1965 – When Syd Barrett joins the band its name is changed to Pink Floyd and it begins to experiment with sonic effects.

1966 – For the launching of the underground periodical *International Times*, Boyd and Hopkins organize an event at the Roundhouse with Pink Floyd and Soft Machine. They decide to continue with these shows at the Barney Club, later called UFO Club.

1967 – In September the group plays for the last time at the UFO Club, which closes down a month later.

The Pink Floyd: left to right, Roger Waters, Syd Barrett, Nick Mason and Rick Wright.

soundtrack, Pink Floyd would become the key band at the UFO Club in the following months. The show, on December 23, wasn't just a concert, but the first big test for Pink Floyd in the field of multimedia, special effects (both audio and visual); it was the first attempt at opening the path that Pink Floyd would perfect over the course of the following years, towards a total rock spectacle. The British underground set up shop at the UFO Club and Pink Floyd became the band of the new cultural revolution.

Monterey:
The First Great
Rock Gathering

[June 16-17-18, 1967]

The first major festival in rock history took place in Monterey, California, from June 16 to 18, 1967. That year wasn't random. 1967 was the year in which youth culture that was born as the dawn of the 1960s reached it's height, exploding all over the world, driven by the Californian utopia according to which the world could be re-drawn with naïve, simple, but revolutionary concepts: equality, joy, creative and, obviously, love for all, from all. In San Francisco especially, the Bay Area's hippy families opened free stores where money was not used and goods could be obtained by bartering. A few youth associations opened the first free clinics that offered free medical assistance, while groups of young lawyers organized alternative legal studios to support the movement's battles in the courts as well. Universities (especially UC Berkeley) became organizational centers for this new reality where there were no recognized leaders, where direct democracy was rigorously adopted and where violence was still far off. Suddenly it seemed that everything had to be debated and every certainty had to be doubted: family, the government,

HISTORICAL NOTES

1967, January 14 – Leary, Ginsberg and Ferlinghetti participate in the Human Be-In, which takes place in Golden Gate Park, San Francisco.

1967, June 10 – The Mamas and Papas's single "San Francisco (Be Sure To Wear Flowers In Your Hair)," the manifesto of hippy counterculture, is released.

1967, June-September – The Haight-Ashbury neighborhood in San Francisco becomes the hub of the Summer of Love and the hippy movement.

1968 – The documentary film *Monterey Pop*, directed by D.A. Pennebaker, is released.

The Who at the Monterey Pop Festival on 18 June 1967.

the military, work, culture. Youth culture seemed to take the upper hand, seemingly able to impose its agenda, its desires and expectations. "We want the world and we want it now," yelled Jim Morrison in that extraordinary year of 1967, and hundreds of thousands of young people yelled along with him, from Milan to Berlin, from London to Tokyo, in an explosion of desire and creativity that hasn't been equaled. In January, there had been the "Human Be-In," where poets such as Allen Ginsberg, activists such as Jerry Rubin and Abbie Hoffman and musicians like the Grateful Dead met in San Francisco's Golden Gate Park for the "general tests" of what would be the first major rock festival in history: Monterey in 1967.

200 thousand young people organized, for the first time, to listen to their music, the music which identified them, that which kept time to the beat of their revolution, that which signaled the definitive break with the world of adults, with the "establishment." In Monterey, hippy counterculture took the stage in all its colors and sounds. And rock made that counterculture its mistress with the Who, as they smashed their instruments on stage, with Jimi Hendrix who set his guitar on fire in front of the crowd in the most exciting rite in the history of rock, with Paul Simon and Art Garfunkel who presented their wonderful melodies, with the Indian sounds of Ravi Shankar next to the soul of Otis Redding and the blues of Janis Joplin and the Animals, with San Francisco's rock families in full force, Jefferson Airplane, the Grateful Dead, Quicksilver Messenger Service, as well as Electric Flag, Moby Grape, Al Kooper and the Paul Butterfield Blues Band, Steve Miller, Canned Heat, and soul with Booker T and Otis Redding. It all took place in front of tens of thousands

of young people, living together for three days, camped in front of the stage. In 1967, rock music became "the" music for the world of young people, a sound that could describe the realities and dreams of a movement that was much bigger and broader than what could be seen in the streets, in the newspapers and television channels that followed the ferment of new generations with curiosity and concern. It was broader because it also involved those who stayed at home, those that didn't yet have the courage to take to the streets, grow their hair long or dress in a certain bizarre way. It was the year in which dreams seemed to become reality and youths from every part of the world felt the infinite exhilaration of what was called storming heaven.

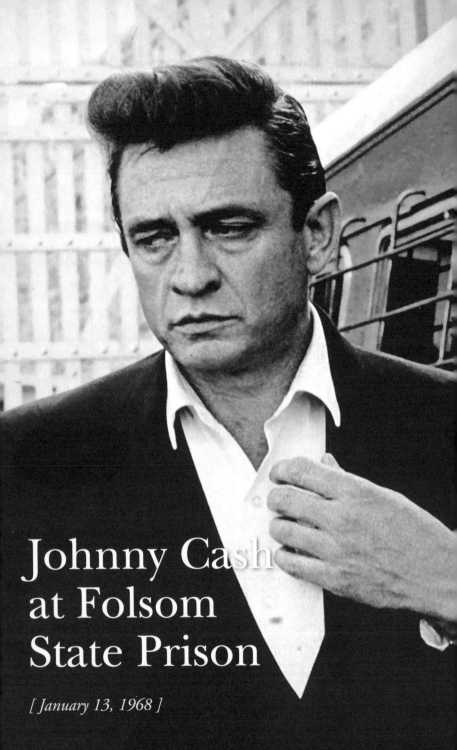

Johnny Cash
at Folsom
State Prison

[January 13, 1968]

Johnny Cash wasn't just a country singer. Nor was he just one of the fathers of rock 'n' roll. Nor was he just the voice of the marginalized, of the defeated and downtrodden, of those who have done more unjust things, than just things, in life, that have a pricey bill to settle with life. No, Johnny Cash was probably one of the greatest voices of the twentieth century, an author and performer of extraordinary strength, a colossus of popular music equal to Woody Guthrie, Bob Dylan and few others. And, if there was an event that not only demonstrates Cash's greatness but that also changed the direction of popular music forever, transforming it into something more, it was Cash's concert at the maximum security prison in Folsom, California on January 13, 1968.

When Cash passed through the prison gates he already had thirty-odd years and a long and adventurous personal history behind him. Different from all the other greats of American music of the era, he had lived through true pain, loss and suffering, just like the detainees that crowded the hall to listen to him sing. He knew their lives because, in many ways, it was his life too. He knew what they were feeling because

HISTORICAL NOTES

1955 – After seeing the movie *Inside the Walls of Folsom Prison* he writes "Folsom Prison Blues" and becomes an advocate of prison reform.

1958 – He gives his first free concert in San Quentin prison in California. He repeats the concert in 1969 and it is recorded by Columbia in the album *Johnny Cash at San Quentin*.

1968 – Cash gives two concerts in the Folsom prison canteen and the closing song is "Greystone Chapel," written by an inmate. Johnny Cash *At Folsom Prison* sells 3 million copies in the USA.

Johnny Cash entering Folsom prison to perform in his fourth concert for inmates.

he had felt it too. And he knew that songs, despite appearances, speak the truth, much more than books and poetry. He knew that art, his art, was mixed with blood and sweat, with the dust of the streets, with the darkness of alleys, with pain, suffering and love. He knew that those listening to him in prison didn't need to be "entertained," because for them, free time doesn't exist and they don't want a simple concert. What the audience wanted was something that they understood in their hearts, sung by someone who really knows how, with stories that everyone could recognize, in which they could recognize themselves. And that day in Folsom, Johnny Cash didn't bring his "best of" to the stage, the songs for which he was already, rightly, famous. Instead, he brought those that count, those that have something to say, those that tell stories that the detainees could tell. He knew he was, for once, their voice...even if he was a star, having moved on from Sam Phillips' Sun Records, having climbed the charts, dominated theaters, crossed America far and wide with his guitar, and having also found the love of his life, June Carter. In short, he's not like them, but he knows them, he could have been there too, instead of on the other side. And he knew it.

Cash had dreamed of recording an album in a jail, since the time he wrote "Folsom Prison Blues" in 1955, but he was never able to convince his entourage, even if he had played in various prisons starting in 1957, when he performed at Huntsville for the first time. When Bob Johnston became his producer in 1967, the project took shape. Cash was looking for an event that would be a turning point in his career: his life had changed, he had beaten his drug addictions, he had a new, deep love and all that was missing was a "strike" that would put his musical adventure, which had also been devastated by drugs, back on its feet. At Columbia, his record label, they were skeptical, supporting the project without enthusiasm and with little money. However, he had his friends at his side, especially Carl Perkins, the Statler Brothers, his longtime band (the Tennessee Three), and his new love, June Carter. Rehearsals lasted three days, at the El Rancho Motel in California, then came the concert at Folsom State Prison, which then became an extraordinary album, signaling the final transition to the popular song that becomes truth and is also the witness to and the banner of this truth. From this album onwards, the difference between those who lie and those who don't, in pop music, became definitively clear. And from Folsom onwards it would be clarified forever. In this way, truth runs through the chords of "The Long Black Veil," or "Give My Love to Rose," or "The Wall," or "Green, Green Grass of Home" – not because he who wrote them wrote truth, but because he who interpreted them, Cash, made them so. With this, the history of pop changed definitively. Also, when he joked with the detainees in "25 Minutes to Go," or in "Flushed From the Bathroom of Your Heart." Cash was magnificent, perfect, complete, moving, ironic, and captivating. And, with "Folsom Prison Blues," he represented himself and his audience, which became, for a moment, a single entity.

James Brown:
The Night that
Soul United
America

[April 5, 1968]

On April 4, 1968, the United States of America witnessed one of its darkest days, when Martin Luther King, Jr. was assassinated in Memphis. The next day there were protests and riots in many cities; African-Americans, downtrodden and betrayed, took to streets all over the country and in a few cases violence erupted. A James Brown concert was planned for the evening of April 5, at the Boston Garden, in the center of the city, with twenty thousand, mostly young, African-Americans expected to attend the event. The mayor, the liberal Kevin White, who had just been elected the previous year, was extremely worried. The night before, there had been a few clashes in some parts of the city, but the concentration of so many black youths in the center of Boston could have brought about much more serious trouble.

The city was divided in two: on one side were the white neighborhoods, where many residents strongly opposed Mayor White's politics of desegregation, and on the other side of the white center were the black Roxbury and South End neighborhoods. The choice was a difficult one, if not downright impossible. Canceling the concert to avoid any possible incidents probably would have embittered the souls of African-Americans even more, causing even more serious trouble; allow-

HISTORICAL NOTES

1963 – He sings at the concert for the March on Washington and continues to support civil rights all his life, with concerts, sponsoring and educational programs.

1966 – At the March against Fear he holds a charity concert at Tougaloo College.

1968 – In June he begins a tour for the troops in Vietnam. In August *Say It Loud (I'm Black and I'm Proud)* is released, becoming the anthem of the civil rights movement.

2008 – The documentary *The Night James Brown Saved Boston* directed by David Leaf is released.

City councilman Thomas Atkins (left) and the mayor of Boston Kevin White (right) conversing with James Brown backstage during his concert at Boston Garden.

ing it to happen would have meant, for White, pitting himself deliberately against Boston's white population, which had openly asked for the event to be suspended. It was left to Thomas Atkins, the first black man elected to the city council, to solve the dilemma, suggesting to the mayor that he let the concert play out but also to convince a local TV channel to broadcast it live, for free. White immediately contacted the directors of WGBH, who quickly accepted the idea and hurriedly organized the unexpected broadcast. They then spoke with James Brown and after a quick financial negotiation (to compensate the artist for the tickets that would be refunded), he accepted the proposal. White held a press conference in which he invited the citizens of Boston to watch the concert from their houses and, in the following hours, thousands of people returned their tickets.

On the night of April 5, at 9pm, Brown and White got on stage at the Boston Garden and the mayor spoke to the nearly two thousand people present and to the hundreds of thousands of people at home: "Now I'm here tonight, like all of you, to listen to James. But, I'm also here to ask for your help. I'm here to ask you to stay with me as your mayor and to make Dr. King's dreams a reality in Boston. This is our city, and its future is in our hands – tonight and tomorrow and in the days that follow. Martin Luther King loved this city and it's up to our generation to prove his faith in us. So all I ask you tonight is this: let us look at each other here in the Garden and back at home, and pledge that no matter whatever the other communities might do, we in Boston will honor Dr. King in peace." And then it was James Brown's turn.

It was a crazy bet, that of trying to unite an entire city under the banner of music, to extinguish the flames of rage with the soul and funk of one of the greatest African-American artists of all time. Brown knew that the evening would be a difficult one, but, as always, he was ready to give 100% of himself. He also felt the same rage that other African-Americans felt, he also was sick and tired of the racism that still saturated American society, he was also becoming aware, day after day, of the need to be part of the change. His band followed him, with strength and emotion, when, by no accident, he started the concert with "Get It Together." His set was passionate and warm, with "There Was a Time," "I Got the Feeling," and "It's a Man's Man's Man's World." The songs came one right after the other and the city slowly emptied. People returned home to listen to Brown and his music, to be united by music. Then came the great covers, "When a Man Loves a Woman," "Chain of Fools," "I Heard It Through the Grapevine," and "Soul Man." The crowd was in ecstasy, but at a certain point a group of guys tried to get on stage, only to be pushed back by the police. The air turned ice cold, the band stopped, everything could have exploded unexpectedly. But James Brown intervened, asking the police to leave the stage, then shaking hands with one of the guys. He then took the microphone, saying, "You make me...you're not being fair to yourselves and to me neither. You're not being fair to yourselves and me; we're all the same race. Now I asked the police to step back because I figured I could get some respect from my own people. It don't make sense, are we together or aren't we?" And then, after having beat out the classic "one, two, three, four," Brown started the music up again, launching towards the finale with "Try Me," "Cold Sweat," "Please, Please, Please," and "I Can't Stand It." That night, there were incidents and clashes in more than one hundred cities in the United States, but Boston remained calm. The city stayed home to watch and listen to James Brown – even the level of crime fell significantly – and it was clear to all that "The Godfather of Soul" had saved Boston. A few months later, James Brown recorded "Say It Loud: I'm Black and I'm Proud." That night had changed the course of things for him as well.

The Hair Revolution: *Hair* Debuts on Broadway

[April 29, 1968]

C an a musical change the world? Certainly not, but it can, without a doubt help change habits and customs, suggesting a different way to live and, obviously, by putting on a show. This is true of *Hair*, which came to the stage for the first time on April 29, 1968 at New York's Biltmore Theatre amid endless controversy. What was defined as "America's First Tribal Love-Rock Musical" immediately became a success, bringing a young – very young – audience, that certainly didn't frequent musicals, to the theaters of Broadway (and those of London as well, a few months later) to follow the aforementioned pacifist story and a handful of great rock songs whose topics revolved around concepts such as pacifism, free love, the use of soft drugs and the fight against racism. *Hair* was a musical that revolutionized musical theater first for the topics it presented, then for the all-important fact that it featured a live rock band instead of an orchestra and, last but not least, for its improvisational and creative style, resembling street theater of companies such as the Living Theater. There are few other musicals that have followed the path of *Hair* successfully, starting with *Oh! Calcutta!*, written

HISTORICAL NOTES

1967 – The musical makes its off-Broadway debut at Joseph Papp's Public Theater, with lyrics by James Rado and Gerome Ragni, and music by Galt McDermot.

1968 – *Hair* opens on Broadway with Rado, Ragni, Paul Jabara and Diane Keaton. Others who later perform are Ben Vereen, Keith Carradine, Barry McGuire, Ted Lange and Meat Loaf. The show has a run of 1,750 consecutive performances up to 1972.

1979 – Miloš Forman, flanked by Ragni and Rado, directs a liberal film adaptation of the musical.

The cast of Hair *on stage under a huge American flag.*

by Kenneth Tynan with the collaboration, of, among others, Sam Shepard, Jules Feiffer and even John Lennon, where the theme of sexuality was treated explicitly, taking the stage for the first time on June 17, 1969 at the Eden Theater in New York; followed in the early 1970s by the triumph of Andrew Lloyd Webber's *Jesus Christ Superstar* in 1971; and *The Rocky Horror Picture Show* in 1973. These are the "masterpieces," the fundamental rock musicals that would then find different modes of expression in the work of groups like the Who, with their cinematic version of *Tommy*, and Pink Floyd, with their stage adaptation of *The Wall*. But *Hair* remains the progenitor because it was able to capture the flavor, the feeling and the unrest of an era in which people truly believed that the world could change and that songs, long hair, pacifism and love were the seeds that would bear the flower of a legendary "Age of Aquarius."

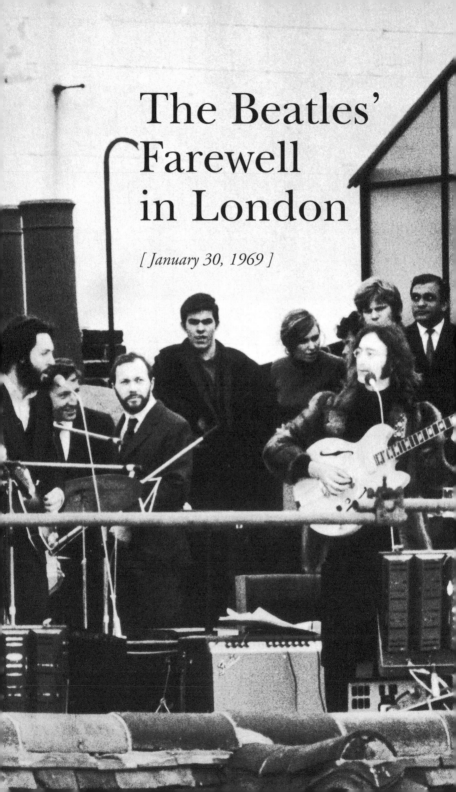

The Beatles' Farewell in London

[January 30, 1969]

The goodbye, the departure, the final farewell: the Fab Four were aware they had reached the end of their rock journey when, on January 30, 1969, they went up to the roof of Apple headquarters for their last public concert. Behind the scenes, it was obvious that the Fab Four had reached the end of the road.. They all agreed on the need for a "last time," and they wanted to write the last chapter of the Beatlemania history. But their desires reflected their personalities. For Paul McCartney, the best thing to do was to return to the beginning, to the Cavern, and close the magic circle that was their story. John Lennon wanted to widen their perspectives, astonish and provoke as always: he was aiming for Africa, with maybe a concert in the desert, to underline all the distance there was between their music and simple entertainment. Ringo was thinking about the present: maybe a concert in London, maybe a festival in which the Fab Four would headline after a day of music. For George Harrison, however, none of it mattered: music was, by this time, an inner voyage and putting it on display wasn't the most important thing.

In the end, the answer was right above their heads. They went up to

HISTORICAL NOTES

1966 – The band's last live show is held at San Francisco, during the Beatles' 1966 US Tour.

1967 – Brian Epstein dies. Relations among the members begins to deteriorate.

1969 – Shooting of the documentary film *Let It Be* commences in the Twickenham Film Studios and is then transferred to the Apple Studio. It ends with the famous concert on the roof.

1970 – One month after the band's break-up the film has its world premiere in New York and debuts in England a week later.

The Beatles on the roof of the Apple Studio building in Savile Row, London.

the roof of the building at 3, Savile Row, near Piccadilly Circus. And, from that roof, they were launched straight into history. In the mid-afternoon, they began to play – without having given anyone forewarning. They played for 42 minutes. People began to look up, intrigued by the sound.

Crowds immediately begin to gather. The Internet was still a science fiction fantasy, but word traveled fast.

Paul and Ringo arrived first, closely followed by John and George. Everything was ready; they didn't even need to tune their instruments. They started with "Get Back," with Paul singing. They were filming the event and every aspect of the production had been studied in minute detail. After the first chorus, the sequence was entirely dedicated to the skyward looks on the faces of Londoners passing by, far below. "It's the Beatles!" you can read on one pair of lips, belonging to a woman in the building across the street, as she watches with eyes wide open. They really got going with their second song. "Don't Let Me Down" almost seemed like it was a request from the police that had started to pass by. "Don't throw me from the roof." Lennon's voice was fabulous and the rooftops of London had never had a soundtrack like it. Anyone wishing to dive into the mystery of music, in its ability to act on the passage of time, must watch them play this song from that roof. Paul's looks of complicity seemed to break the distance and the tension that existed between him and John. Billy Preston was also there, playing the keyboard. And in the end, the police intervened. Scotland Yard ordered their officers to interrupt that "horrible racket." The Fab Four stopped. John approached the mic and said "Thanks everyone…I hope we've passed the audition."

The Doors: Poetry and Rebellion.
The Scandal in Miam

[March 1, 1969]

By this time, he was dissecting, inch by inch, the plane bent towards his self-destruction. Entrusting everything to his words, you become a patrol among demons, ghosts and absolute nostalgia. Everything under the spotlights. At the start of 1969, Jim Morrison was no longer the angel in black leather that, in the last two years, had shown the United States and the world what it meant to take the connection between rock and rebellion seriously. At the start of 1969, Jim Morrison was tired, frustrated and overweight. He wanted to escape, to flee, to be that which he had always wanted to be: a poet, and nothing else. But the car that was the Doors was already in high gear and it would have been hard to jump out without crashing.

Miami, March 1, 1969: there are fifteen thousand people at the Dinner Key Auditorium. The heat wave and humid air made it feel like a scorching hot swamp. It was the perfect place for the umpteenth appearance of the Lizard King. The fifteen thousand people are there for this – to witness the almost "mystical" event put on by the band from Los Angeles. But the four

HISTORICAL NOTES

1965 – The Doors is formed at Los Angeles. Morrison chooses this name for the band as a tribute to Aldous Huxley's *The Doors of Perception*.

1967 – The first album is released. It includes the legendary "Break on Through (to the Other Side)" and "The End". More than one million copies of the single "Light My Fire "are sold.

1969 – After the period of ostracism triggered by the incidents in Miami, the group resumes its concerts at the Aquarius Theatre in Hollywood.

1991 – Oliver Stone's movie *The Doors* is released on the twentieth anniversary of Morrison's death.

An intense portrait of Jim Morrison.

band members are late to get on stage and they continue to delay. More than an hour's wait. Why? Because Morrison is having one of his special days. He fought with Pamela, his fiancée: they had planned a trip to Jamaica, but had to cancel it since all the band's concerts can't be canceled. Jim became Jimbo, the fruit of a perverse equation: increased depression equaled increased alcohol and LSD. The flight to Miami was transformed into a trip to hell. When he got off the plane in Miami, Jim could no longer stand. He arrived at the Dinner Key Auditorium and the other three members of the Doors glared at him. "He's wasted again," "let's play without him," they whispered. But Jim smiled at them and got on stage. A black, wide-brimmed hat, long beard, eyes half open to the audience and the concert started. The groove laid down by the Doors was devilish, as if the tension between Morrison and the rest of the group was pushing the music into uncharted territory. Jim doesn't just sing, but "slays" every hit that the group has on the set list. He forgets the words, the changes, and he can't keep time with the band, but the crowd is going crazy just the same.

Then came the moment that would mark the group's future, since for the Doors, there is before and after Miami. During "Five to One," Morrison seems like he's in ecstasy, motionless on stage, bathed in light. He screams: "You're all a bunch of fuckin' idiots." The music continued, stronger, and Jim continued with his tirade. The temperature continued to rise, up until "Light My Fire," when Morrison walked up to Robbie Krieger, the group's guitarist, got down on his knees and simulated fellatio. Hell breaks loose, the concert transforms into a Dionysian ritual. Still on stage, Morrison starts to undress. A few people say they saw him expose his genitals. The singer is then dragged off the stage, the priest to officiate the bacchanal of rock.

Over the following days, the press campaign was furious. The Miami police made up the most civil element against the group. So began the lengthy trial that would shatter the relationship between the Doors and the entire world that revolved around music. The tour was canceled. They would not be invited to Woodstock – Morrison was too dangerous. However, they would continue to be influential: in the two following albums, *Morrison Hotel* and *L.A. Woman*, Jim hones his poetry and the group rediscovers the blues roots of their own acidic music. Those were two small miracles, but the times of "we want the world and we want it now," were over. Morrison would continue to slip further and further down. He tried to save himself; he tried to find peace in Paris, attempting to escape from the effects of the trial in Miami. The story of his end is one that everyone knows. And the concert in Miami will remain where the Doors definitively sealed their fate.

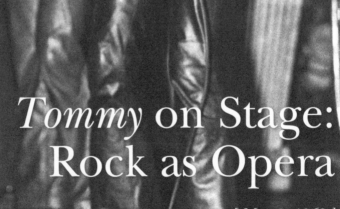

Tommy on Stage: Rock as Opera

[May 1, 1969]

Rock became an adult, or rather, it had been an adult since 1967, when the Beatles tried to build a kind of concept album with *Sgt. Pepper's Lonely Hearts Club Band*, an operation that was never fully completed. It became an adult with the growth of psychedelia, with the work of Jimi Hendrix and Pink Floyd, with the songs of Bob Dylan. But no one had yet tried to write a rock opera, a complete, complex work with a single story told through different songs. At the time, Pete Townshend was racking his brain about the matter and, instinctively, he felt that the classic structure of a rock song was no longer sufficient to contain the stories that he wanted to tell. He had already tried with, "A Quick One, While He's Away," to take on longer, more complex compositions and, like the Beatles, the Beach Boys, Bob Dylan and many others, he was thinking about the best use of an album, of 33 revolutions per minute, which allowed for the creation of not just a sequence of disconnected singles, but a more complete and ambitious discourse.

So, in 1968, he set to work on a rock opera, which he discussed in many interviews at the time, slowly bringing into

HISTORICAL NOTES

1961 – John Entwistle joins Roger Daltrey's The Detours, followed a year later by Pete Townshend.

1964 – The band changes its name to The Who. Keith Moon replaces Doug Sandom.

1965 – Their debut album *My Generation* reaches second place in the UK charts.

1969 – The double LP *Tommy* is released after the Soho premiere.

1970 – The band's last show (performed again only during the 1989 Reunion Tour) is held at the London Roundhouse.

1975 – The movie *Tommy* directed by Ken Russell is released.

Roger Daltrey performing on stage.

focus the themes and characters of *Tommy* – the story of a blind, deaf and mute boy and his redemption through his ability to play pinball. The band started to record the album's songs in September of 1968 and in March of 1969 the work was complete. The first live performance, the first test of *Tommy* in front of an audience, came on May 1, 1969, in one of the most famous jazz clubs in the world: Ronnie Scott's Jazz Club, in the heart of Soho, London. The differences between this and a normal rock concert were many, especially the fact that the opera (even if it wasn't exactly an opera since there were no actors on the stage, everything being sung by Daltrey alone, there were no costumes or staging, and we should call it a 'song cycle' instead) was played out in its entirety, one song after the other, thus asking the classic rock concert audience to have a decisively different state of mind. This was also because the opera, to be comprehensible when played (live as well as on the album), had complete songs accompanied by instrumental tracks, such as the splendid "Overture," and a few fragments that serve as a reminder, or explanation, for the narrated events, choices that radically changed the way in which the concerts were presented to the public. And then there was Daltrey, who had changed both his way of singing, choosing lower tones, as well as his stage presence, often impersonating Tommy in an entirely credible way, thus overthrowing the mechanism of identification between singer and audience. And that's not all: Tommy represented, metaphorically, the events taking place in the world of young people from the 1960s onwards, with all its baggage of dreams and hopes, its struggles and, obviously, also its risks, anticipating their defeats and disillusionments.

The concert at Ronnie Scott's allowed Townshend to test

the opera's inner workings, its flow on stage, the possibility for improvisation that could arise from the interplay between Entwistle and Moon. To take the necessary steps, the band played five songs from their normal repertoire, then began the entire execution of *Tommy*, without interruption. The volume was much higher than usual, as Daltrey said, to "encapsulate" the entire feeling of the story and from that night on it would always remain that loud, helping define the band's sound. The reaction from press and public was overwhelming; it was a perfect test. Their recording sessions finished at the end of March, by mid-April they had started to play parts of the work for the first time, in Bolton. During May, they had done a few more runs, cutting out a few pieces. Ronnie Scott's was the first official, complete performance – the first of another 160 and more over the next two years, including the one which would become legendary at Woodstock and the one record-ed on *Live at Leeds*, with which the Who would change the course of rock history.

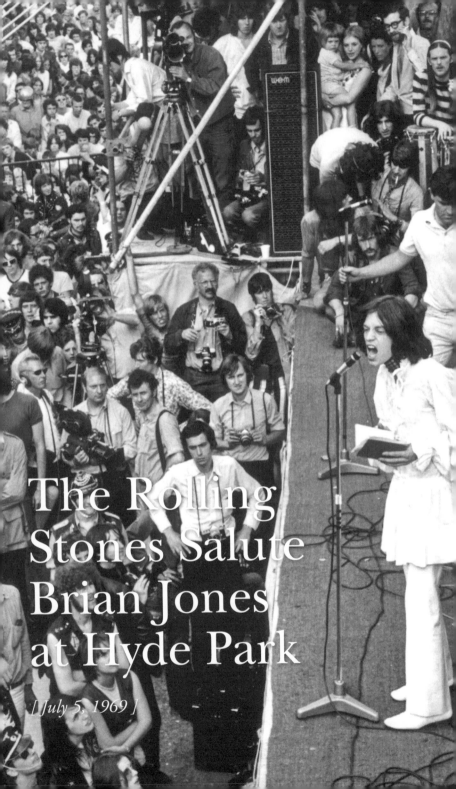

The Rolling Stones Salute Brian Jones at Hyde Park

[*July 5, 1969*]

The densest forty-eight hours in the life and career of the Rolling Stones. Forty-eight hours in which Jagger & Co. would visit the deepest abyss and then re-emerge into the light. It was to be a new start, and it was in every way. Just a week before that July 5, the concert in Hyde Park was to signal a new phase for the group. A phase without Brian Jones, the heart, soul and engine of the band's early days. The band wanted to formalize a quasi-consensual separation in front of their public. Metaphorically speaking, Brian was already elsewhere, as a person and as a musician, suspended almost perpetually in a state of altered consciousness.

On the night of July 3, that metaphor would become terribly real, taking shape in a never-to-be-erased stain on the skin of the Rolling Stones. The guitarist was found drowned in the swimming pool of his home outside London. He was the first member of the "27 Club" – rock angels who died at that age. He was to be joined by Jimi Hendrix, Janis Joplin, Jim Morrison, Kurt Cobain and Amy Winehouse.

On that afternoon in July of 1969, there were 500 thousand people in

HISTORICAL NOTES

1967 – Brian Jones' excesses begin to damage his relationship with the rest of the band.

1969, June – After the recording of *Let it Bleed*, Jones is replaced by guitarist Mick Taylor.

1969, July – After the Blind Faith show at Hyde Park Jagger decides to imitate them and organizes a free concert to introduce Taylor, but in the end dedicates it to Brian Jones, who dies two days before. This is Taylor's first public concert before the band's 1969 American Tour.

2001 – *The Stones In The Park*, with material from the Hyde Park concert, is released on DVD.

Mick Jagger reading some lines from Shelley's Adoais in memory of Brian Jones.

the most beautiful park in London. It was a party with mixed in melancholy. The band's genius spirit still seemed to be with them. His musical intensions are still present, the enormous effort he took to move, album after album, the axis of the Rolling Stones, taking them from pure and simple rock to include influences from other musical genres. And it was no coincidence that in the three albums that would follow, Mick Jagger and Keith Richards, now in control of the group's aesthetics, would reinforce their return to their original territory: *Let it Bleed* was being recorded, and Jones had contributed to only two songs. Then came *Sticky Fingers* and *Exile on Main St.* This was the trilogy that the Rolling Stones, without Brian Jones, would deliver to the history of rock. Even without Brian, the need to move forward was never questioned. That was made immediately clear on July 4, the night before the show. The group had just gotten back from his funeral when they announced: "We won't be canceling the concert, we'll still play: it will be our way of remembering Brian." And they did so with what may be considered one of their most important concerts.

The biggest rock 'n' roll band in the world got on stage shortly after dusk. Opening for them were King Crimson, Roy Harper and Alexis Korner. Mick Jagger, dressed entirely in white, dedicated a few verses from Shelley's *Adonaïs*: "He is not dead, he doth not sleep / He hath awaken'd from the dream of life." Mick holds back his tears while hundreds of white butterflies are released. The music starts to flow: "Honky Tonk Woman," "Mercy Mercy" and "Love in Vain." In "Sympathy For The Devil," a multitude of African percussionists joins the group. The Rolling Stones detach from their demons and so begins their golden era.

In fact, their golden era was opaque and murky, full of vice and excess. But it was also full of simply amazing music. It would have been difficult not to think of Jones when Sticky Fingers came out, two years later. The first three songs: the wretched lyrics of "Brown Sugar," the heroin that takes away awareness and energy; then the sulfurous suspension of "Sway," those trademark verses by Brian Jones that arrive in the second stanza when you notice the song's strings, "Ain't flinging tears out on the dusty ground / For all my friends out on the burial ground / Can't stand the feeling getting so brought down / It's just that demon life has got me in its sway;" followed by "Wild Horses," which was the song "prompted" by Mick Jagger and Marianne Faithfull's relationship, and which would become the quintessential song about how painful certain separations can be.

Three Days of
Peace and Music:
The Legend
of Woodstock

[August 15-16-17, 1969]

Three days of peace, love and music, three days of the Aquarian Exposition, the Woodstock Music and Art Fair was held in the fields of Max Yasgur's farm, near Bethel, Sullivan County, from August 15 to 17, 1969, fifty miles away from the originally planned location of the festival, in Woodstock, New York. It was the height of the American movement in the 1960s and also, in many respects, the beginning of the end of the dream. Organizing the festival was a company called Woodstock Ventures, formed in February of 1969 by two financial partners, John Roberts and Joel Rosenman, and two creative contributors, Michael Lang and Artie Kornfeld. The first one to have the idea of organizing the festival was Lang, who lived in the artistic community of Woodstock, a sort of hippie retreat that had become famous in the world of rock for its proximity to Big Pink, where Robbie Robertson and The Band were located. Lang had designed the project to be much more grandiose than it actually became. For example, in addition to the concert, the project was to include the construction of a large recording studio in the area, which the festival was intended to launch.

HISTORICAL NOTES

1969 – The festival hosts 33 rock, folk, soul and blues bands and soloists. Despite the huge crowds there are no incidents.

1970 – *Woodstock: Music from the Original Soundtrack and More*, the album recorded live, is released.

1994 – The Woodstock '94 festival, celebrating the 25th anniversary of the original one, is held at Saugerties and draws over 300,000 spectators.

1999 – The third edition is a purely commercial operation that is costly, has poorly planned logistics, and is marked by various episodes of violence.

The Woodstock Music and Art Fair took place near Bethel, New York.

A few weeks after having established the company name as Woodstock Ventures, it was clear that the festival could not be held in any of the areas around the town due to lack of space, hostility from local residents, bureaucratic red tape and so on. Slowly, the location where the festival would see the light of day was changed, moving increasingly further away from Woodstock. However the name was kept, one of the few things that did not change into something radically different than the initial propositions for the entire event, as remembered by Jack Curry, author of the book *Woodstock, The Summer of Our Lives*.

There were many people working at the festival, a few of whom were experienced, expert promoters and concert professionals, and many – lots – were hippies that simply came to lend a hand. It wasn't the first festival that had been organized in the USA, and in the same summer, many other events dotted the American night sky. Yet, thanks to who-knows-what magical aligning of the stars, even before the official event's program was published, the word-of-mouth in what was called the counterculture scene – among hippies, rock fans and young people – caused expectations to grow drastically. Lang and his associates were expecting a crowd of 100 thousand people, and they put tickets on sale at eighteen dollars for three days, or six dollars for each day of the concert. But by two days before the event, the vast area of Yasgur's Farm had turned into an enormous amphitheater with the sixty-five thousand people who had arrived without having paid for a ticket. Being unable to ensure any sort of real control over the entrances of such a vast area, the four partners of Woodstock Ventures thought it best to declare the festival to be a free concert (which only served to increase the number of attendees, not only from New York but from all over the United States). A large number of the security guards enlisted by Woodstock Ventures were in fact made up of other hippies and young people, and the only job instructions they were given was to be nice, to help those in need as much as possible, and to try, above all else, to avoid causing any commotion. Essential to the success of the festival was the collaboration of The Hog Farm, one of the biggest and most effective hippie communes of the time. They were the ones, starting on August 9, to help the organizers clean the festival area, prepare the campsite, buy immense quantities of whole grain rice that was then freely handed out to the hundreds of thousands of hungry young people that were arriving and, in particular, to intervene in the many problems that the kids in the audience had with drugs. Those who have seen the film will remember their leader, High Romney, who bent over backwards on stage to tell jokes, give directions and advice, make announcements and keep the large sea of humanity that filled the area calm.

At noon on August 14, the two main access routes to the Yasgur's farm were already completely blocked by a veritable river of cars and the first protests by the local population began. An incredible gridlock was created on all the streets in the early afternoon, and similar problems were happening in the town of Woodstock, where many concertgoers wound up, unaware of the change in venue.

In theory, by the morning of August 15, everything was ready for the start of the festival, and the program was to include performances by Joan Baez, Arlo Guthrie, Tim Hardin, Richie Havens, The Incredible String Band, Ravi

Shankar, Bert Sommer and Sweetwater. At 5pm, an hour later than the planned start time, the festival got started with Richie Havens. He was forced to go on stage first, given that none of the other artists on the lineup had arrived yet thanks to the giant traffic jam blocking the entire area. To resolve the problem, a few helicopters were rented to allow the artists to reach the concert area and also to bring supplies. In the meantime, the zone was declared a disaster area, and all radio stations began to advise listeners not to show up. However, more than 500 thousand people had already reached White Lake. Despite problems such as the lack of food and water, the situation was perfectly calm and, after Havens, Country Joe McDonald took the stage. He was supposed to play on Sunday but, given the absence of other musicians (and of his own band), he went on stage to fill the void, singing a few songs that would become festival classics, including "I-Feel-Like-I'm-Fixin'-to-Die," perhaps the most political moment of the festival, a song against Vietnam that opened with a collective and liberating "fuck" yelled along with the entire audience. After Country Joe, it was another artist's turn, John Sebastian, who had arrived as a tourist at the festival but who was compelled to go on stage since the scheduled artists still hadn't arrived yet. Then it was the turn of an almost unknown folk singer, Bert Sommer, followed by the Indian music of Ravi Shankar, accompanied by the rain. After the rain there was more music, with Melanie Safka (another un-planned act), Arlo Guthrie, Sweetwater, and, closing the night, Joan Baez. Everything, despite the problems, had gone well.

Saturday, however, started out with bad news: an attendee sleeping in his sleeping bag in a camp not far from the festival had been crushed by a tractor. Despite the accident, the situation on Yasgur's farm remained calm and without tension, as if under a spell, even if it was really thanks to the heavy use of drugs, especially marijuana and lysergic substances that helped create that atmosphere of good vibrations that lingered throughout the three days of the festival. What happened there has been abundantly documented in Michael Wadleigh's documentary: thousands of tents, a giant commune where everything was shared, small alternative markets, free love, drugs to expand one's consciousness as Ginsberg suggested – all of which, in short, marked the audience at Woodstock as something radically different from the daily way of life of America's children. And the music, naturally, especially the music, was like a giant emotional glue for an endless series of magical moments.

The program of the second evening was incredibly rich, and the show was opened by an unknown band, the Quill, followed by Carlos Santana's band, which immediately became famous after their performance. On Saturday afternoon, reporters from all the main American newspapers and TV channels arrived, creating even more buzz around the event. Among the 500 thousand youths, in the meantime, tranquility reigned and the majority of problems faced the small hospital in the festival's campground, mainly to assist those who had taken too many drugs. The program, meanwhile, went on with Jefferson Airplane; the great Janis Joplin in one of her last shows; Canned Heat; the legendary champions of the psychedelic sound of California, the Grateful Dead; the black music of Sly Stone; the beautiful performance by Creedence Clearwater Revival; and a memorable performance by the

Who. It was during the concert by the Who that the skirmish between Pete Townshend, the group's guitarist, and Abbie Hoffman, one of the leaders of the American movement, took place. Hoffman wanted to get on stage during the Who's performance to read a statement on the liberation of the political activist, poet and musician John Sinclair, and Townshend, in response, threw him off stage, hitting him with his guitar. Even if everyone had witnessed the scene, no one protested or took up a defense of Hoffman, and the danger that this violent act would cause of series of dangerous chain reactions was never realized.

Sunday was a day of rain, of a great sea of mud throughout the entire concert area, whose bill opened with the young and passionate Joe Cocker and by his rhythm 'n' blues. After the rain, Country Joe played, this time with the Fish, and at dusk it was Alvin Lee's Ten Years After, followed by the Band and Blood Sweat and Tears. Then came the on-stage debut of Crosby, Stills & Nash (and Young) "This is only the second time we've performed in front of people. We're scared shitless." as Stills would say when they introduced themselves, followed by the long night with the Butterfield Blues Band. At the dawn of Monday morning, when part of the audience had already left the festival, Sha Na Na would climb on stage and, for the grand finale, came Jimi Hendrix and his famous version of "The Star Spangled Banner."

Without a doubt, these were three great days of rock music, and a few of the performances have become legendary, boosted with the help of the film. A few would have become famous anyway, especially that of Jimi Hendrix, which came after the festival was officially over. In front of a few hundred people, the guitarist distorted the notes of the national anthem until it became a desperate act of indictment against the Vietnam War. Others became legendary for mythic processes, such as the "rain chant," the chant from the soaked crowd after the violent downpour on the second day: a reverse rain dance, that became a sort of alternative hit. Many musical careers began at Woodstock, and a few ended as well. But every group, every musician, on those three days, represented not just himself, but a space in the young people's universe, an idea, a dream, a different adventure. Every musician and every note played at Woodstock carried weight; they became a part of the history of American culture and the "counterculture" of young people in the 1960s.

Altamont:
The Dream
Becomes
a Tragedy

[December 6, 1969]

Rock has died many times. It may be that an event is able to raze to the ground all the dreams, hopes and ambitions that a bass, a guitar, a drum set and a singer can embody. In an instant. In an evening. Rock died when the plane carrying Buddy Holly crashed. And, it dies every time that a star, perhaps a young one, disappears after having burned up his existence.

For contemporary popular music, December 6, 1969, is a day to circle in red. On that day, all of the 1960s, those years that were full of grace, instantly stopped living. The heart of liberty and psychedelia stopped beating. Freeing oneself through music, reaching the Promised Land, riding atop rhythms and songs: after that night, it no longer seemed possible.

It was nothing more and nothing less than a collision with reality. With malice for its own sake, with pure, indiscriminate, absolute violence. It happened at the Altamont Speedway in California, where the Rolling Stones organized their own personal festival, which was advertised as the Woodstock of the West. But, the air people breathed that day wasn't entirely full of love, music and

HISTORICAL NOTES

1969 – Four months after Woodstock the Rolling Stones organize the Altamont Speedway Free Festival, a free concert that concludes their 23-date tour of the United States. At Altamont the violent Hells Angels kill one spectator and the Stones do not return to the US for three years.

1970 – The documentary *Gimme Shelter* by Albert and David Maysles, featuring the last weeks of the Stones' tour, is shown *hors concours* at the 1971 Cannes Film Festival.

1973 – The Altamont Festival is revived three years later.

The violence of the Hells Angels at the Altamont Speedway.

peace. There were 300 thousand people; the air they were breathing was full of tension. Even now, it's enough to look at the images of *Gimme Shelter*, the documentary about the event.

That evening four people died. And, it was one of those deaths that would change the history of rock. It was a story of Hells Angels, a motorcycle gang recruited to maintain order at the concert. They didn't want money, just the equivalent of 500 dollars in their favorite fuel: beer. They got drunk, became aggressive, and, as predicted, they did everything but maintain order. Even a few musicians, including Marty Balin of Jefferson Airplane, were attacked by these angels from hell. The Grateful Dead refused to play, and the atmosphere was that which precedes a tragedy.

The Hells Angels were uncontrollable. They began roaming around, passing through the crowd on their choppers. Not even the Rolling Stones were safe: Jagger was attacked by a fan, just as he got off the helicopter that had brought him to the concert. And, what shouldn't have happened, happened while the Rolling Stones were playing "Under My Thumb." Eighteen-year-old Meredith Hunter tried to get up on to the stage. Hells Angels pushed him down. Shortly after, Meredith tried again, this time, allegedly, with a pistol. Hells Angel Alan Passaro saw it and reacted: he stabbed Meredith Hunter to death. Other Hells Angels furiously attacked the corpse. It's all over now, baby blue. The dream is over and a dark cloud would extend over the Rolling Stones and all the main players of the time. For a few years, rock would change its tune, becoming introverted, exploring personal spaces rather than being a public appeal for liberation. And, if it was all about a dynamic whose origin cannot safely be traced to Altamont, it's certain that that concert represented a grasping of the collective consciousness, especially that of the rock establishment, of how "dangerous" music could be if not delivered carefully and safely.

But it didn't end there. Immediately after the episode, Jagger let the Hells Angels know he didn't want anything more to do with them. The gang was furious. They decided to kill him. At least, according to Mark Young, a former FBI agent.

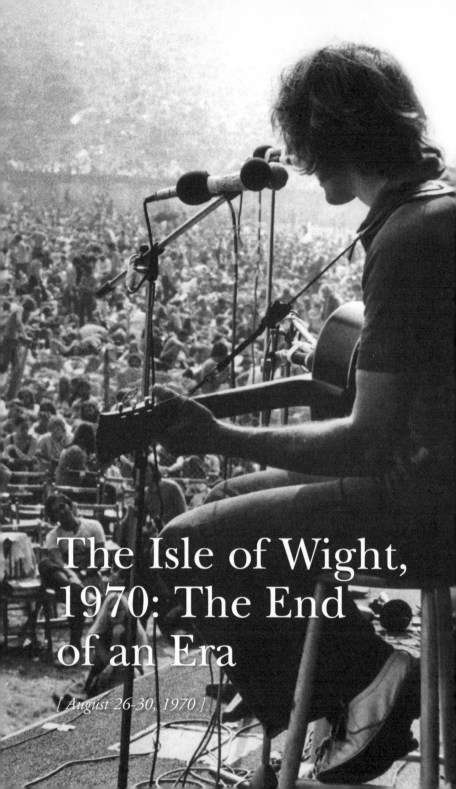

The Isle of Wight, 1970: The End of an Era

[August 26-30, 1970]

If you had to choose only a handful of concerts to film, record and send into orbit to make an alien civilization understand what rock 'n' roll is, the Isle of Wight Festival from 1970 would definitely be on the list without a second thought. Along with Woodstock, the four days of concerts along the English coast signaled the height – and the end – of the hippie dream of the 1960s. That dream that had nothing abstract about it, which was based on a concrete desire to transform everyday life into a vessel of poetry, gentleness and music. Life was to be a colorful vehicle of freedom.

And even if this 1970 edition was only the third, it certainly was a defining moment in the history of rock: the arrival point of the Flower Power bus. From August 26-30, 600 thousand people witnessed many unrepeatable moments. Among the many was the second to last live performance by Jimi Hendrix and the last European concert for the Doors with Jim Morrison. That would be enough, but there was so much more: the Who, Joni Mitchell, Jethro Tull, Free, Joan Baez, Donovan, Emerson, Lake & Palmer and Leonard Cohen brought the best

HISTORICAL NOTES

1968 – The first edition of the festival features a concert of the Jefferson Airplane with an audience of 10,000 persons.

1969 – Two weeks after Woodstock, the two-day festival draws 200,000 spectators.

1970 – The huge crowds attracted by this extraordinary line-up of bands brings about serious economic and legal problems, and the festival is interrupted for 32 years.

1997 – The movie *Message To Love: The Isle of Wight Festival*, directed by Murray Lerner, is released.

2002 – The festival is held at another location on the island.

Ralph McTell on stage at the Isle of Wight Festival.

that rock had to offer to the stage in those days. Which for many is equivalent to the best that rock has ever offered in the span of its history.

But beyond the "recognized" stars, the Isle of Wight Festival provided the chance for the rock population to stumble upon that which is easily defined as the musical group that in the 1970s represented nothing other than the avant-garde in its purest form: Miles Davis and his band. Following the release of *In a Silent Way* and *Bitches Brew*, he was practically able to perform a miracle, that of hypnotizing 600 thousand people to then transport them in a musical voyage of more than half an hour that – lucky for us today – was recorded almost perfectly.

When Miles Davis got on the stage at 5:30pm on August 29, almost everything had already happened: clashes with the security guards, endless controversies over the ticket price (only fifty thousand people paid the three pounds sterling entry fee) and the on-stage tears of Joni Mitchell, worn out by the chants coming from the audience. Miles Davis entered the stage like a shaman, a concentrated look on his face, grim, looking only sporadically at the crowd. Hunched over on his trumpet, he immediately started to suggest directions to his band, small musical phrases that would instantly change the direction of that lava-like musical flow. It was lava generated by a series of talents, that seeing them all together was almost unbelievable. Keith Jarrett and Chick Corea on the keys as was possible only a few other times, Gary Bartz on sax, Dave Holland on bass, Jack DeJohnette on drums and Airto Moreira on percussion. For thirty-five minutes the audience was simply silent, floored by the "strangest" music ever to come out of the speakers at a rock festival. It was a "micro-history lesson in jazz," as Keith Jarrett would call it, years later.

The concert on the Isle of Wight is also important for another reason: from the start it entered into the imagination of rock fans all over the planet. During the 1970s, it was no longer possible to repeat those oceanic gatherings and the mood of rock itself plummeted towards intimism, losing sight for some time of the communal inspiration that characterized it throughout the 1960s.

The Farewell of the Electric Angel: The Death of Jimi Hendrix

[September 18, 1970]

F ive years and four albums. A flash, an immense, luminous flare that changed the destiny of rock forever. This was the extraordinary career of Jimi Hendrix. James Marshall Hendrix began playing in rhythm and blues bands at the start of the 1960s and he was soon hired to play in the bands of highly visible artists of the time, such as Ike Turner, Little Richard, Wilson Pickett, Jackie Wilson, Sam Cooke and many more. In 1964 he moved to New York, where he collaborated with the Isley Brothers, John Paul Hammond, King Curtis and, most notably, Curtis Knight, with whom he wrote a few songs and recorded several tracks on his album. Hendrix's first true band of his own was formed in 1965, Jimmy James and The Blue Flames, with which he played in many clubs in New York. It was during a concert at the famous Cafe Wha? that producer Chas Chandler, former bassist for the Animals, decided to bring Hendrix to England and record an album with him. Young Jimi arrived in London and in September of 1966, with Chandler's help, he got his band – the Experience – on its feet with Mitch Mitchell on drums and Noel Redding on bass. Just a few weeks

HISTORICAL NOTES

1966 – Jimi Hendrix becomes famous in England thanks to his concert at the Bag O'Nails in London.

1969 – He ends the Woodstock Festival with a historic performance, accompanied by the new Gypsy Suns and Rainbows band, which breaks up only one month later.

1970 – On September 17 Hendrix poses for the photographs for his new album, *The Cry of Love*, which will be released a year after his death.

1997 – The third version of the album is released with the title *First Rays of the New Rising Sun*.

A photograph of Jimi Hendrix taken on 3 September 1970.

137

of practice and the group was ready to play live: an early concert was held in Paris, at L'Olympia, as the opening act for Johnny Hallyday, in October.

In December of the same year, the first single was released, "Hey Joe." Their success was immediate: the single reached number six in the UK charts and the group was invited to be the opening act for the Who at the Saville Theatre. Their second single came out in March of 1967. It was another classic, "Purple Haze," and it anticipated the release of their first album, *Are You Experienced*, by a few weeks. The album stayed in the charts for a good thirty-three weeks, climbing up to second place behind the Beatles' *Sgt. Pepper's Lonely Hearts Club Band*. In June of 1967, the Jimi Hendrix Experience made their debut in the United States, at the Monterey Pop Festival, to great acclaim. In the same month, the group started a tour as the supporting band for the Monkees, but after just seven concerts, Hendrix and his band, considered too wild for the Monkees' audience, interrupted the tour. In mid-1967, the band returned to the studio to record their second album, *Axis: Bold as Love*, which was released in December of that year, reaching fifth place in the UK charts. Their concerts and tours multiplied and with their success, the tension and pressure on Hendrix increased. In June of 1968, the group returned to the studio to start recording their third album, which included collaborations with musicians such as Steve Winwood and Jack Casady. Hendrix had changed a lot by then: drugs, which circulated in large quantities among the band members, often led him astray. The sessions lasted many months and the album, *Electric Ladyland*, was released in October of 1968, becoming one of the most important albums in the history of rock. The album's original cover was censored due to a photograph depicting a group of nude women, but it was, nevertheless, a great success.

In December, the tension between Hendrix, Mitchell, Redding and Chas Chandler reached breaking point: Chandler left their management and the group officially disbanded shortly after. They still played together until June of 1969, at which point Hendrix began working with Billy Cox, an old friend from the military, and with drummer Buddy Miles. In August of 1969, Hendrix performed at Woodstock with the Gypsys Sun and Rainbows, performing last, on the morning of the fourth day, in front of a few hundred people. However, his version of "The Star-Spangled Banner" would go down in history. In January of 1970, Hendrix performed in a concert with Buddy Miles and Billy Cox, the Band of Gypsys, with whom he recorded a live album. However, the experience didn't last long; Hendrix had become impossible, hot-tempered and always dissatisfied. The guitarist returned to the stage with Mitchell and Cox for a series of concerts: a few of them excellent, such as that at the Berkeley Community Center in May, others mixed, such as that for the Isle of Wight Festival, and yet others were terrible, such as the group's last performance, at the Isle of Fehmarn Festival in Germany. On September 18, 1970, Jimi Hendrix was found dead in his girlfriend's apartment, having choked his own vomit, caused by the use of barbiturates. With him died the idea of rock, free, wild, electric, unstoppable and, more than anything else, a musical genius that had not only radically innovated how to play the electric guitar, but who had paved the way for the great musicians that came after him, from Miles Davis to Prince.

Rock Shows Its Heart: The Concert for Bangladesh

[August 1, 1971]

It's hard to imagine an event with a greater scope than this, in the 1970s. And, until Live Aid, in 1985, no rock event like it had ever been staged before. Because the Concert for Bangladesh, organized by George Harrison and his friend Ravi Shankar, with two shows at Madison Square Garden in New York on August 1, 1971, was the first great rock gathering inspired by a humanitarian cause, blazing a trail that has continued to this day and down which rock music and charity walk arm in arm. But it also laid down the rules for the creation of a multi-media event, a concert that could become a triple album and a film, just as with Woodstock, but for a good cause: that of helping and supporting the people of Bangladesh who had been struck by a powerful cyclone in November of 1970. Not only that, but the country had been engaged in a long, bloody war with Pakistan to win their independence, which was followed by a terrible famine, with the ten million refugees that had escaped to India literally reduced to starvation and decimated by cholera. It was Ravi Shankar who motivated George Harrison to do something to help Bangladesh, in the first few months of 1971, and Harrison, busy with many other projects (including his collaboration with John Lennon for *Imagine*),

HISTORICAL NOTES

1971 – After the single "Bangla Desh," in only a few weeks Harrison manages to organize a charity concert, the first US show Dylan performs in since 1966. In December the triple LP recorded live is awarded a Grammy.

1972 – The New York premiere of the movie *The Concert for Bangladesh*.

1973 – The release of *Living in the Material World* coincides with the establishment of Harrison's Material World Charitable Foundation. Proceeds from the LP and the single "Give Me Love" go to the foundation's charities.

George Harrison accompanied by the band formed for the concert. The drummer was Ringo Starr.

began to work tirelessly on it in the first half of June, immediately involving Ringo Starr, Leon Russell, Billy Preston, Eric Clapton, Badfinger, Klaus Voormann and Jim Keltner. Clapton's drug problems cast doubt on his participation until the last minute and Harrison, to play it safe, arranged for Peter Frampton to practice all of his guitar parts, while Klaus Voormann coached Jesse Ed Davies on the guitar parts as well. Harrison had to make quite an effort to get Bob Dylan on stage as well, since he hadn't played live for a few years, his last appearance being in 1969 at the Isle of Wight Festival, and getting the participation of the other two Beatles, Lennon and McCartney, proved just as difficult. Lennon had initially agreed to the project, but two days before the concert, due to a fight with Yoko, he left New York and didn't participate in the event. McCartney, on the other hand, immediately declined, saying that the relationship between him and the Harrison-Lennon unit was still extremely tense and that the presence of Allen Klein at George's side in the event's organization made everything even more difficult. For Harrison, the entire operation was equally difficult, not just because he had never organized anything of the kind before but also because this was the first time that he would go on stage alone, without the Beatles, as a leader.

After a day of practice, the first of the two concerts was to start on the afternoon of August 1, 1971, followed by a second concert in the evening. The set included an introduction of forty-five minutes of Indian music, played by Ravi Shankar with Ali Akbar Khan, Alla Rakha and Kamala Chakravarty, then, after a brief interval that included the projection of a documentary about what was happening in Bangladesh, the stage was occupied by Harrison's band of twenty-four musicians, a "full Phil Spector/

All Things Must Pass rock orchestra," as the former Beatle called it.

Today, after having seen many other rock events, this one almost seems "normal." But just think for a moment about the extraordinarily exceptional quality of the event: Harrison brought, live, for the first time, songs that the Beatles hadn't ever played in concert (such as "While My Guitar Gently Weeps," with Clapton as the soloist, "Something" and "Here Comes the Sun"), Bob Dylan returned to the stage for the first time in two years, and for the first time in the USA, with his repertory from 1966. Clapton had fallen entirely victim to heroin and it was only by a miracle that he was able to get on stage. Ringo had just achieved great success as a solo artist with "It Don't Come Easy." And, for the first time, two Beatles played live with Bob Dylan.

Aside from the music in the two sets (one in the afternoon and one in the evening), which was beautiful, the extraordinary thing was the impact on mass communication that the event created. All media outlets, in order to report the event, also had to show conditions in Bangladesh, and the attention of the audience, thanks to the participation of the rock stars, allowed millions of people to become familiar with the problems of a place in the world that they probably didn't know existed the day before. It was a demonstration that, even if the dreams of the 1960s were fading, rock had held on to its potential; in fact, it was able to do unimaginable things, to stimulate people's consciousness, to provide information, to move substantial economies, to create "awareness" and at the same time proactively intervene. The Concert for Bangladesh was the foundation upon which the great events of the following years were built, but it was also an extraordinary closure of the 1960s. Rock, after 1971, would be reinvented, permanently.

Jesus Christ Superstar: The Musical Becomes Rock

[October 12, 1971]

It was in 1970 that a certain double album arrived in record stores: *Jesus Christ Superstar* by Andrew Lloyd Webber and Tim Rice, with the voice of Ian Gillan as Jesus. The album was a resounding success, so much so that within just one year, it would become a theater show that debuted on Broadway in 1971 and opened in Europe in 1972. One year later, a film appeared in cinemas which was destined for great success and which would unleash an equally broad set of controversies: *Jesus Christ Superstar*, directed by Norman Jewison.

"The album is still extraordinarily strong and the theater show is always revived with old and new cast members, but the years do not weigh on a film that, even if remaining intensely linked to the era in which it was made (in the height of the planetary explosion of hippies, the aftermath of the revolution of 1968, in a decade, the 1970s, in which the clash between generations was even stronger than the one before it), has not lost any of its powerful emotional charge and it remains, if we can use the term, "revolutionary."

Jesus Christ Superstar changed a lot of the rules for musicals, after also having drastically renewed those of musical theater as well, upon its debut on the stages of London's West End.

HISTORICAL NOTES

1969 – Release of the single "Superstar," a year before the LP *Jesus Christ Superstar* is released.

1971 – The American premiere is held in Kansas City, Missouri and the Broadway debut takes place at the Mark Hellinger Theatre, where it will run until 1973. The musical is banned in South Africa due to its 'profanity'.

1972 – The London premiere at the Palace Theatre; Russia composer Dmitri Shostakovich is in the audience. A year later it plays at the Théâtre de Chaillot in Paris.

1973 – Norman Jewison's film version of the musical is released.

Yvonne Ellima (Mary Magdalene) and Ted Neeley (Jesus) in a scene from the movie.

The film, sung in its entirety without any spoken dialogue, presented the life of Jesus as if created by an action-theater company, constantly playing with the ambiguity between what was on stage and what was reality. Thus, there were many scenic innovations – the use of music (strictly rock and soul) was different even from other "hippie" musicals such as *Hair*. Then there was the choice, which became the source of much criticism, to represent Jesus and his disciples as a group of hippies, to tell the story of the last seven days of Christ's life from Judas' perspective and to represent Jesus primarily as a man, pairing him with a visibly enamored Mary Magdalene.

The heart of the film's success, which garnered two Golden Globe nominations, is in the music, in a series of songs that would lead the soundtrack to sell more than seven million copies and to be, even today, greatly loved by the public. The star of the first version of the musical, the original recording of the album, from 1970, was Ian Gillan, the legendary singer from Deep Purple, dressed in Jesus' clothes. Gillan has said that singing in *Jesus Christ Superstar* was one of the best and most satisfying moments of his career. Lloyd Webber and Rice had heard his voice in "Child in Time" and they called for him. He went to Webber's apartment, where he was played the melody to Gethsemane on the piano and Rice told him the lyrics. Despite being very nervous, everything went well in the end. Two years later, Norman Jewison once again thought of him for the cinematic version, but in the meantime Deep Purple's success had grown exponentially, and it was impossible for Gillan to take the part. The role of Jesus, which everyone got to know at the movie theater, went to Ted Neeley, who became very popular despite a lot of criticism for his combination of a "hard rock" vocal style with generous use of falsetto and

Lloyd Webber's melodic structure. The third famous Jesus from the musical was Jeff Fenholt, who was the first to hold the role in the theatrical version and who was a great success on Broadway.

Jesus Christ Superstar was the first attempt, and a very successful one, to insert counterculture into mainstream pop, to transmit new messages, in an open alternative to religious tradition but in perfect sync with the culture of a younger generation, using many of the tools of mass communication: music, theater and film.

The film triggered countless controversies when it arrived in movie theaters, and there were worldwide protests and disturbances by reactionaries, super-Catholics and right-wingers that arranged protests in front of these movie theaters, trying to stop the film from being shown. With the passage of time, *Jesus Christ Superstar* was able to earn a prominent place not only in the history of musical film and the hearts of a less orthodox and bigoted audience, but also in the hearts of a religious audience that has understood how Lloyd Webber's and Rice's interpretation was anything but blasphemous and anti-Semitic.

The fact remains that *Jesus Christ Superstar* was, together with *Hair*, a work that contributed fundamentally to the renewal of the musical genre, be it in the theater or the cinema, establishing new, freer and more creative production standards and bringing rock to center stage. It allowed an entire generation to rediscover musicals and their language, while paving the way for a new legion of artists who were able to create works that in the following decades would always take account of the innovations Jewison brought to film and that Lloyd Webber and Rice brought to theater. From that moment on, the theatrical space of rock became the stage, paving the way for artists that, like David Bowie, would push it all to extreme, yet genius, outcomes.

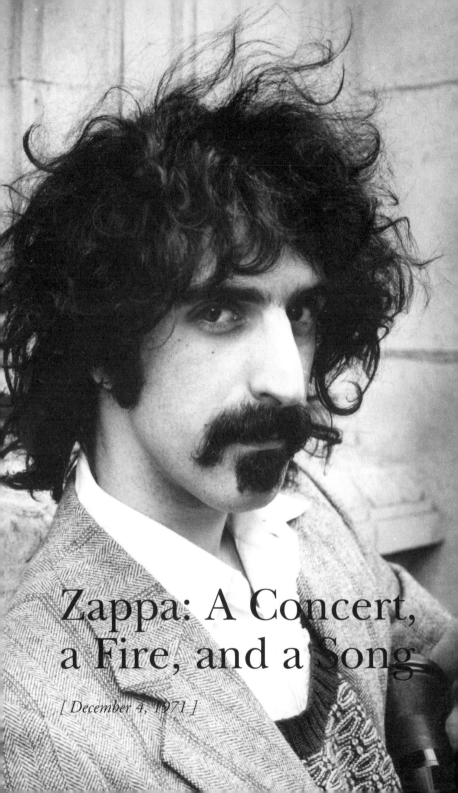

Zappa: A Concert, a Fire, and a Song

[*December 4, 1971*]

Y ou may be able to find it, online or in some tiny store that still has rock relics or treasures. An album – a bootleg to be exact. The cover will strike you instantly: it's the farthest thing from sobriety. There is Frank Zappa with a red scarf, wearing nothing more than leopard print briefs and surrounded by plants, looking straight at the camera, hard-nosed. It's called *Swiss Cheese/Fire!* and it's not just a simple, pirated tape of a concert by the genius from Baltimore, like the thousands of others in circulation. It is the audio testimony of the fiercest concert in the history of contemporary music. And that's not a metaphor.

Montreux, Switzerland, the evening of December 4, 1971: in the city's casino concert hall Frank Zappa was, as usual, enveloping his European fans with a sonorous magma of guitars and nonsense, of solos and provocation in their purest form. It all happened during "King Kong": someone, who was much too excited, pulled out and fired a flare gun. Just a few minutes later almost the entire building was engulfed in flames. The best description was by Zappa himself, in an interview a few years later, stating that somebody in

HISTORICAL NOTES

1966 – *Freak Out*, the double LP that marked The Mothers of Invention's recording debut, is released.

1967 – Their first European tour takes place. Two years later Zappa leaves the band.

1970 – Zappa reunites the band in order to play with the Los Angeles Philharmonic Orchestra directed by Zubin Mehta at UCLA.

1971 – Premiere of the film *200 Motels* and of the double LP with the movie's sound track. The European tour begins. After the famous fire at Montreux, Zappa has to rent the band's equipment for the next concert, held in London, during which he has been pushed from the stage and is seriously injured.

Frank Zappa in a 1971 photograph.

the audience had pulled out a Molotov cocktail or shot a flare into the rafters, which were made entirely of wood and fabric. It happened in an instant, everything caught fire in a second. Naturally, the concert was stopped and the facility's manager, Claude Nobs, the mastermind behind the Montreux Jazz Festival, managed to rescue dozens of fans before the entire casino collapsed to the ground. Tragedy had been avoided.

But the importance of that concert for rock comes via another band. Because, that night, right in that Swiss town, Deep Purple were in the mobile studio that they rented from the Rolling Stones, working on songs for their new album. They were, like everyone else, incredulous about what happened. Incredulity broken by one of the most famous guitar riffs of all time: "Smoke on the Water," which Deep Purple composed on that very night. A song inspired by the news that went straight into history. The final verse tells us just how it was composed: "We ended up at the Grand Hotel / It was cold, empty and bare/ But with the Rolling Stones truck thing just outside / Making our music there/ With a few red lights and a few old beds / We make a place to sweat / No matter what we get out of this / I know we'll never forget / Smoke on the water, fire in the sky."

In short, there's no denying it: Frank Zappa, in addition to indelibly making music history, contemporaneously also contributed to the inspiration of one of the milestones of the 1970s. "Smoke on the Water" would become nothing other than the workhorse of Deep Purple and would take them on a world tour the following year. And that tour was the one in which one of the most important live albums of the 1970s was recorded: *Made in Japan*. But that's a whole other story, a different concert to remember.

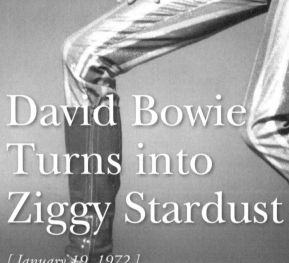

David Bowie
Turns into
Ziggy Stardust

[January 19, 1972]

From persona to person, he has lived through almost half a century of rock. He's been the Thin White Duke, his incarnation as a pop star with backcombed hair, wearing the wide, bright jackets of the 1980s – the musician that was entirely dedicated to pushing the boundaries of rock in the 1990s. But, it's much more likely that David Bowie will be remembered for his first alter ego, Ziggy Stardust, who, in London in the early 1970s, simply represented something that no one had ever seen before: rock wearing a mask. There were already musicians who wore make up, just think of Little Richard. Sequins and the like had already been cleared by Marc Bolan and the world was already full of rock stars in black leather, from Jim Morrison to Alice Cooper. But, Bowie's project was different: rock was on a crash course with theater and the result was the first "character" of contemporary popular music: Ziggy Stardust.

The creation of Ziggy came about during the early dates of Bowie's 1972 tour. On January 19, 1972, three days before the famous interview in *Melody Maker* in which he stated he was gay, Bowie was busy with rehearsals for his Ziggy Stardust Tour, at the Royal Ballroom in

HISTORICAL NOTES

1970 – During the US tour to promote his third album, *The Man Who Sold The World*, Bowie conceives an imaginary character called Ziggy Stardust.

1971 – He begins to write the songs for this new project and releases the first versions of "Moonage Daydream" and "Hang On to Yourself."

1972 – Bowie's first official tour, The Ziggy Stardust Tour, begins at the Toby Jug in Tolworth to promote *The Rise and Fall of Ziggy Stardust and the Spiders from Mars*, released in June.

David Bowie as Ziggy Stardust in London.

Tottenham, London. He stopped to talk to a few journalists, telling them that the layout would be shocking, but very theatrical, with costumes and choreography, something never tried before. And so it was. From his first appearance, it was clear that Bowie wasn't just performing: he embodied the audience's imagination. He gave a systematic framework to insights that were scattered about, as he would many other times throughout the course of his career. He shone a light on an entirely different world, and a world that was absolutely closed in on itself, equipped with its own logic, in front of the eyes of his fans. Bowie's fantasies, dreams and nightmares were arranged in an order that had a lot to do with chaos.

He said he wanted sound and images to line up, and they did. "Sound and Vision." The rise and fall of Ziggy Stardust was a spectacle of its own, Bowie's face dissolving into that of the alien he had created. A spectacle that moved through "Five Years," "Moonage Daydream," "Starman," through "Hang On to Yourself," and the title track. Perfect pop song structures that were played, at times, in the style of the Velvet Underground or echoing Berlin in the 1930s. Everything was dressed in "ultra-violence, in Liberty fabrics" as Bowie himself defined it. And the mask the singer used allowed him to speak about the unspeakable, of his own split consciousness and of unpronounceable desires, and to put all those contradictions, oppressed by genteel English society at the time, on stage. Young Londoners (and thus those worldwide) expected nothing less: Ziggy, the liberator, fallen to earth to transform a horrible world into the sublime and acidic light of art.

It was Ziggy-mania. In concert after concert, in country after country, from 1972 to 1973, Bowie laid down the foundations of his empire. He did so only then to destroy them, on the night in which he decided to say goodbye to Ziggy, to free himself from his mask – only to wear another. Only to search out new territory, without any pretense of authenticity, without any intention of being himself. Bowie or ambiguity. One of the darkest and most attractive zones in the entire history of rock.

Deep Purple:
The ABCs
of Hard Rock

[August 15-16-17, 1972]

R oger Glover, who with his bass has always been the rhythmic motor of Deep Purple, defined it as the "most honest album in the history of rock," since the technicians that recorded the songs in the set list of *Made in Japan* didn't do anything except position microphones and press record. There was no subsequent studio intervention, no attempt to make the sound anything other than what the spectators heard live. At the time, in 1972, this was already newsworthy.

Three concerts: August 15 and 16 in Osaka, and August 17 at Tokyo's Budokan. Hours of music to choose from for those seven songs that would end up on the double vinyl album that influenced, perhaps more than any other, the idea of how much energy live hard rock could unleash. There are moments in *Made in Japan* that are still, today, part of the collective imagination of every self-respecting hard rock fan. Ian Gillan's yell in "Child in Time," his call & response with guitarist Ritchie Blackmore during "Strange Kind of Woman," the drum solo in "The Mule." And, obviously, that which has come down through history

HISTORICAL NOTES

1968 – After their debut album *Shades of Deep Purple* and the single "Hush," in October they release *The Book of Taliesyn*. They begin their US tour.

1969 – Release of *Deep Purple*, the last album of the original band.

1970 – *Deep Purple in Rock*, the first LP with Ian Gillan as vocalist and Roger Glover at the bass, marks a turning point for them in Europe.

1971 – *Fireball* peaks to number one on the English charts.

1972 – Their Japanese tour begins at the Festival Hall of Osaka. *Made in Japan* sells millions of copies.

Deep Purple performing in 1972.

as the best version ever played of "Smoke on the Water," the song that Deep Purple wrote the day of the fire at the Casino in Montreux, Switzerland, during a Frank Zappa concert.

It's an album that even today, more than forty years later, defines the reputation of Deep Purple. A rock machine, definitely theatrical and likely to make an impression, that continues to shake sports arenas and stadiums around the world. It's a reputation based particularly on their fans' involvement in the show. And everything begins from those three nights, especially from the concert at Budokan. As Glover said, "twelve or thirteen thousand Japanese kids were singing along to 'Child in Time.'" All the way on the other side of the world, and still so many people knew the words to the songs.

So, the riffs. It's not hard to imagine: every self-respecting guitarist has spent at least a few hundred hours holed up in his room to listen, understand and reproduce everything that Ritchie Blackmore put in that album. Simply in a state of grace, the guitarist made occasional errors to develop new directions. He played solos that have yet to see their equal in inspiration, putting his riffs over the foundation of that genuine wall of sound that you can feel with every listen of *Made in Japan*.

And, for every disk that has entered history there is an entire series of legends that follows. The main one that relates to *Made in Japan* is that about the existence of films documenting the concerts. It's all false; they do not exist. Just do a little research online to see how much such images would be worth.

In conclusion, if there is a concert that still, today, correctly guides and establishes the tastes of hard rock fans, without a doubt it is *Made in Japan.* Just consider one thing: in January 2006, Dream Theater, contemporary followers of Deep Purple, celebrated their idols with two concerts in Japan where they exactly – slavishly even – reproduced the album's track listing. Everything on it is perfect, brilliant, played to perfection. But it has nothing to do with the original release, which remains a hard-to-avoid milestone, obtaining top ranking on all the charts that specialized magazines dedicate to the best shows in the history of rock. It's an album that should always be listened to with the speakers blaring, jumping around, accompanied by reckless headbanging, without any fear – ethical or aesthetic – of appearing like an old dinosaur from an era of rock that is by now in its sunset years.

The Future of Rock is on Stage: Bruce Springsteen in Boston

[May 9, 1974]

The phrase has gone down in history: "I saw rock and roll future and its name is Bruce Springsteen." It was written by Jon Landau, at the time a music critic, after having seen the Boss' concert at the Harvard Square Theater in Cambridge on May 9, 1974, publishing his thoughts in Boston's *The Real Paper* on May 22. Bruce Springsteen had met Landau in Boston in April, on the occasion of another concert, and the two struck up a friendship. But, the evening of May 9 was different.

The Boss and his band had opened a concert for Bonnie Raitt, two sets, one in the early evening and one later in the evening. Landau took part in the latter one and his experience of the concert was one that, as those who have seen a Springsteen concert love to say even today, changed his life. Life was certainly about to change for both of them. Landau's changed immediately, as he himself explained in the article: "I saw my Rock 'n' Roll past flash before my eyes. And I saw something else: I saw rock and roll future and its name is Bruce Springsteen. And on a night when I needed to feel young, he made me feel like I was hearing music for the very first time."

HISTORICAL NOTES

1972 – Springsteen forms the E Street Band and signs a contract with Columbia Records.

1973 – His debut album *Greetings from Asbury Park, NJ* is released, receiving praise from the press; but sales are modest.

1975 – His third album, *Born to Run*, the result of long, hard work in the recording studio, is an international success and is awarded the gold and platinum records.

1984 – He releases *Born in the USA*, which sells 30 million copies throughout the world, half of which in the USA alone.

Bruce Springsteen during a show.

Springsteen played for little over an hour, in a show that mixed rock, folk, rhythm and blues, and much more, in a unique way, as Landau underlined in his article: "Springsteen does it all. He is a Rock 'n' Roll punk, a Latin street poet, a ballet dancer, an actor, a joker, bar band leader, hot-shit rhythm guitar player, extraordinary singer, and a truly great Rock 'n' Roll composer. He leads a band as if he has been doing it forever. I racked my brains but simply can't think of a white artist who does so many things so superbly." Simply put, Landau was right: Springsteen played everything, rock, folk and soul, in the vein of Van Morrison but with a lot more Rock 'n' Roll, suburbs and American streets in his veins. He played "New York City Serenade," "Kitty's Back," and "I Sold My Heart to the Junkman" from the repertory of Patti LaBelle & the Bluebelles, "The E Street Shuffle," "For You," "It's Hard to Be a Saint in the City" and according to some, even the first execution of "Born to Run."

Both their lives changed that night: Landau became Springsteen's producer and one of his dearest friends and advisors, which he still is today. As Springsteen himself said of Landau: "His creative ability as a producer, an editor, speech-writer earlier this evening, his ability to see through to the heart of matters both professional and personal, and the love that he's given me has altered my life forever.

And the truth is that, seeing the work that Landau and Springsteen did together after that night, they also changed the lives of everyone who truly loves rock 'n' roll.

Peter Gabrie[l
Says Goodby[e
to Genesi[s

[November 20, 197[

Progressive rock was one of the most beloved styles of rock. Appearing at the end of the 1960s, its creative trajectory ended in the middle of the following decade. The start of the end for Genesis dates to November 20, 1974, when they began their last tour with Peter Gabriel, at Chicago's Auditorium Theater, bringing their most complex and ambitious work to the stage: *The Lamb Lies Down on Broadway*. The tour wasn't only the height of creativity for Gabriel and his band, for its rich and awe-inspiring musical structure, but also for the band's and the singer's ability to build a complete, theatrical show with costumes, scenes and projections that were intended to make the story more compelling and comprehensible.

The story of *The Lamb Lies Down on Broadway* revolves around the figure of Rael, a young Puerto Rican juvenile delinquent, who lives in New York and who is forced to face an extraordinary voyage in order to rescue his brother John. The story is surreal and symbolic because, as demonstrated by the presence of a mannequin dressed exactly like Peter Gabriel, by his side on stage, Rael's search for his brother

HISTORICAL NOTES

1965 – The Garden Wall, the original nucleus of Genesis, is formed.

1969 – Decca releases *From Genesis to Revelation*.

1972 – *Foxtrot* released. During the tour of the same name Peter Gabriel begins to wear costumes, drawing inspiration from the lyrics. This marks the beginning of his spectacular, theatrical performances.

1975 – After a long worldwide tour Gabriel leaves Genesis and concentrates on experimentation, ending up by embracing world music.

1976 – He records his first four solo albums. Success arrives with "Solsbury Hill," which narrates his break from Genesis.

Peter Gabriel during the last Genesis tour in which he took part.

is nothing other than the search for a missing part of himself. This voyage brings Rael to face various difficulties, but also to confront the problems of contemporary society.

In the first part of the show, Gabriel was dressed simply as Rael, in a t-shirt and jeans, while the second part the show became decidedly more complex, with various costume changes, some of which were quite elaborate (for example, that during "The Lamia" or the famous "Slipperman"). There were numerous special effects, a few of which were particularly spectacular, such as in the final song, when Gabriel appeared on stage, amid strobe lights, after a large explosion, once again dressed identically to the mannequin. Both of them stood still, unmoving on the stage, making it difficult for the audience to make out which was the real Gabriel.

The first concert in Chicago was met with enthusiasm, even if often, like most of the rest of the tour, not everything worked perfectly: not the costumes, not the projections, not the special effects. The star of the show was Gabriel, with his expressiveness, his great vocal strength, and his theatricality, even if the music played during the show had been entirely composed by other members of the band, who all were at their peak when playing live, perfectly balanced between technical ability and creativity.

The Lamb Lies Down on Broadway was the final episode of a great season of progressive rock; the newer generations were progressively less interested in the depth of messages, the complexity of structures and the richness of compositions. And, Gabriel himself was no longer at ease within the group's dimensions. Halfway through the tour he decided to leave Genesis, which he announced a few months after the last performance of The Lamb, on May 22, 1975, at the Palais des Sports in Besançon, France. Soon after, punk would arrive and rock would shed its skin once again.

Blood, Sex and Games:
The Rocky Horror Picture Show

[March 10, 1975]

It wasn't certain, in 1975, that music and cinema sealed their union with *The Rocky Horror Picture Show*. During the 1960s, "musical cinema" did nothing but develop. Just look at the series of Elvis Presley films that were often nothing more than long video clips where the narration takes second place to the King's songs, or the great tribute that rock paid to the soundtracks of cult films of that era, beginning with *Easy Rider*. They're images that lose their force and evocative power if you try cutting out the music. Or, again, the first, pioneering attempts to film rock concerts and events to preserve the memory of them, Woodstock in particular. But one thing is certain: it is only with the story of Brad and Janet, the protagonists of *The Rocky Horror Picture Show*, that music and image were put on the same plane, in an attempt to give life to a kind of total art.

And, it is in this context that the key factor comes into play, the one that has made that magic union between cinematography and rock 'n' roll possible: the Broadway musical. It was the start of the 1970s and rock was the new fuel needed to get the musical vehicle back into gear, which had become weighed down by its own

HISTORICAL NOTES

1974 – In the wake of the great success enjoyed by Richard O'Brien's musical (1973), shooting on location of the movie version begins in England.

1975 – *The Rocky Horror Picture Show*, directed by Jim Sharman, is released.

1976 – At first the movie does not do too well, but it eventually becomes a cult film. The fans begin to return regularly to the movie theater to re-enact the various scenes.

1981 – Release of the sequel, *Shock Treatment*, directed by Jim Sharman and starring Richard O'Brien and Patricia Quinn.

Left to right: Little Nell, Patricia Quinn, Tim Curry and Richard O'Brien on the set.

baggage of musical formulas taken directly from 1950s American musical tradition. *Hair*, *Jesus Christ Superstar* and *The Rocky Horror Picture Show* represented the three steps that Broadway made towards rock. For that matter, Bob Dylan and the Beatles, established in their ability to lead the course of popular art, had not taken steps forward in vain. And it's a short leap from the musical to the big screen. Three stories inspired by the conquest of freedom, especially the freedom of expression, that would easily play in a country that in the 1970s was going through a kind of decline from the point of view of a hypothetical future, of new roads, for mass culture.

The Rocky Horror Picture Show fulfilled one need: that of the retreat of every form of Puritanism, of every tendency towards bigotry, of every sterile moralism making a comeback in regard to sexual behavior. It is no coincidence that Brad and Janet, newlyweds, start their personal descent into the glam-pop underworld by listening to Richard Nixon's speech on the radio in which he communicates his resignation to the nation. Out with Vietnam, out with conservatives, out with the hypocrisy of a society now split between public, hypocrit-ical virtues and private behaviors that were vices only in the notepads of conformists. *The Rocky Horror Picture Show* is the metaphor that stokes the fire of sexual liberation. Here, disguised as an apologia for transvestism and bisexuality. The only forms able to unhinge the puritanical horror that was so well represented by Grant Wood's *American Gothic*, the painting that runs throughout the development of the film.

In short, how could you not but want to be present at the show's premier, at the Belasco Theater on Broadway, that March 10, 1975? How could you not want to mix with that crowd of fans that finally took over the projection halls not just to reinforce their private tastes, but also to publicly demonstrate their own ambitions for freedom? It may be considered excessive, this *Rocky Horror Picture Show*, but you can't help but read it as one of the greatest moments in which mainstream pop culture once again was diverted toward the underground, again enriched by the expressive force of those who used art as the only way to express themselves – all without forgetting how perfect the soundtrack is, to the images that scroll before our eyes. Because, as in this case, rock isn't just a soundtrack, but the backbone of that cry for freedom.

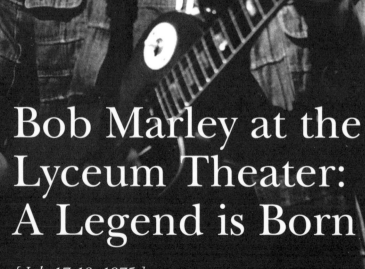

Bob Marley at the Lyceum Theater: A Legend is Born

[July 17-18, 1975]

In the UK, in mid-1975, the vast majority of young people professed one musical faith, that of progressive rock. Genesis, Yes and the like: long instrumental suites, an iron pact between rock and classical, themes and lyrics that delved into the roots of Celtic myths. That was the new look chosen by rock after the grace of the 1960s and the collapse in the first part of the decade. It was an electric, baroque spaceship that very few were unwilling to board. But that reality of instrumental, dreamlike flights was substituted in just two nights by another collective dream and another voyage, brought from a magic rite, officiated by a young priest that came from Trench Town, Jamaica, the former outskirts of the Kingdom. On July 17 and 18, 1975, Bob Marley's singing picked rock up, stripped away its certainty and led it down other roads.

On that afternoon in July, only one thing was certain: that no one had ever seen "such strange" people in the center of London, outside the Lyceum Theater, one of the most beautiful theaters in the English capital. Three thousand Jamaicans perfectly mixed in with English youths, all of them there to listen to who they considered

HISTORICAL NOTES

1963 – Marley forms The Wailing Wailers with his friends Bunny Livingston and Peter McIntosh (and, later, Peter Tosh).

1972 – The band signs a contract with Island Records. *Catch a Fire* is released and is a huge international success, selling over 10 million copies.

1974 – Livingston and Tosh leave the band. The Bob Marley & The Wailers band is formed and releases *Natty Dread*.

1975 – Release of *Live!*, the album recorded live during the historic concert at the Lyceum Ballroom in London. Reggae revolutionizes rock.

Bob Marley during a concert.

to be their spiritual father. Almost no one had a ticket, but everyone wanted to attend. The police tried to intervene, but there was nothing to be done: two doors were torn off their hinges and the crowd was free to enter. Those who got in witnessed a memorable concert, recorded by the Rolling Stones' mobile recording studio. Bob Marley was at his peak. He had just released *Natty Dread*, the album that would consecrate him as an international star. The atmosphere that night was indescribable. Dennis Morris, a concert photographer, summarized it as such: "That night, everyone present decided to become a Rastafarian." "Lively Up Yourself" and "No Woman No Cry" carried the audience and popular music to new territory – exotic, uncontaminated. Rock rediscovered what holiness meant; it became the entry to a free paradise in the heart of the West that would find its disciples in England: without that concert, the Clash, the Police and dozens of other groups would simply never have existed.

It wasn't just about bringing the world of reggae to the West. In those two concerts, Bob Marley almost seemed to leave his own history and origins behind. He was able – and this is what makes it magical – to cover his songs with a fresh coat of paint, transforming them from the diary of a rebel on a voyage to an ecumenical calling. He did just that on those two nights in London. On one hand, he relied on electricity; he contaminated his band's entire sound with what rock had been teaching for the last twenty years. And on the other, he staged an infinite call & response with the I Threes, his three backup singers, according to the dictates of his soul. It wasn't just an addition, but pure alchemy. Marley was able to extract, from all the musical genres that he went through, all the elements that sound "messianic." He absorbs them and he injects them into an entirely new musical fabric. Rock takes mankind's future as its subject, re-establishing his being as the best way to arrive to the Promised Land, without naivety, dogma or canons. Redemption Music, the vehicle of liberation, started that July day in London.

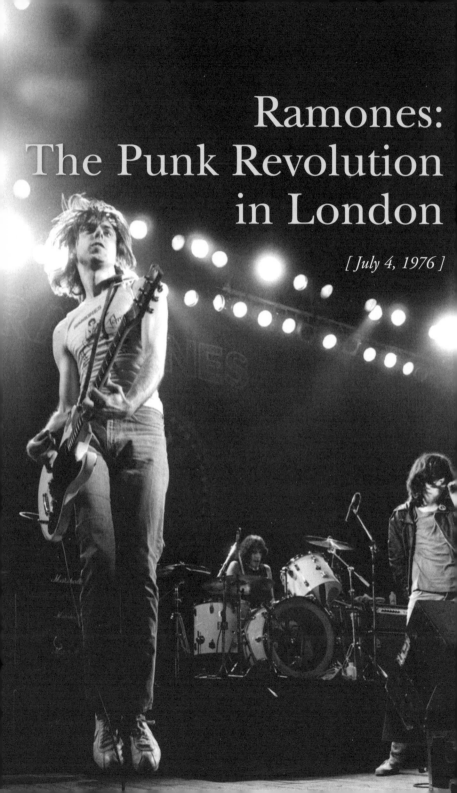

Ramones:
The Punk Revolution
in London

[July 4, 1976]

One might ask why highlight a Ramones concert in London as one of the fundamental events that changed the course of rock, and not one of their seminal concerts at CBGB in New York, the temple of new rock that saw its birth and growth? Because, even if it is true that the Ramones were among the fathers of punk, their direct descendants, those to whom they ideally gave life, were born on July 4, 1976 at London's Roundhouse when the four young Ramone "brothers" arrived to shock the capital city, still crushed between the residue of prog rock and glam, in front of a public that was ready to exploded. In front of the band that night were the fans that, after that concert, decided that they didn't want to do anything else. Present that night were future members of the Sex Pistols, the Clash, the Pretenders, Adam & the Ants, Siouxsie and the Banshees and the Damned. On stage were four musicians that, as *Melody Maker* would write at the time, played minimalist music: a few chords, super-fast rhythms, absolute immediacy, obsessive simplicity, the zero grade of rock with an extremely high impact. In one night, the rock played by the Ramones swept away a decade of intellectual,

HISTORICAL NOTES

1974 – Their first gig is at the Performance Studios.

1976 – *Ramones* is released, followed by *Leave Home* and *Rocket to Russia* the following year. They start their first tour abroad, performing at the Roundhouse as support for the Flamin' Groovies, marking a turning point in the evolution of English punk rock.

1980 – *End of the Century* released. Tension begins among the band members; there are disputes about which direction the group should take and personal conflict among the members.

1996 – Their last concert takes place in Los Angeles. The Ramones disbands.

Left to right: Johnny Ramone, Marky Ramone and Joey Ramone.

thought-out music that searched for art and deep expression and replaced it with rock that was punk, that rummaged haphazardly though the catalog of rock 'n' roll and surf through the quintessential music of young people, and then slammed energy in its purest form into the face of the audience without mediation or discussion. In fact, the Ramones (Joey, planted in front of the microphone, Dee Dee on bass, Johnny on guitar, both arrayed on the sides of the stage in a wide-legged stance, and deadpan behind his drum set) didn't give any hint of emotion, enthusiasm or passion. They were savagely concentrated on their set, where there was practically no pause between one song and the next, aside from the time to say "one, two, three, four" and start again.

They had done so since 1974, when they decided to band together and play what they could, with little technical expertise but with the desire to change things, to bring enjoyment back to the heart of rock. They managed to do so, releasing their first album in 1976, a few months after the release of another essential album for new rock, *Horses* by Patti Smith, changing the rules of the game once and for all. Sid Vicious, Mick Jones, Chrissie Hynde and Siouxsie Sioux, to name just a few of the many kids that packed the Roundhouse, got the message: you could play even if you weren't technically competent, you could sing even if you didn't have a powerful voice, you could be on stage in ripped pants, without being beautiful or covered in make up, without lights and colored smoke, without large amplifiers, as long as you had something to say and you wanted to play for others without any distance between the stage and the crowd, without any big difference between band and audience. This was punk as it was starting its journey, two years that would overwhelm the entire world of rock.

The End of the 1970s: The Last Waltz for the Band

[November 25, 1976]

There could be no better eyes than those of Martin Scorsese to show us and tell us about this last act: the last waltz for the quintessential band of American rock in the 1960s and 1970s. Robbie Robertson, Rick Danko, Richard Manuel, Levon Helm and Garth Hudson – the group that every musician would have wanted supporting him. It was November 25, 1976, Thanksgiving Day, and, at the Winterland Arena in San Francisco, the Band said farewell to their audience. They did so by inviting to the stage a parade of stars that hadn't been seen since the days of Woodstock. Everyone was there to pay tribute: Neil Young, the Staple Singers, Joni Mitchell, Muddy Waters, Emmylou Harris, Ronnie Wood, Ringo Starr, and, especially, Bob Dylan.

The Band was, in particular, Bob Dylan's band, the musicians that had accompanied the prophet of rock throughout his electric turning point, who had composed and recorded with him that timeless marvel, *The Basement Tapes*. It was by playing with Bob Dylan that they developed their sound, the epitome of rock. Just think of Bob Dylan's tour of England in 1966, of those furious versions of "Like a Rolling Stone" and "Tombstone Blues."

HISTORICAL NOTES

1964 – Robbie Robertson, Richard Manuel, Garth Hudson, Rick Danko and Levon Helm form the Levon and the Hawks band, later known as The Band (1968).

1965 – They become famous when Bob Dylan hires them as a support band for his tour of the US.

1968 – *Music from Big Pink*, their first album, is released.

1976 – *The Last Waltz* is their farewell concert. The band reunites from 1983 to 1999.

1978 – Martin Scorsese's documentary is released.

Neil Diamond, Dr. John, Joni Mitchell, Neil Young, Rick Danko, Van Morrison, Ronnie Hawkins, Bob Dylan and Robbie Robertson during the concert.

It was a sound that immediately became an archetype, a code.

It was that very code that was celebrated on that evening in November of 1976. The decision had already been taken and the group had chosen Martin Scorsese – who was already on the path to glory and, as an assistant director, had helped make the Woodstock documentary – to film their last concert. And in those timeless images, there is all the force and gentleness of American rock.

The unforgettable concert began with a series of the band's songs: "The Weight" and "The Night They Drove Old Dixie Down." These were timeless songs, already classics, played on that occasion with a particular zeal that, if possible, made them even more poignant. All of this while in the other rooms of the venue, Lawrence Ferlinghetti – not exactly someone random – captivated the audience, who were offered a Thanksgiving Dinner as he performed. But the miracle, the reason that concert went straight into the annals of rock history, came with the arrival of the guests on stage. It's enough to go back and watch two performances: that in which Neil Young, accompanied by Joni Mitchell, sings his version of "Helpless;" and then the choral moment, when Bob Dylan comes on stage to play, with everyone present, his unsurpassed and unsurpassable version of "I Shall Be Released." It will still give you goose bumps.

And it is to Bob Dylan that one of the event's back-stories is linked. The singer had agreed to be part of the show but he didn't want to be filmed by Scorsese. There was nothing personal.. The fact was that Bob Dylan, busy with his tour, was shooting his own film, *Renaldo and Clara*, and he didn't want the Band's concert to come out in theaters first. He got what he wanted and, indeed, *The Last Waltz*, Scorsese's documentary, came out in 1978. A documentary considered by many to be the most beautiful film ever made about rock. It was important for its style more than anything else: continuous feedback between live shows, archival film and conversational moments with the group. It was a canvas that Scorsese would amplify in all his films relating to music, from *No Direction Home*, dedicated to Bob Dylan himself, to his wonderful documentary about George Harrison. Images and music, those of *The Last Waltz*, that continue to be a pure and simple lesson in rock.

The Sex Pistols:
Anarchy in the U.K.

[December 9, 19

I 1 On December 1, 1976, the Sex Pistols were invited, together with other punk members of the Bromley Contingent, including Siouxsie Sioux, to Bill Grundy's television program at Thames Television, in London. The segment doesn't last long and ends with the Sex Pistols telling the host to go to hell, spouting swear words and insults, which wasn't quite the norm on television in the 1970s. The scandal they caused was enormous; the front pages of the newspapers spoke only of them and the explosion of the punk phenomenon. A few days earlier, on November 26, the Sex Pistols had released their first single, "Anarchy in the UK," focusing the attention of every English adolescent on them. The single's release and the growing interest in punk pushed Malcolm McLaren, the band's manager, to organize a tour, the Anarchy Tour, which assembled the best of punk: the Sex Pistols as the headliner, the Clash, Johnny Thunders and the Heartbreakers from the United States and, for the show in Manchester and a few other venues, the Damned, who were also fresh from the release of their first single, "New Rose." It goes without saying that the controversy that arose after the incident on television made the tour almost impossible.

HISTORICAL NOTES

1975 – Formation of the band: Johnny Rotten, Steve Jones, Paul Cook and Glen Matlock (replaced by Sid Vicious in 1977).

1976 – EMI releases their first single, "Anarchy in the UK."

1977 – "God Save the Queen" is released. The band is faithful to its controversial notoriety, often using obscene language when referring to the music industry, consumer society, the royal family and the Holocaust.

1978 – At the end of their turbulent US tour Rotten leaves the band, which breaks up the following year.

Sid Vicious and Johnny Rotten during a concert. The words "Gimme a fix" are on Vicious' chest, carved with a razor.

The media followed the Sex Pistols wherever they went and just the news of their arrival in a city unleashed immediate protests. Fearing mishaps, the vast majority of clubs and concert halls, on the tour, decided to cancel the shows, and often protest demonstrations were held in front of the venues where the concerts were to take place, such as at the Castle Cinema in Caerphilly, Wales. It got to the point where a few workers in EMI's plant refused to work on the production of the single. The statements made by English politicians were not much different and a few of the most conservative among them even came to wish death upon the group's members. This was the official tour calendar, as the Sex Pistols remember it on their website:

12.03.76 Norwich University, Norwich – CANCELED
12.04.76 Kings Hall, Derby – CANCELED
12.05.76 City Hall, Newcastle – CANCELED
12.06.76 Leeds Polytechnic, Leeds – PLAYED!
12.07.76 Village Bowl, Bournemouth – CANCELED
12.09.76 Electric Circus, Manchester – PLAYED!
12.10.76 Lancaster University, Lancaster – CANCELED
12.11.76 Stadium, Liverpool – CANCELED
12.13.76 Colston Hall, Bristol – CANCELED
12.14.76 Top Rank, Cardiff, Wales – CANCELED
12.14.76 Castle Cinema, Caerphilly, Wales* – PLAYED!
12.15.76 Apollo, Glasgow, Scotland, UK – CANCELED
12.16.76 Caird Hall, Dundee, Scotland – CANCELED
12.17.76 City Hall, Sheffield – CANCELED
12.18.76 Kursaal, Southend – CANCELED
12.19.76 Civic Hall, Guildford – CANCELED

12.19.76 Electric Circus, Manchester* – PLAYED!
12.20.76 Town Hall, Birmingham – CANCELED
12.20.76 Winter Gardens, Cleethorpes* – PLAYED!
12.21.76 Woods Centre, Plymouth – PLAYED!
12.22.76 400 Ballroom, Torquay – CANCELED
12.22.76 Woods Centre, Plymouth* – PLAYED!
12.23.76 Paignton, Penelope's Ballroom – CANCELED
12.26.76 The Roxy, London – CANCELED

Live, the Sex Pistols were a force of nature that was expressed in all its primordial energy; Cook, Jones, Matlock and Lydon were far from incapable, but they reduced the need for technical ability to a bare minimum. In doing so, they gave off a message, loud and clear, that anyone else, who wanted to, could take a guitar in their hands and follow their lead, the exact opposite of progressive rock, which was super-technical, complex and impossible to play without a deep understanding of the instrument. They stood on the stage just like any other guys in the audience would have, paying no attention to anything but entertaining and having fun, making a racket at the loudest volume possible, and singing about what they had inside, what they saw before their eyes: a world that sucked, without prospects or a future. They had an extraordinary ability to involve the audience, an explosive gift for rage and irony, and they were just like the guys in front of the stage, as was evident to anyone who went to their concerts. They were "dangerous" because they brought rock back to the streets, because they were rebellious and they didn't follow any of the established rules, because they set their audience, no longer seated and still, free to go crazy.

The concert in Manchester is probably the one, of the seven realized tour dates, that deserves to be remembered, not just for the cast – the Clash, Johnny Thunders and the Heartbreakers, the Damned – but also for the audience. From that concert, like the previous Sex Pistols concert held at the Free Trade Hall in Manchester, in June, you can say that Manchester's punk and post-punk music scene was born. The Buzzcocks (Howard Devoto and Pete Shelley), for example, was born of the concert on June 4, while of the many who attended the concert of December 9, several came out totally changed by the event, giving a different shape to their music. In retrospect, Joy Division/New Order, Mark E. Smith's the Fall, the Smiths, the Buzzcocks/Magazine, Slaughter & the Dogs and dozens of other bands were formed by that concert which featured the explosive Sex Pistols, the devastating Damned, the young Clash and the more experienced Heartbreakers, and which would make a fundamental mark on British rock history.

The Death of the King: "Elvis Has Left the Building"

[August 16, 1977]

There's a song by Neil Young, released in 1979 in two different versions, the acoustic version of which goes: "My my, hey hey / Rock and roll is here to stay / It's better to burn out / Than to fade away." It goes on to remind us that "The king is gone but he's not forgotten / This is the story of a Johnny Rotten". Neil Young, tow years after the death of Elvis Presley, celebrated the myth and the legend, linking the old, dead king with his heirs. On August 16, 1977 – while punk was exploding in England with all of its nihilist and rebellious charge, while Johnny Rotten, the leader of the Sex Pistols, spit on everything that the youth culture had expressed up to that point and tried to put a tombstone on the history of rock 'n' roll – Elvis, the king, awaited his end within the walls of his castle in Memphis, in his own private "grace land," in his virtual garden of Eden where even the memories of his real life seemed fake and artistically recreated. There is a strange synchronicity in these events, between the end of rock as heralded by punk and the death of Elvis Presley. It was as if in that year, in 1977, the end of youth itself, the end of the dream handed down by Presley and many others after him (such as Bob Dylan, the Beatles, the

HISTORICAL NOTES

1968 – "The 1968 NBC Comeback Special" is the venue of Elvis' return to the music scene after almost ten years spent acting in mediocre movies and recording soundtracks.

1969 – RCA releases *From Elvis in Memphis*. Presley seems to foretell his coming death in the track "Long Black Limousine."

1973 – Elvis's health worsens because of drug use and obesity.

1977 – He holds his last concert at the Market Square Arena. Two months later, the day before he is to begin another tour, Elvis dies at Memphis.

One of Elvis's last appearances before his death on 16 August 1977.

Rolling Stones all the way to Bruce Springsteen) had been in the spotlight. The sad artistic end of Elvis Presley in the 1970s, his spectacular and essentially useless concerts for audiences in Las Vegas and his jackets with sequins and spangles, was exactly what punks wanted to destroy; they represented everything that rock was not, only they were unable to break it down but, on the contrary, all that rock had managed to solidify, was to turn into an institution, a market and an "establishment." Elvis was the "enemy." But, at the same time, he was the legend, the origin, the be-all and end-all, the clamorous glint that sparked the youthful fire of the 1960s, the grandfather.

It was not the punks or the freaks of the preceding decade who mourned his passing. It wasn't even the kids from the 1960s, who had already placed Elvis among the old stuff to be saved as a memory. But the pain was there and it was a collective pain. It was an older, deeper America that mourned the death of its special child, of that boy from Tupelo who wanted to become king and that was now mocked by his own subjects, his own children. Elvis represented America, once young and rebellious, but now fat, drugged, sleepy, unable to look at itself in the mirror, to understand what its dreams were, where its children had ended up, those "flowers" that Joan Baez and Bob Dylan sang about, broken by the war in Vietnam, by the lies of Richard Nixon, by the gunshots that had killed JFK, Martin Luther King, Jr., Malcolm X and the students at Kent State University. Elvis was the "system" and death arrived, in the end, to save him, to anchor him forever in his youthful image. It hadn't always been so: Elvis really had been the king of rock 'n' roll, the most famous and noble of its founding fathers, the hips that had awoken young Americans of the 1950s from their slumber, showing them the road to happiness, the way to freedom, the path of generational release on the wave of music that had shaken the foundations and the habits of pop.

In the almost forty years that have passed since his death, Elvis has, perhaps, been in the spotlight perhaps more than ever. If it is true, as J. Edgar Hoover said, paraphrasing an old, racist American proverb, that "the only good rocker is a dead rocker," Elvis' image has become even more powerful than when he was alive. His image remains "pure", uncontaminated, freshly rebellious and transgressive. The gyrations of his hips, referred to in countless films on television, his music, that innovative fusion of black and white sound, that subversive joy that emanated from his early songs, has reached us intact precisely because Elvis' demised "physique" had stopped the real Presley from dispelling his heritage, because the industry managed by his wife was able to commercialize the best of Elvis and slowly erase the worst images of him, the memories to be forgotten. Many of his songs, even some from his darkest period, far from the unwieldy presence of the real Elvis, come to us today with a truly incomparable force, originality and energy, and are still used by many young people as the compass to orient themselves in the vast sea of rock. Without Elvis, popular music would have been very different; without Elvis, the youth of this world wouldn't have been what we have known. With his legend, his image, still present among us, rock will never truly die. It will remain eternally young, electric and rebellious, ready to fight, as Neil Young said, against the "rust that never sleeps" and which corrodes the dreams and hopes of generations of young people around the world.

Rock Against Racism: Punk Becomes Combat Rock

[April 30, 1978]

It wall all thanks to Eric Clapton – a great guitarist and a political conservative – who in August 1976, from the stage during a concert in Birmingham, drunkenly declared his support for Enoch Powell, a right-wing English politician and champion of England's battle against immigration. The era was also politically problematic in England because the neo-fascists of the National Front had upped the level of confrontation with immigrants throughout the country, causing various altercations. In response to these events, Rock Against Racism was founded, an association of English musicians with the goal of combating racism and increasing awareness among musicians and audiences alike.

The largest demonstration organized by Rock Against Racism (an association to which many English punk, reggae and new wave artists belonged at the time) came on April 30, 1978: a long march from Trafalgar Square, organized with the Anti-Nazi League, ending with a big concert in Victoria Park. Nearly 100 thousand people came together in front of the stage to listen to the Clash, Steel Pulse, the Ruts, Sham 69, X-Ray Specs and the Tom Robinson Band, while a second march moved to arrive at Brockwell Park, in south London, to listen

HISTORICAL NOTES

1976 – Red Saunders and Roger Huddle form the Rock Against Racism (RAR) band. From 1978 to 1981 hundreds of concerts are organized to combat the wave of racism and the neo-Fascist National Front in England.

1978 – 100,000 persons march from Trafalgar Square to the East End for the Victoria Park concert, which is repeated shortly afterward at the Manchester carnival.

1982 – *Combat Rock*, the Clash's fifth album, is released and earns a gold record.

Paul Simonon and Jimmy Pursey, the vocalist of Sham 69, on stage at the Rock Against Racism festival at Hackney.

to Stiff Little Fingers, Aswad and Elvis Costello. It was the defining affirmation of new rock: aware, rebellious, focused, ready to shake up young people and English politics, ready to speak out, loud and clear. Punk had shaken music and English society; a new generation had already come forward, enraged and irreverent, with a completely different look and attitude than the older generation. No more long hair and hippie attitudes, but a deep desire to make noise and cause a scandal. But the punk of 1978 was no longer that of its early years, the Sex Pistols had reached the end of their path and many things had changed in two years. There was a new awareness, the desire to change things, the desire to put rock back at the center of youth culture with a wave of commitment that grabbed all the musicians of the younger generation. The two generations convened on that day; there were militants and old hippies, those for whom the dream of rock's ability to change the world still wasn't dead. And there they were, in large numbers, in front of the stage, ready to pogo up and down and make some noise. They were the ones to occupy the stage, to enthusiastically support the bands on stage, to signal, with their presence, an event that was no longer the child of the 1970s, but a new reality.

Rock Against Racism rallied tens of thousands of people on that day, and for the Clash, the standard-bearers of "combat rock," rock that wanted and could once again be militant and rebellious, it was their consecration. They had recently released their debut album and in the two preceding years they had crossed England far and wide on the wave of the punk revolution, turning the entire spectrum on its head. They were a strong team, with the guitar and creativity of

Mick Jones, the rhythm that hovered between punk, rock 'n' roll and reggae sustained by Paul Simonon and Topper Headon, the overwhelming voice and guitar of Joe Strummer, the rebellious and brazen front man who could easily compete on an even footing with all the other band leaders of the new generation. The conclusion of their set with "White Riot," yelled by Joe Strummer, with the complicity of Jimmy Pursey of Sham 69, was the loud cry of a generation that didn't want to stand still any longer and declared the end of the 1970s with a gathering that had nothing in common with the flower children and all the rest of Woodstock. At Victoria Park, English new wave was born, the new wave that in the following decade would change the face of music around the world, creating a second "British Invasion" in America and dictating the new rules of rock.

The Grateful Dead Play in front of the Pharaohs

[September 14-15-16, 1978]

The Grateful Dead were, with Pink Floyd, the trailblazers of the most visionary and fantastic rock in history. Who else, then, between the two bands, could have put on the most spectacular and incredible concert possible? After all, it was, simply, giving substance to the visions that they had been chasing for more than ten years – years in which their music had always remained a vehicle aboard which they faced any and every type of mental voyage. With that, in September of 1978, the Grateful Dead departed for what would become their most symbolic performances: three days, three concerts, at the foot of the Egyptian pyramids. Their music, played under the gaze of the most mysterious being in history, the Great Sphinx of Giza. Enigma upon enigma, note upon note, symbol upon symbol. Pure Grateful Dead style.

On September 14, 15 and 16, the Grateful Dead began their "occupation" straightaway: Ken Kesey and the deadheads immediately climbed to the top of the pyramid of the Great Pyramid to hoist the group's flag, the famous white background with a red and blue skull with a lightning bolt running through it. A "cosmic connection" commented Jerry Garcia, the

HISTORICAL NOTES

1965 – The band is formed in Palo Alto, California and becomes the vanguard of hippy counterculture, famous for their eclectic style and for the Deadheads, the faithful fans who followed them on their tour. For 30 years they hold live concerts throughout the world, attracting millions of spectators.

1973 – The band's record label, Grateful Dead Records, is established and releases *Wake of the Flood*.

1995 – The band breaks up after the death of Brent Mydland (1990) and Jerry Garcia (1995).

Jerry Garcia (né Jerome John Garcia) relaxing.

mind and soul of the band. More serious was the comment from the Egyptian Ambassador to the United States, Ashraf Ghorbal, stating that it was an absolute first for the annals of modern music, a unique chapter in the historically friendly relationship between the two countries. It was a chapter that would continue into the following days: on September 17, 1978, with the mediation of President Jimmy Carter, Egypt and Israel signed the Camp David Accords, putting an end to the Yom Kippur War that began in 1973.

But let's return to the music. The start of the first concert would send a chill up your spine. At sunset, with the profile of the pyramids on the horizon, Jerry Garcia "hid" with his guitar behind the PA system. On one side of the stage, in the dark, there was the profile of the Great Sphinx. Then the first notes, hypnotizing, emanating from the Cairo Youth Choir. And slowly, adding to the sounds being made by the Egyptians, the phrasing of Garcia's guitar began to creep in.

This alone would be enough. But it was only the beginning of three days in which the Grateful Dead anchored all their creativity and all their virtuosity in transforming live performances into difficult to reproduce, unique moments in time. They even added astral phenomena: the third concert started with a lunar eclipse in progress.

The Hammer of
the Gods on Stage
at Knebworth

[August 4, 1979]

The Twilight of the Gods always brings ill omens and so much dark material with it that it is difficult to control. Or, if you will: before curling up in a black hole, a star always reaches its maximum height of brightness. Metaphors aside, in August of 1979 Led Zeppelin were unanimously considered faded, extinguished, strange animals belonging to another era of rock. And you have to understand that England in those days was all punk and new wave, musical genres that were created precisely to erase what Zeppelin represented in the previous ten years. Away with solos and any sort of complexity. But on the evening of August 4 of that year, 200 thousand people stood in front of the largest Witches' Sabbath ever put on stage – a pagan rite with which Led Zeppelin, by then on the wane, once again reached the heights in which they had pushed hard rock before imploding forever.

They had not played in their native England for two years. And those weren't easy years. The slow erosion of personal relationships, an increasingly difficult to manage "bandwagon," the crossfire of music critics and fans from their early days. The poison arrows from their colleagues. And then

HISTORICAL NOTES

1969 – *Led Zeppelin* is released: a combination of blues, folk, rock and heavy metal recorded at the Olympic Studios. *Led Zeppelin II*, with a more explicit hard rock style, is released.

1974 – The band establishes Swan Song Records and the following year release their first double album, *Physical Graffiti*.

1979 – The two concerts at the Knebworth Festival mark their return to live performances after a two-year hiatus.

2007 – Their last concert is held at the O2 Arena in London. There are more than 20 million requests for tickets in 24 hours.

Led Zeppelin on stage at Knebworth in 1979. Left to right: Robert Plant, John Bohnam and Jimmy Page.

you have their recent albums ever made, never reaching the heights of those from their golden age. In short: a decline. Everything was wiped away for those three hours in which, in the English countryside, Led Zeppelin would show the world their power and crystalline class. The concert in Knebworth was rehearsed with care. At the end of July the group played for two consecutive nights at the Falkoner Theatre in Copenhagen: general tests, Danish fans used as guinea pigs, to try out the set list for their return to the UK. Then the four closed themselves into a movie studio to work on the show's light display. They then met again on the afternoon of August 4 for a quick sound check.

Their entrance is one of wide-open eyes and gaping mouths. The initial notes of "The Song Remains the Same" are covered up by a superhuman roar. Fans new and old paid due tribute to the four pioneers of hard rock. Robert plant would later say he didn't think it was possible for Led Zeppelin to still play well enough to satisfy the audience's expectations. It took him the first half of the evening to realize that he was there and that it all was really happening – even if he thought his voice was choked by nervousness. Whether they believed it or not, something good was happening for sure. Put the concert DVD in the player and after the required listening to "Black Dog," "No Quarter," "Since I've Been Loving You" and "Kashmir," skip directly to Jimmy Page's solo that comes before "In the Evening." The guitarist and his bow, in a pyramid of lasers. An electric symphony, dense with dark musical territory, which was simply meant for the annals of rock. And that's before we even mention the final song, a devastating version of "Communication Breakdown."

The voyage of Led Zeppelin ended that night. Their management was no longer able, due to exaggerated heroin use, to manage the band's affairs. The growing friction between the members of the group, followed by the death of John "Bonzo" Bonham. Zeppelin's Coda. They left the rock stage and immediately entered the world of legend. And that concert is connected to their return, that Celebration Day of December 10, 2007 at the O2 Arena in London: that which today remains – and with all probability will remain – the group's last performance. A little game: compare the two versions of "Stairway to Heaven," that of 1979 in Knebworth and that of 2007, and come to realize that through the passage of time and history, are nothing against those who, even for just a moment, thanks to the music, find themselves looking into another, timeless, classic dimension. For this reason, whenever and wherever, it's necessary to go back and listen to and watch Led Zeppelin again: to understand how dense and outside the rules of time a guitar riff can be.

In the Heart
of Florence,
Patti Smith
Leaves
the Stage

[September 10, 1979]

"Florence was our last gig. We arrived and I hit the streets, searching for Michelangelo's *Unfinished Slaves*. There were thousands of kids camped out in the narrow streets of the city center. What the hell was going on? I passed by a newsstand and saw my face on the cover of every magazine. Followed by hordes of screaming girls wearing jackets and ties, I tried to get to Hotel Minerva on the back streets. I holed up there for hours, downing one espresso after the other. Our last gig. In a football stadium. Kilometers from Michelangelo."

It was the summer of 1979 and Patti Smith and her band had released *Wave*, their fourth album, shortly before. Patti Smith was the goddess of new rock – anarchic, poetic, rebellious, emotional, idealistic. All that the generation of 1977 could love.

In Italy, punk had little impact, but the new rock coming from America had become the soundtrack to a generation on the move, sandwiched between the desire for revolution and the terrible reality of the Red Brigade. Smith was already a star of the new wave – thousands of people attended her concerts in Europe and the USA – but the difference between her two Italian concerts was unfathomable, leaping

HISTORICAL NOTES

1975 – Her first album *Horses* is released by Arista Records, followed by *Radio Ethiopia* (1976), *Easter* (1978) and *Wave* (1979).

1979 – After a show in Bologna she performs at the closing concert of the Festival dell'Unità in Florence. This is her first Italian tour, after which she leaves the stage (except for rare appearances) for 16 years to dedicate her time to her family.

1994 – After her husband's death she takes the advice of her friend Allen Ginsberg and resumes her artistic career.

Patti Smith's concerts in Bologna and Florence were simply fantastic.

from the five to ten thousand that she was used to, to sixty thousand in Bologna and fifty thousand in Florence. The stadiums were packed with young people to bear witness, with their faith, to rock that they still believed could change the world, become part of history and change its course, expressing forceful, political and social content that was in-line with the new times, in-line with change. In front of them was a thin, gritty poet, who loved to combine beat poetry and verses by Arthur Rimbaud, but also declared her love for Pope Luciani (who preached that music is reconciliation with God), causing a scandal among rock's more militant audience. The two concerts were extraordinary; Patti Smith gave the most of her creativity and strength, but the controversy, the tension, the enormous crowd, her being followed by TV cameras and journalists, covering the front pages of newspapers and weeklies, the role as the "high priestess of rock" was all too much for her.

She who had recorded a masterpiece like *Horses*, giving a crucial jolt to sleepy American rock. She who with *Easter* one year before had warmed the hearts of the world, singing "Because the Night," written based on the notes and thoughts of Bruce Springsteen. She who had set fire to New York nights playing at CBGB or Max's Kansas City, who had danced in the rooms of the Chelsea Hotel with her friend Robert Mapplethorpe, who lived on Ginsberg's literature and poetry, she who had joined rock with art like only the greats can – she, as she descended from the stage in Florence, decided she'd had enough. And so it was. Patti Smith didn't just descend from that stage, but from all stages; she abandoned music and rock, retiring with her husband, the former MC5 member Fred "Sonic" Smith, had two children and, until her husband's death in 1994, wouldn't play again.

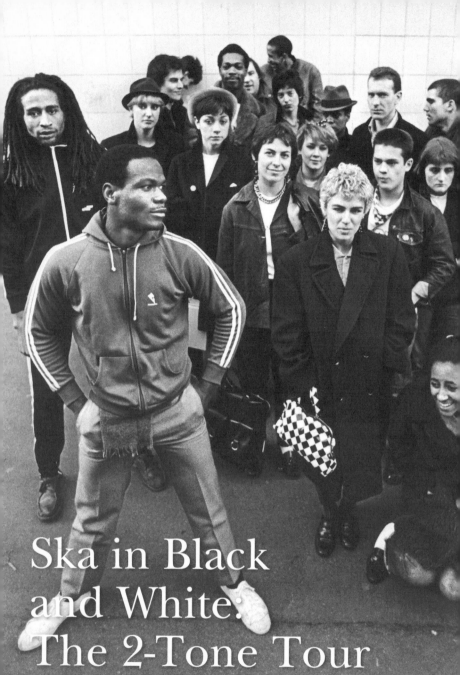

Ska in Black and White:
The 2-Tone Tour

[October 1979]

C oventry, England, has never been considered the center of the world. Yet, at the end of the 1970s, it became the center of a musical revival that radically changed the color of music, first in England and then, slowly, around the world, bringing reggae's ancestor, ska, born in Jamaica many years before, to the center of attention..

A small record label was founded in Coventry, 2-Tone Records, by Jerry Dammers. Dammers, a producer, musician and cultural organizer, saw the possibility for a comeback for ska, music originating in Jamaica in the 1960s, created by a group of artists that wanted to link the rhythmic traditions of Jamaica with soul and rhythm and blues. Coventry was the right place; there was a strong community of people from the West Indies, and Jamaican music – reggae, calypso and obviously ska – was heard on the streets and in the clubs. Passionate about music and a musician himself, Dammers, an art student, started his first band, the Automatics, in 1977 with a few others, shortly afterward changing their name to the Specials. In order to release their first single, "The Gangsters," Dammers also started his own independent record

HISTORICAL NOTES

1977 – Formation of the multiracial band The Specials, the leading exponent of the ska revival in England.

1979 – At Conventry their leader Jerry Dammers founds 2 Tone Records, the hub of the ska movement. He organizes the 40-date 2-Tone Tour featuring The Specials together with Madness and The Selecter. The tour is inaugurated at the Top Rank in Brighton to a full house. In November they make their TV debut in *Top of the Pops*.

1986 – The movement has outlived its innovative drive and 2 Tone Records closes down.

The members of the 2 Tone Records band, formed in Coventry in 1977.

label, 2-Tone Records. On the B-side, the single had a song by another local ska band, the Selecter. With this single, the season of "ska revival" opened with a bang, which also saw the forming of other excellent bands such as the Beat, Madness, the Bodysnatchers, Bad Manners and Dexys Midnight Runners.

In the short span of a few months, the "dance craze" swept the UK. It was a happy yet engaging wave, since the Specials' songs, both those that evoked the Jamaican ska tradition as well as those wonderful songs written by Dammers and his companions (especially Terry Hall, Lynval Golding and Neville Staple), interpreted, in an original way, the dissatisfaction of a generation that didn't see itself reflected in the status quo and which yearned for a different reality than that of the UK under Margaret Thatcher. The 2-Tone logo, with a stylized mod in black and white, reflected the reality of multi-racial bands, grown up in neighborhoods where tensions were always on the rise, but where the desire to overcome barriers, beat them down with the help of music, were much stronger. The recovery of original ska (and especially the great trombone work of Rico Rodriguez, friend of the members of the Skatalites, a legendary Jamaican ska band) in this new form, revitalized, explosive, engaging, had its moment of true triumph with the tour of 1979, with the Specials, Madness and the Selecter traveling around the UK. The set offered the entire spectrum of possibilities of the new breed of ska: on one side, there was the Selecter, leaning more towards reggae, based on strong central rhythms around which keys and guitars lighten the mood and make a perfect counterpoint; on the other was Madness, with their strong ties to traditional soul and rhythm and blues filtered through the best of Jamaican ska, but also with solid roots in British pop, in English songwriting that from the Beatles onward had changed the groove of popular music, and animated by a sound and solid silliness that transformed each of their concerts into a brilliant party. And at the center of it all were the Specials, a band that could send an audience into ecstasy – an audience that didn't just want to dance, jump and move around to the pulsating rhythm of Jamaican music but also wanted to put their bodies and minds in sync. They wanted to dance and think, singing songs that weren't just fun and sweat inducing, but songs that also left room for reflection. The 2-Tone Tour opened a completely new season, it inaugurated the 1980s, because it erased the rage without a future of punk and brought music back to the streets with a perspective of change. The 2-Tone Tour, with its extraordinary mix of enjoyment and responsibility, didn't just put ska in its place again on the road map of popular music, a place from which it hasn't ever moved, but it paved the road for that which would come in the following decade, leading directly to Live Aid, to rock that once again discovered its ability to be a positive force for change in the world.

Rock's Darkest Day: The Death of John Lennon

[December 8, 1980]

Lennon had withdrawn from the scene five years prior, in 1975, to leave that vortex of success, creativity, excess, tension and drugs that had pushed him, in the five years since separation from the Beatles, to not only write masterpieces such as "Imagine," but also towards self-destruction. However, he was still John Lennon, a central figure in youth culture, an extremely loved (though still extreme) figure, contradictory and legendary, libertarian and adventurous. But with the birth of Sean, he discovered the role of a father that he had essentially refused with his first son, Julian. He discovered the love of a family that he had been denied as a youth; he discovered the pleasure of staying in one place, New York, instead of the constant movement around the world, isolation rather than worldliness.

Five years of musical silence that were about to be interrupted by the release of *Double Fantasy*, a new album in delicate colors with the eternal couple on its cover: John and Yoko. The wait for John Lennon's return was long and after the album's big release, John and Yoko had started down the road of promotion, interviews, photo sessions and meetings. And that's how he was to spend the

HISTORICAL NOTES

1980 – One month after the release of *Double Phantasy*, Mark Chapman shoots and kills John Lennon. Thousands of fans spend the night in front of the Dakota Building, where Lennon lived, singing his songs.

1982 – In his album *Jump Up!*, Elton John dedicates "The Man Who Never Died" and Empty Garden (Hey Hey Johnny) to John, as does Queen with "Life is Real (Song for Lennon)" in their album *Hot Space*.

1985 – The Strawberry Fields Memorial, dedicated to the memory of Lennon, is inaugurated in Central Park.

John Lennon fans the day after the murder of the former Beatle in New York.

day of December 8: Lennon and Yoko had welcomed the photographer Annie Leibovitz into their home for a photo session destined for the cover of *Rolling Stone* magazine, then in the afternoon the crew of RKO arrived to record a radio interview with him and Dave Sholin, a DJ from San Francisco. Once the interview was over, John and Yoko left the Dakota Building, where they lived in New York (and where Yoko Ono still lives), to go to Record Plant Studios to remix "Walking on Thin Ice." At the entrance there were, as always, some fans and curious people waiting for him. Among them was twenty-five-year-old Mark Chapman, who asked for an autograph with a copy of the new album in hand. Lennon stopped and signed the disc, an event that would be immortalized by the photographer Paul Goresh, who was also waiting for Lennon. After a few hours, just before 11pm, John and Yoko returned home. Getting out of the car, Lennon was approached by Chapman, who had been waiting for his return, who said, "Hey, Mr. Lennon" and then fired his pistol five times, hitting John Lennon four times. A police squad immediately came to his aid, but he died a few minutes later while being transported to Roosevelt Hospital. There was no funeral, his body was cremated and his ashes were scattered. Thus, there is no tomb for John Lennon, but only a memorial in Central Park, as requested by Yoko.

For many, it was like losing a friend, a loved one with whom they had shared important moments of life, in a way that no other rock star had been able to equal. There was the awareness that the world had unexpectedly lost something important. From that moment on, without John Lennon, the world seemed more desolate, emptier, to everyone. A crazy man had killed him, Mark Chapman, who was obsessed with Lennon but also with fame, the search for celebrity, a disturbed young man that had planned his actions because he felt betrayed by John Lennon, that now saw him as a swindler, a traitor, a millionaire that pretended to be a revolutionary. He had killed a symbol, a dream, an image. But in reality, he had killed a man, an artist that was able to give shape to hope, a musician that had, with the Beatles, decisively contributed to changing the world. December 8, 1980 changed history for popular music, it changed history for popular culture and it changed history for every one of us.

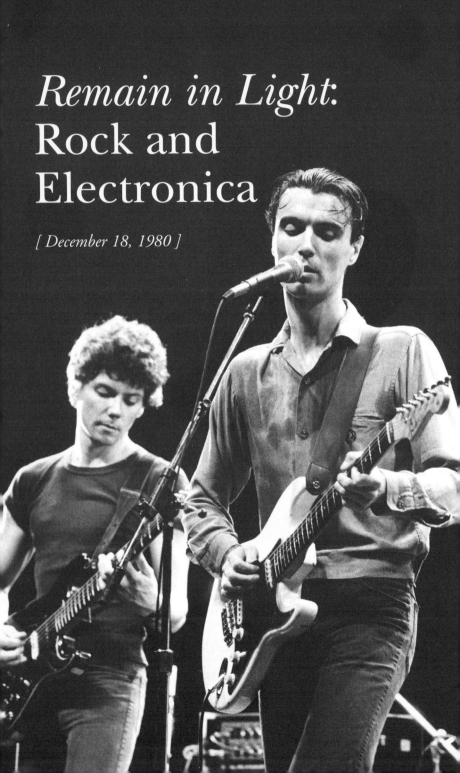

Remain in Light:
Rock and
Electronica

[*December 18, 1980*]

There are concerts that are watersheds in the history of music, that definitively mark a "before" and "after." To these ranks belong the concerts of the tour following the release of *Remain in Light*, the fourth album by Talking Heads, in 1980. You could, and should, say that it is the album that is the watershed, that it is what officially opened the a new decade, what radically changed the idea of music itself, the way it's written, thought about, executed and listened to. But it is its incarnation, its translation from a reproducible, mechanical product, a disc, to a physical, natural event that made everything even more extraordinary and fantastic. Let's try to explain: *Remain in Light* is, without a shadow of a doubt, the essential album to understanding the decade that opened in 1980, the seminal album that would influence, in one way or another, the production of a large part of popular music in subsequent years, fruit of a course that had brought Talking Heads from their first concerts in the clubs of New York to become, with the help of Brian Eno, the most important band of the time. David Byrne, Chris Frantz, Tina Weymouth and Jerry Harrison, after three albums in which their creative and artistic growth was, literally, exponential, created a

HISTORICAL NOTES

1977 – "Love Goes to Building on Fire" is released by Sire Records, the band's historic label. After a tour with the Ramones, they release the memorable *Talking Heads: 77*.

1978 – The collaboration with Brian Eno begins with *More Songs About Buildings and Food*.

1980 – Sire Records releases *Remain in Light*, the band's fourth album. A harbinger of world music, it is a fusion of rock, funk, new wave and African music.

Jerry Harrison and David Byrne performing in Hollywood, California.

work that combined, as was said at the time, "metropolis and desert," deep Africa and the heart of Manhattan, the super-technology of the recording studio with the naturalness of voices and percussion, imagining the world of the future (the digital revolution and the Internet were still far away) in which the distance between cultures, languages, human beings and histories is eliminated – a hyperrealist and post-modern construction that has an irresistible appeal. It was the height of intellectualism, of an operation studied in the tiniest detail by the band and Eno, joined with the height of fun, funk and soul. Yes, because the music of *Remain in Light* breathes and has a heart that is always beating. Pop-art and Africanism, afro-funk and electronica, atmospheric music and tribal music, rock, soul and new wave, post-punk and radicalism, disco music and frenzied dance, reggae and avant-garde: they all become one in a project made of influences that involved all musical knowledge in 1980. Arab, African, Western, Eastern combined in songs that don't have one specific harmonic structure, but are, instead, based on a solid and layered rhythmic structure. Over all this are David Byrne's lyrics and vocals, songs that often become choral with superimposed choruses and sermon-like voices. It all was done by cutting, pasting, and superimposing track over track, a work of sonorous alchemy that exalted the role of the recording studio as a musical instrument, to the highest degree.

How then to stage this and turn it into a concert? The four Talking Heads certainly weren't enough and, in fact, to take the project on the road, they became nine in number, adding Adrian Belew, an eclectic, genius guitarist (fundamental for many rock masterpieces of the 1980s), Bernie Worrell, keyboard player of Funkadelic, Busta Jones, a bassist that came from Eno's entourage, percussionist Steve Scales, fundamental for translating the album's complex rhythm structures during a live setting, and the backing vocalist Dolette McDonald. With this set-up, they went on stage, offering a show that was incredibly involving, fun and danceable, but at the same time meticulous, avant-garde and innovative in every aspect. It is difficult to recount that which for the public of the era was a sort of initiation. Going to see the Talking Heads of *Remain in Light* was like taking a quick trip into the future, being transported into a parallel reality, a borderless world, a rhythmic and sensual universe in which everyone could find their own place, emotional and vital. Live, the album's complexity became an overwhelming rhythmic ebb and flow that captured listeners, from the start, in a celebration of the power of music and rhythm that seemed to be without precedent, just as one can still see in the recording of their December 18, 1980 concert in Rome made by Italian television and released as a DVD. Whoever has seen Talking Heads live knows that there is a "before" and an "after" that concert. The music we listen to today started there.

PINK FLOYD

THE WALL

Pink Floyd's *Wall*: Creativity, Passion and Freedom

[June 17, 1981]

"I hate Pink Floyd," were the words that, in 1978, stood out on t-shirts worn by Johnny Rotten of the Sex Pistols. England had been conquered by punk, and the rock of Pink Floyd, like that of all the great groups that had dominated the scene up until then, seemed to be over. The "new wave" was about to take center stage and the music of Waters, Gilmour, Mason and Wright seemed old and destined to disappear. But instead, just in that moment, Pink Floyd was about to complete one of the greatest masterpieces of rock history, despite the enormous tensions they were going through: a complex and fascinating project that would see the light of day one year later, in 1979, called *The Wall*. The work, presented several times live and becoming a film in 1982, directed by Alan Parker, and starring Bob Geldof, is one of the most ambitious projects in the entire history of rock, not just for its musical compositions (twenty-six songs, four sides for a colored vinyl album that came out in 1979), but especially for the live show in which the band was slowly hidden from the audience's view by the construction of a wall.

HISTORICAL NOTES

1979 – Release of the rock opera *The Wall*, the first phase of a project by Roger Waters that includes live spectacles and a movie.

1980 – The 31-concert tour to promote the record begins. There are signs of tension among the band members.

1982 – The movie *Pink Floyd – The Wall*, directed by Alan Parker and screenplay by Waters, makes almost 20 million dollars.

1983 – Release of *The Final Cut*, the last album with Roger Waters.

1985 – Waters leaves the band.

1995 – The Wall breaks up.

The poster of The Wall, *considered the most incredible show in the history of rock.*

For just a handful of concerts, at the dawn of the 1980s, at London's Earl's Court Exhibition Centre, it became the most incredible show that the history of rock had ever imagined. Certainly, others before Pink Floyd had brought "rock operas" to the stage. But never before had anyone imagined such a technical setup and such scenery, to the extent that the tour was only about thirty dates in Europe and the USA, due to the difficulty and enormous costs of the structure that had to be built up and broken down every time.

Roger Waters wanted to symbolize the wall that separated him from the public, the wall that restricts our freedom, all walls – imaginary, physical, personal, collective – that make our lives difficult or impossible, walls that should be torn down and destroyed, on the stage. And he wanted to do so by telling a partially autobiographical story in which personal memories (the death of his father on the beach at Anzio during the Second World War, and the unsatisfying role of a rock star) were mixed with collective histories (protests against authoritarianism in schools, and the search for freedom). But it is the music, the mature, rich and fascinating rock of Pink Floyd that immediately transformed *The Wall* into a resounding success, in spite of the new wave that was changing the world of music at the end of the 1970s. In London, the audience was stunned by the complexity and richness of the show which brought the great dream of rock to the stage for the first time – rock that managed to be a comprehensive and multimedia artistic language, where thought and art are as essential as entertainment and amazement. After *The Wall*, rock became electronic and new wave arrived. These were all things of little interest to Pink Floyd, which they would demonstrate live with a show that had nothing to do with the zeroing of punk or the minimalism of new wave. Here, for perhaps the last time, everything was big, magniloquent, profound, truthful – a show that loudly signaled the difference between band and audience, represented by the wall that covered the group, but also by the show itself.

Nevertheless, the concert featured memorable songs, such as the beautiful "Comfortably Numb," where David Gilmour's guitar shines once again, as well as singles able to climb the charts, such as "Another Brick in the Wall," ballads such as "Nobody Home," and even more articulated and complex tracks such as "Run Like Hell," which became even more epic, legendary and magnificent during the live show. *The Wall* also signaled the end of Pink Floyd's heroic era. Rick Wright was "fired" by Waters during the recording; fights with Gilmour became more frequent and harsher; the band, as a creative unit, ceased to exist; and, after these concerts, it would no longer have the same four-person line-up of Roger Waters, David Gilmour, Nick Mason and Richard Wright. Despite all this, *The Wall* remains one of the highest points in the history of Pink Floyd, a true rock masterpiece.

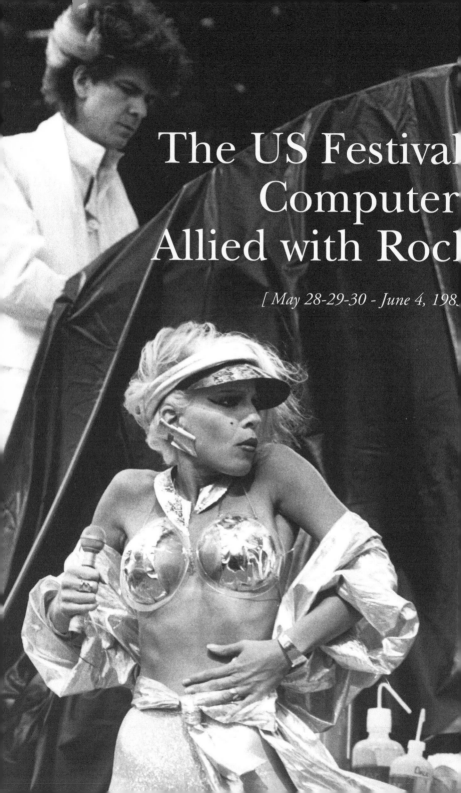

The US Festival
Computer
Allied with Rock

[May 28-29-30 - June 4, 198.

What else could be expected from the co-founder of Apple? It's simple: order and creativity. Genius and reason. Just read the set list of the 1983 edition of the US Festival, thought up and produced by Steve Wozniak, to discover how the "best friend" of Steve Jobs also applied the philosophy of Apple to the organization of one of the biggest music festivals in the 1980s, the precursor to all the mass gatherings of the decade. Calling it the Woodstock of the 1980s isn't an exaggerated comparison. Four days, divided by musical genre: new wave, metal, rock, and folk. Every day with its own strong internal rationale: old and new stars of the genre. Order? Creativity? Delegated entirely to the artists, especially called upon by Wozniak to lead rock along the road – of no return – to meet technology. The computer era of rock started here.

And, following Wozniak's nerdy intelligence, we'll also go in order. The first day began on Saturday, May 28, a day dedicated to new wave, which, in those days, was at the height of its imperialistic phase. INXS, Oingo Boingo, the English Beat, Stray Cats, Men at Work, and the last concert by the Clash with Mick Jones in particular. In a harsh twist of fate, it was the concert with the biggest audience that the "Guns of Brixton" had

HISTORICAL NOTES

1982 – Steve Wozniak organizes and sponsors an event that combines music and state-of-the-art technology at Glen Helen Regional Park in San Bernardino, California, hiring the most famous bands of this period.

1983 – Nine months later he organizes another festival featuring the leading names of four different musical genres. The event draws around 700,000 spectators, 375,000 of whom are there on Heavy Metal Day. Wozniak spends over 10 million dollars.

Chuck Wild and Dale Bozzio performing during the US Festival.

ever played to. In fact, Wozniak chose as the location of his festival – and of his technology-packed stage in particular – the Glen Helen Regional Park just outside San Francisco.

So, the stage. Perhaps it is the real reason that the US Festival will live on through history. Dimensions never seen before, two towers of screens as high as the third story of a building off to the side of the structure, plus a central maxiscreen, like those used for football games. The structure itself was a living organism, made of tunnels and stations where workers used devices that could change the topography of the stage, between songs. It had an amplification system of 400 thousand watts and, at night, lasers that lit up the enormous valley. But let's get back to the music.

Twenty-four hours later came Heavy Metal Day. Lace blouses and mascara and the back-combed hair of 1980s metalheads were right at home. Queen Riot, Mötley Crüe, Ozzy Osbourne, Judas Priest, Scorpions – everything that moved under the heavy metal sun. Sure, Iron Maiden were absent and Metallica had just released their first album. But Van Halen were there to ensure no one felt the absence of the present and future, in one of their best live shows. To show how metal could, to the detriment of its "subversive" charge in comparison with the mainstream, enter the canons of the new rock of the 1980s.

Let's push the needle to go on to what surely was the best day – not just because it was simply dedicated to rock. Sure, there were the Pretenders and Stevie Nicks. But this day belonged to U2 and David Bowie. Perfect performances. The four-piece from Dublin, in front of an oceanic crowd, lined up the best versions ever played of "The Electric Co." and

"Sunday Bloody Sunday." The White Duke brought his new image and his pop breakthrough into focus, presenting the songs of *Let's Dance* live. Then came the day dedicated to folk, put at the end, almost to accompany everyone home after having unloaded their adrenaline rush in the prior three days.

Too bad that it had to stop there. But the US Festival was a real financial abyss for Wozniak. A good dose of economic programming had to be added to the order and creativity. But the addition to the history of rock was secured.

Madonna Departs to Conquer the World

[April 10, 1985]

The numbers, you have to start with the numbers. And since we're talking about Madonna, it is necessary to deal with her ability to create and influence styles, slogans and attitudes. But to understand what Ms. Ciccone's arrival on the contemporary pop scene meant, the numbers are absolutely necessary. And there's no better numbers than those relating to her first tour, titled, it goes without saying, "The Virgin Tour": with just two albums behind her, in April 1985, Madonna launched her first series of concerts in North America. Forty dates, 200 thousand tickets sold. Those for the double concert at Radio City Music Hall in New York – eighteen thousand of them – were grabbed up in thirty-three minutes. And, in particular, one shirt was sold every six seconds. In the dictionary of pop, all that's written under "debut with a bang" is: see "The Virgin Tour" of 1985.

Just think, Paul Grein, one of the greatest critics for *Billboard*, had predicted only six months of time in the spotlight of American show business for Madonna. In the end, it was a slightly hasty judgment. Madonna was Madonna since the mo_ ment of her appearance: a perfect, complete, classic icon. And in those forty concerts the queen of pop

HISTORICAL NOTES

1983 – Sire releases her debut album, *Madonna*, followed by *Like a Virgin* a year later, which sells 25 million copies.

1985 – Madonna begins her first concert tour in North America to promote the two albums: the first three concerts held at the Paramount Theatre in Seattle are performed to a full house. In July she takes part in Bob Geldof's *Live Aid famine relief concert.*

1987 – She leaves for her Who's That Girl? world tour. 130,000 fans welcome her at the Parc des Sceaux concert.

Madonna during The Virgin Tour at Radio City Music Hall, New York.

would put her seal on her success that up until that moment had existed entirely in the media. And it was quite clear that the reason for her success certainly wasn't her musical ability. Just go back and watch the DVD dedicated to this tour. Madonna's strength was – and still is – that of laying down the law in terms of style, starting with the very first date on April 10, 1985.

Madonna created a model. She took the entire surface of punk and rock, reinforcing it with an imposing dose of brazenness, then added deadly singles and the game is over. The result? Madonnamania: hundreds of thousands of young girls that copied her moves, style and attitude. Girls that took, from her songs, the necessary ethic to move ahead in the 1980s, in that hedonistic present that seemed like it would never end. And then, of course, they also borrowed her armor of necklaces, earrings, crosses, loud colors, mascara, eye shadow, lace gloves and headbands. Not just frills, but integral elements, signs of recognition for an entire generation. As Madonna remembers, it, she saw all those girls dressed like her and it seemed just entirely crazy. Not just that. From that moment on, Lady Ciccone would represent the archetype of every future pop star, the touchstone for every potential new star.

"Will you marry me?" Thus began the performance of "Like a Virgin" in that tour. Dressed as a bride, Madonna came down the stairs toward the stage accompanied by two male dancers, offering the audience the chance to celebrate an indissoluble marriage with the new version of pop. A marriage that still endures today: solid, colorful and always impressive.

Does the story end here? No, of course not. Because that tour deserves to be remembered for another reason: for three young rowdy New Yorkers that opened Madonna's concerts with their personal, unforgettable reinterpretation of hip hop known as the Beastie Boys. In short, who knows how many people went to see Madonna and came home with the deep desire to learn more about a completely different story.

HFORD & SIMPSON ☐ JOAN BAEZ ☐ BEACH BOYS ☐ BLACK SABBATH ☐ THE
S ☐ CSN ☐ DURAN DURAN ☐ BOB DYLAN ☐ FOUR TOPS ☐ HALL & OATES ☐
AS PRIEST ☐ EDDIE KENDRICK ☐ PATTI LABELLE ☐ KENNY LOGGINS ☐ MADC
I ☐ OZZY OSBOURNE ☐ JIMMY PAGE ☐ TEDDY PENDERGRASS ☐ TOM PETTY &
NT ☐ POWER STATION ☐ THE PRETENDERS ☐ REO SPEEDWAGON ☐ DAVID RI
PLE MINDS ☐ RICK SPRINGFIELD ☐ ROD STEWART ☐ TEARS FOR FEARS ☐ TH
L YOUNG ☐ ADAM ANT ☐ BOOMTOWN RATS ☐ DAVID BOWIE ☐ PHIL COLLIN
☐ BRIAN FERRY ☐ ELTON JOHN ☐ HOWARD JONES ☐ NIK KERSHAW ☐ PAUL
EN ☐ SADE ☐ SPANDAU BALLET ☐ STATUS QUO ☐ STING ☐ STYLE COUNCIL
E WHO ☐ PAUL YOUNG ☐ BRYAN ADAMS ☐ ASHFORD & SIMPSON ☐ JOAN BAE
☐ THE CARS ☐ ERIC CLAPTON ☐ PHIL COLLINS ☐ CSN ☐ DURAN DURAN ☐
OATES ☐ THE HOOTERS ☐ MICK JAGGER ☐ JUDAS PRIEST ☐ EDDIE KENDRICK
☐ MADONNA ☐ PAT METHENY ☐ BILLY OCEAN ☐ BILLY OCEAN ☐ JIMMY
I PETTY & THE HEARTBREAKERS ☐ ROBERT PLANT ☐ POWER STATION ☐ THE
DAVID RUFFIN ☐ RUN DMC ☐ SANTANA ☐ SIMPLE MINDS ☐ RICK SPRINGFIELD
S ☐ THOMPSON TWINS ☐ TINA TURNER ☐ NEIL YOUNG ☐ ADAM ANT ☐ BO
L COLLINS ☐ ELVIS COSTELLO ☐ DIRE STRAITS ☐ BRIAN FERRY ☐ ELTON JOHN
☐ PAUL McCARTNEY ☐ ALISON MOYET ☐ QUEEN ☐ SADE ☐ SPANDAU BALLE
COUNCIL ☐ U-2 ☐ ULTRAVOX ☐ WHAM ☐ THE WHO ☐ PAUL YOUNG ☐ BRYA
JOAN BAEZ ☐ BEACH BOYS ☐ BLACK SABBATH ☐ THE CARS ☐ ERIC CLAPTO
URAN ☐ BOB DYLAN ☐ FOUR TOPS ☐ HALL & OATES ☐ THE HOOTERS ☐ MI
KENDRICK ☐ PATTI LABELLE ☐ KENNY LOGGINS ☐ MADONNA ☐ PAT METHEN
☐ JIMMY PAGE ☐ TEDDY PENDERGRASS ☐ TOM PETTY & THE HEARTBREAKERS
N ☐ THE PRETENDERS ☐ REO SPEEDWAGON ☐ DAVID RUFFIN ☐ RUN DMC ☐
RINGFIELD ☐ ROD STEWART ☐ TEARS FOR FEARS ☐ THOMPSON TWINS ☐ TIN
T ☐ BOOMTOWN RATS ☐ DAVID BOWIE ☐ PHIL COLLINS ☐ ELVIS COSTELLO ☐
ON JOHN ☐ HOWARD JONES ☐ NIK KERSHAW ☐ PAUL McCARTNEY ☐ ALISON
U BALLET ☐ STATUS QUO ☐ STING ☐ STYLE COUNCIL ☐ U-2 ☐ ULTRAVOX ☐
G ☐ BRYAN ADAMS ☐ ASHFORD & SIMPSON ☐ JOAN BAEZ ☐ BEACH BOYS ☐

Live Aid:
The World
Becomes One

[July 13, 1985]

C CLAPTON ☐ PHIL COLLINS ☐ CSN ☐ DURAN DURAN ☐ BOB DYLAN ☐ FOUR
ERS ☐ MICK JAGGER ☐ JUDAS PRIEST ☐ EDDIE KENDRICK ☐ PATTI LABELLE ☐
T METHENY ☐ BILLY OCEAN ☐ OZZY OSBOURNE ☐ JIMMY PAGE ☐ TEDDY PENI
BREAKERS ☐ ROBERT PLANT ☐ POWER STATION ☐ THE PRETENDERS ☐ REO S
DMC ☐ SANTANA ☐ SIMPLE MINDS ☐ RICK SPRINGFIELD ☐ ROD STEWART ☐
S ☐ TINA TURNER ☐ NEIL YOUNG ☐ ADAM ANT ☐ BOOMTOWN RATS ☐ DAV
STELLO ☐ DIRE STRAITS ☐ BRIAN FERRY ☐ ELTON JOHN ☐ HOWARD JONES ☐
ALISON MOYET ☐ QUEEN ☐ SADE ☐ SPANDAU BALLET ☐ STATUS QUO ☐ ST
TRAVOX ☐ WHAM ☐ THE WHO ☐ PAUL YOUNG ☐ BRYAN ADAMS ☐ ASHFORD

It's difficult to refrain from exaggeration, but the impact of Live Aid on culture at the time was truly incalculable. For the first time, thanks to rock, the world became one big village for one long day. The fact that this came about due to rock could not have been otherwise, because of the universality that it had achieved throughout its history. It was the music of young people worldwide, and, for better or worse, it was the biggest expressive force, which was still able to shake people's general indifference by mobilizing them to help the world's hungry. From Band Aid (the group that created the Christmas album in England to benefit Ethiopia) to Live Aid, the crescendo was dizzying. In a few months, it had been possible to build, for humanitarian reasons, the greatest show imaginable, a concert that, in an instant, overshadowed the most famous mega-events of the past. It was no longer about 100 thousand people, or even the 500 thousand of Woodstock. Thanks to being broadcast live, hundreds of millions of people – nearly a billion – were able to 'attend' the concert simultaneously. For once, television allowed us to witness an unforgettable

The poster of the Live Aid concert held at JFK Stadium in Philadelphia, Pennsylvania on 13 July 1985.

day as it was taking place. It seemed like a miracle, but in a few months, the world of rock had come to know a solidarity and unity that had been unthinkable just a few years earlier. Just think of the atmosphere that settled upon Wembley and Philadelphia and be amazed. There was no jealousy, no one competing to be the center of attention; everyone was willing to play with everyone else, especially Phil Collins, who, physically, was ready to unite the world by traveling from one side to the other, by Concord, so that he could play in both shows. In other words, everyone was determined to make the day as special and as original an event as possible, and not just a sequence of rock stars in search of worldwide promotion. The example set by Elvis Costello was true for everyone; he wanted to sing just one song by the Beatles, "All You Need is Love." It was a highly symbolic choice, not only because it was the most exquisitely pacifist song recorded by the Beatles, but also, for those who remember, the song which inaugurated Mondovision in 1967, giving the first hint of a new era of communication that had its most important moment on this day. But, there's another episode that summarized the day: U2's performance. Bono, the group's singer, quoted a few of the most famous songs of old rock, including "Ruby Tuesday" by the Rolling Stones and "Walk on the Wild Side" by Lou Reed, as if to underline the historic and collective feeling of the day. Then, by surprise, he asked if it would be possible to have a girl get up on stage. Seeing that it would be too difficult, at one point, he climbed over everything and jumped down from the stage, to grab a girl and then hug her and kiss her, most likely followed by the emotion of everyone watching the non-stop broadcast. Here, the separation between stage and audience, the symbolic gesture of the embrace between Bono and the girl, which became the great embrace of the entire concert, among all the artists with the entire audience, and was, perhaps, the most beautiful and intense moment of the day.

With the arrival of the greats – from Sting to Paul McCartney – Live Aid increasingly became a sensational and unrepeatable festival, surely the biggest that rock has ever celebrated. Nothing compares to it. Nothing in the world has ever been able to unite the population of the entire planet in this way, including the Slavic countries and Russia, which were still closed off on the other side of the Iron Curtain, but who were present at the festival with their contribution of various films. And, watching the event on television had a certain effect, making one feel part of an audience that spanned the globe from California to Siberia, including everything in between.

Rock was represented in all of its genres, even that of the past, its roots, the foundation of rock culture: the Who reunited for the occasion, as well as the surviving members of Led Zeppelin. Plus, there were all the special combinations born of the occasion: the Beach Boys, who were able to rekindle the "Good Vibrations" of the past; Bob Dylan, with the unlikely help of Keith Richards and Ron Wood; David Bowie with Mick Jagger; Black Sabbath; Joan Baez; Crosby, Stills, Nash & Young; Carlos Santana; B.B. King; Elton John; Eric Clapton. Then there was the new wave, from post punks to new romantics, the Style Council, Adam Ant, Ultravox, Spandau Ballet, Elvis Costello, Duran Duran, and metalheads like Judas Priest and pop stars such as Wham!, as well as rock heroes from the 1970s – Bryan Ferry, David Bowie, with Queen ready to send the audience at Wembley Stadium into ecstasy, and the supergroup USA For Africa led by Lionel Richie ready to thrill the JFK Stadium, all thanks to rock music's surprising return to a commitment to human rights. It was rock that managed to teach a lesson in humanity to the entire world. In just one day, Bob Geldof was able to unite the entire world for a good cause, all in the name of rock. And rock proved to be the single, greatest, worldwide language capable of speaking about justice, sharing, love and peace. Once again.

When Wembley Became Queen's Royal Palace

[*July 12, 1986*]

They had passed, unscathed, through the cyclone of punk; they had understood, earlier than many others, which way the wind of 1980s pop was blowing. And, they hit the jackpot, not losing anything with their historic audience, the one they brought together in the glam, glitter and ambiguity of London of the 1970s. In the mid-1980s, Queen could call themselves the English band par excellence: the only one still able to pack stadiums across the world. And their concert on July 12, 1986 at Wembley Stadium marked their zenith, the apex of a career built on the solid foundation of Freddie Mercury's voice and the musical invention of Brian May, Roger Taylor and John Deacon.

They had warmed up over the course of their "Magic Tour" that had already brought them to half of Europe. They arrived at the Wembley venue in a form and spirit that was really beyond the norm. Especially when thinking about the singer, because with that night, with those songs, Freddie Mercury would deliver one of the greatest front-man performances ever in the history of rock. Live at Wembley '86 is no more and no less than a

HISTORICAL NOTES

1973 – EMI releases the band's debut album *Queen*.

1975 – *A Night at the Opera*, the band's most representative album, which combines rock and opera, is released. The tour of the same name begins, with 77 concerts throughout the world.

1986 – The Magic Tour, the band's fourteenth, begins in order to promote *A Kind of Magic*. The historic 1992 concert at Wembley leads to the release of the album *Live at Wembley '86*. The tour ends at Knebworth to an audience of 125,000 fans. This is the band's last concert with Freddie Mercury.

Freddie Mercury wore a robe and crown in all the Queen concerts.

rite founded on collective hypnosis, and Mercury is the high priest capable of leading the eighty thousand fans by the hand. Taking them by the hand and accompanying them on a thrilling musical journey for one of the last times before starting his painful, hopeless battle against AIDS.

Live at Wembley '86 exists both as an album and as a video. Forget about the disc and go straight to the images. They are a compendium, a small encyclopedia that contains the phenomenology of a perfect frontman, a lesson given to posterity on how to act on stage. There are many key moments in the concert and every song offers up a small marvel. But, in a few moments, you can literally see and perceive what it means to participate in a concert: to be projected into a dimension beyond, where neither the band nor the audience exists, but only the music that holds it all together.

Mercury's entrance will give you goose bumps even today, every time you watch it. The keyboard intro to "One Vision," and then comes the percussion. A moment of suspense and then comes the guitar riff. And then, here he is, a yellow leather jacket, white t-shirt and pants, his microphone with its half stand. Freddie Mercury appears, a demigod that throws himself straight at the audience. He looks like he's walking a few feet above the ground; he seems to look into the eyes of everyone present. Instantly, he breaks from all forms of theatricality, establishing a visceral connection with the crowd. He launches into a vocal attack and...welcome to rock 'n' roll right in the middle of a decade of plastic. Charisma in its purest form. He calls out to the audience and the audience – as will happen countless times in the following three hours – responds note for note.

Call and response, the nucleus of the feeling of soul music. Because, again, *Live at Wembley '86* is a celebration, a collective chanting in which eighty thousand British citizens passed a hand over a conservative nation, over Margaret Thatcher's empire, and rediscovered the importance of the common dream, community and the sharing of experiences. In "Tie Your Mother Down" all eighty thousand danced on all forms of relapsed bigotry, in "Radio Ga Ga" they applauded in unison, celebrating the messages of freedom that travel through the ether, and in "We Will Rock You" they articulated, as a single entity, the rhythm of an escape from all moralism.

And it's not worth mentioning the live version of "Bohemian Rhapsody": watch and listen, be enthralled by Freddie Mercury, and that's it. What a night it was for all who were lucky enough to be there. The evening was sealed by the chorus of "We Are the Champions," the words and the thing itself found on the same street, since Queen and their audience, that night, were nothing other than champions.

Run DMC and
the Beastie Boys
Rap Invades the Streets

[May 21, 1987

Rap moved to take over Europe. And it would do so with a major tour that saw some of the most revolutionary crews of the new generation, Run DMC and the Beastie Boys, who moved with certainty over the line of crossover between rap, electricity and rhymes, between electric guitars and samplers. And the band's concert in Paris ended with a brawl inside the theater, Paris' beautiful Grand Rex, and a series of incidents outside, with the inevitable broken glass and the arrival of the police along the boulevard de la Bonne Nouvelle, with sirens blaring.

Run DMC were three black men, street rappers and perfect ambassadors of a generation of African-Americans that wanted to conquer their own space on the American stage. The Beastie Boys, on the other hand, were white kids from an American middle class, ex-punk rockers that helped build the most recent incarnation of youthful rebellion that pop music had seen. To orchestrate the success of the two bands, their albums ranking top of the American charts just a few months apart, were Rick Rubin and Russell Simmons. Rubin and Simmons were owners and managers of a small

HISTORICAL NOTES

1981 – The hard-core punk Beastie Boys band is formed in New York.

1983 – Joseph Simmons, Darryl McDaniels and Jason Mizell form the hip hop Run DMC trio.

1985 – In July the Run DMC take part in Bob Geldof's Live Aid.

1986 – The Beastie Boys release their first album, *Licensed to Ill*, which sells 10 million copies in the USA. The two bands play together in the Raising Hell Tour.

1987 – The Run DMC and Beastie Boys perform 31 dates in USA for the Together Forever Tour.

Adam Yauch (MCA), Adam Horovitz (Ad-Rock) and Mike Diamond (Mike D) of the Beastie Boys with Jason Mizell, Darryl McDaniels and Joseph Simmons of Run DMC.

label, Def Jam, which had made the crossover between metal and rap, the hallmark of their style. The idea was simple and effective, absolutely ground breaking, innovative and modern: the music is carried, even during a concert, by a deejay who mixes a series of rock albums on the two turntables in front of him in the best scratching tradition, while the rappers unleash their ultra-fast rhymes over a rhythm pulsating from a drum machine.

The true hit of the season, the song that brought the genre's success, was "Walk This Way," by Run DMC – a crushing guitar riff stolen from Aerosmith, "rapped" with force by the band. But the more overwhelming success was had by the Beastie Boys with their debut album, *Licensed to Ill*. Almost as shattering as the Sex Pistol's first album, the Beastie Boys had reinvented punk.

The conquest of Europe started in Paris, and their show kept all its promises: one consecutive hour of "fucking noise" (as they themselves defined it), opened to the notes of Rocky and immediately launched at full speed into loud, overwhelming rap. They stayed true to their reputation, constantly throwing beer onto the audience, provoking with words and gestures: and the audience, blessed by all this apparent violence and energy, jumped, went crazy, whistled and threw empty cans on the stage. It almost seemed like Belushi's food fight in *Animal House*, and to be honest, the true spirit with which Adrock (Adam Horovitz), Mike D. (Mike Diamond) and MCA (Adam Yauch) carried on their show was precisely that. They yelled in their microphones without caring about the music, they moved about the stage with the grace of three little hooligans, while at their backs a go-go dancer in a cage danced, dressed as Wonder Woman, and at the end of their show, a giant pink penis rose from a box placed at the middle of the stage. Then it was Run DMC's turn, who appeared on the stage looking like all-but-reassuring Black Panthers, who would incite loud, fevered enthusiasm from their audience in no time. Their music was a continuous and ambiguous crossover between black and white, rock and rap, pop and soul, composed of rhythm (black) and noise (white), of tribalism and technology. Until the grand finale, when with "Walk This Way," a real whirlwind of metal and rap, the atmosphere in the Grand Rex, packed to its gills, became truly incandescent until the final fight, when Run got down into the audience to be the first to throw blows, under a dense hail of cans, while on the stage the Beastie Boys and the rest of Run DMC continued singing "Fight For Your Right." Rock is dead; long live rap.

The King of Pop Returns to the Stage

[July 15, 1987]

The first time Michael Jackson went on a solo tour was in 1987: sixteen months, 123 concerts, and four and a half million fans in fifteen different countries. It was a triumph because everyone wanted to see the "King of Pop" in concert. And the show on July 15 at Wembley was the definitive consecration of the legend.

It all began with the stage styled like a giant Aladdin's lamp, rubbed by thirty-five thousand young people, invoking him. He appears, a good sprite for young and old, to the notes of "Wanna Be Startin' Somethin'," and the thing that's starting is, of course, the concert, after a curtain of vaguely apocalyptic lights that anticipated the arrival of this tightrope walker, light and spirited as his music.

Four dancers help him mime this electric dance, perfect and synchronized with a short rhythm, from the shortness of breath that echoed in the stadium, sweeping through without harming the crowd that applauds happily. Jackson holds the stage well, thanks to a career that began at five years old, as we are reminded by "Motown Medley," a souvenir of his past in the band with his brothers. And then after "I Just Can't Stop Loving You," came "Human Nature," perhaps the peak

HISTORICAL NOTES

1984 – After the Victory Tour, the third made by The Jacksons, Michael leaves the band for good.

1987 – Epic Records releases *Bad*, Michael Jackson's third solo work with this label and his seventh album. The Bad World Tour begins in Japan.

1988 – Princess Diana and Prince Charles, together with more than 70,000 other spectators, at Jackson's live concert at Wembley Stadium, London. In 2012 a DVD and a CD of the concert are released posthumously.

Michael Jackson on stage at Rotterdam during his Bad World Tour.

of his inspiration, which came from 1982's *Thriller*, that carried his name to unprecedented heights. The songs flow like video clips, containing quotations of the choreography of Fred Astaire (in "Smooth Criminal") and the tricks of a magician interspersed with firecrackers and sudden disappearances up until the apotheosis of "Thriller," where Jackson emerges disguised as a werewolf from a 1930s-style cloth beach hut to then disappear into thin air and reappear with four dancers dressed as zombies. It was a real circus that, like a rigid screenplay, follows the traces of the video making the viewer feel like he is standing before a giant television. With this, Michael Jackson changed the rules of the game; he altered the idea of a live performance, of a concert, at its base, changing it for good into a show, as demonstrated with "Beat It." In that song, he disappeared among the silver curtains after an inevitable explosion, and reappeared on the other side of the stage on top of a large moveable platform with a cloak flapping behind him like captain EO. The finale, built up in a crescendo, is a sequence of well-known hits. "Beat It," "Billie Jean," "Bad," which was also the title of the tour, and for the encore, "The Way You Make Me Feel" and "Man in the Mirror," a final message about a man that looks at himself in the mirror and thinks if he wants to change the world, he must start with that man in the mirror: himself.

That is, unfortunately, exactly what Jackson was never able to do.

Mandela Day:
The Battle
that Rock Won

[July 11, 1988]

Hedonism, disengagement, "plastic" music, the great music festivals of the 1980s and the rule of carelessness: pop invaded everything. Rock seemed to stand still, to wait, maybe expecting just the right occasion to come back and rebuild, musically, the conflicts around the world reduced to a global village. And it was around a leader turned symbol, around his history, his inherited values, that rock's elite found the motivation and reason to carry the charge. They gave shape and life to the question "Why is Nelson Mandela still in prison?" Madiba and his great spirit have been a symbolic place, the destination of a constant pilgrimage for those musicians who don't intend to "shut up," and who use songs and their participation to denounce the apartheid that governed South Africa. Bob Dylan, Keith Richards, Peter Gabriel and Bono: Mandela's angels.

These angels found themselves together on July 11, 1988, when eighty thousand people participated in "Mandela Day" at Wembley Stadium, while 600 million watched on TV. "We salute you Nelson Mandela, and we want to see you and fellow political prisoners in South Africa freed." This is how, at 12:15pm, Harry Belafonte opened

HISTORICAL NOTES

1985 – Little Steven Van Zandt and producer Arthur Baker launch the Artists United Against Apartheid project to protest against racial segregation in South Africa.

1988 – Eighty-three artists participate in the Nelson Mandela 70th Birthday Tribute concert, which is broadcast in 67 countries.

1990 – Wembley Stadium plays host to Nelson Mandela: An International Tribute for a Free South Africa. Mandela, released from prison two months earlier, gives a speech in which he asks that sanctions against South Africa be maintained.

A boy holds up a banner that calls attention to the theme of the concert: freedom for the leader of the ANC.

the giant event that the world of rock organized to celebrate the leader of the African National Congress' seventieth birthday and to ask for Mandela's liberation after twenty-six years of incarceration. Immediately after, Sting came on stage yelling "Set them free!" and following with his song dedicated to disappeared Chileans. His set was short but emotional, simple yet direct, created just to warm up a crowd that couldn't ask for anything better.

In front of Wembley Stadium, to welcome the eighty thousand visitors, there was no one selling music trinkets, but rather an incredible row of political activists, from militants from British socialist organizations to kids passing out flyers against violence, racism and unemployment. This was a sign of the changing times.

There were no divisions around genre and style; it didn't matter that George Michael was a slick star when he got on stage to sing "Sexual Healing" by Marvin Gaye and he said "I can't say much, since they've restricted us. But the important thing is that you all know why we are here today," to underline the censorship imposed by Fox, which was broadcasting the event in the USA. Sir Richard Attenborough knew this was true when he presented the Farafina Ensemble, an extraordinary group of African dancers and musicians, as did Richard Gere and Whoopi Goldberg who introduced the Eurythmics. Political discourses were reduced to a minimum, the large portrait of Mandela behind those playing and the enormous birthday cake that dominated one side of the stage were enough. The Eurythmics broke barriers on stage, standing beside Boris Grebenshikov, one of the biggest rock stars from the Soviet Union. "We want freedom in South Africa," sang

Annie Lennox, "Happy birthday Mandela," with the strength of tens of thousands of voices ready to sing along in chorus. The music displayed in this great show came from every corner of the world, from aboriginal Australians and the beautiful voices of a South African group, to the soul music of the great Al Green, introduced by a fake, yet entertaining, Michael Jackson, alongside Joe Cocker, Freddie Jackson and Ashford and Simpson, Natalie Cole, and Jonathan Butler. Music was political and being there all day together was political; singing for freedom was political, according to Joe Cocker.

It was a celebration of collaboration as demonstrated on stage by the super group put together by Midge Ure, with Phil Collins, Paul Carrack, Mark Kelly, and Curt Smith, ready to accompany Tony Hadley, Paul Young, Fish, the Bee Gees, Joan Armatrading, Bryan Adams, and Wet Wet Wet.

Absent from the show were all the artists that, refusing the boycott on concerts in Sun City, played in South Africa, such as Queen, Jimmy Cliff, Status Quo and Black Sabbath. There were, however, two great South African artists in exile, Miriam Makeba and Hugh Masekela, and Wembley reserved its longest and loudest applause for them. It is impossible to describe the atmosphere of the stadium as evening slowly fell and the enthusiasm, the warmth and the force of the audience that was living and breathing together to the rhythm of the music arriving from the stage, with Sly and Robbie, UB40, Jackson Browne, Tracy Chapman, Youssou N'Dour, Salt-N-Pepa, Courtney Pine, Derek B, the Fat Boys, and even the great Chubby Checker, up to the grand finale with Peter Gabriel, Simple Minds, Whitney Houston and Dire Straits, and a legendary duet between Mark Knopfler and

Eric Clapton. Obviously, there was no shortage of battle rock "hymns" in favor of Mandela: "Sun City" with Little Steven on the stage, and "Free Nelson Mandela" with Jerry Dammers of the Specials. But the biggest surprise was the unplanned arrival of Stevie Wonder, who was a great musician but also an active fighter for civil rights. Stevie Wonder sent the audience into ecstasy, and even the political figures (Neil Kinnock at the head) stood to applaud what would be one of the most beautiful moments of the day.

The show was unforgettable; rock music, intense in its broadest sense, had once again demonstrated its great capacity for aggregation, brotherhood, humanity, its ability to be the single language spoken by all people, easy to understand, to transmit, to sing, ready to be set into motion to breathe life, once again, into the dream of a better world, united and without racism or violence. "Mandela Day" was the resounding start of a battle that music would fight without respite until victory: that of Mandela's and South Africa's liberation from the slavery of racism.

Rock Takes a Stand in Defense of Human Rights

[September 2, 1988]

When he was young, Bruce Springsteen bought an album – perhaps one by the Rolling Stones – went home, placed it on his turntable and from that moment on his life changed. Through rock music, Springsteen felt free. And rock, at its best, expresses freedom and liberty, which was exactly what Amnesty International aimed to do. Introduced by Springsteen with these sentiments, it was without a doubt one of the most ambitious tours that rock history has ever seen, starting at Wembley Stadium in London on September 2, 1988. The Human Rights Now! would pass through five continents, covering thirty-five thousand miles (56,000 km) in six weeks, on the world tour promoted by Amnesty International to celebrate the fortieth anniversary of the Universal Declaration of Human Rights. The kickoff concert was seen by more than sixty thousand people, who had crowded into Wembley stadium starting in the early afternoon to participate in more than seven hours of music from some of the most important and famous names in rock: Bruce Springsteen, Peter Gabriel, Sting, a young Tracy Chapman and the Senegalese artist Youssou N'Dour, also including vibrant moments such as the duet between Springsteen and Sting. For Springsteen, the tour marked a clamorous

HISTORICAL NOTES

1986 – For the 25th anniversary of Amnesty International, A Conspiracy of Hope tour in the US begins, with a total of six dates. This is the first of a series of concerts this organization will promote in favor of human rights.

1988 – The Human Rights Now! worldwide tour begins: 20 concerts in 15 countries and 5 continents to celebrate the 40th anniversary of the Universal Declaration of Human Rights.

The crowd at the Human Rights Now! concert given in Budapest, Hungary.

change of pace towards social and political engagement, something which he would not abandon in the following years. At
a press conference before the show, he would say that it was
Peter Gabriel who convinced him, who made him understand
the importance of a demonstration such as this. Gabriel had
gone to Springsteen to discuss Amnesty International and the
Declaration of Human Rights and got him to agree to participate. Sure, people wanted to go see a big rock concert, but if
they were able to get their message out to just a few people,
it would be worth it. And as Springsteen said, it's not that
someone doesn't understand why they are there, why they are
dancing at that concert – they still get the message, and music
still can change lives. And even if they couldn't save the world,
saving even just one person was enough.

The tour was one of the most extraordinary projects that
the world of rock ever got off the ground, a trip around the
world in six weeks that touched down in Paris, Budapest,
Turin, Barcelona, San José in Costa Rica, Toronto, Montreal,
Philadelphia, Los Angeles, Tokyo, New Delhi, Harare, San
Paolo and Mendoza, to then conclude at the River Plate Studio
in Buenos Aires. It was one of the most ambitious large-scale
demonstrations for freedom that rock had ever dreamt up.
It was a party without borders that reminded the world that
human rights are sacred, done through music, through rock,
which for entire generations had been the symbol of possibility, change and peace. Nearly sixty-five thousand people
gathered in Wembley Stadium starting at 4pm to applaud
the on-stage arrival of the first of the five artists that would
make up the solid backbone of the tour: Senegalese Youssou
N'Dour. This fascinating and colorful music, deep and light

at the same time, supported by the extremely personal voice of N'Dour, was able to bring life to ancient and modern images and emotions in a marvelous opening set. Throughout the concert, Amnesty International representatives did not appear on stage, discourses were reduced to a minimum, there were no long speeches or rhetoric; there were only tables manned by activists offering materials on the infinite violations of the Universal Declaration of Human Rights. It was a show for awareness, not of fighting or rage, and it did not have that electric charge that made Live Aid or Mandela Day great.

However, the show didn't lack commitment, and it was Peter Gabriel who reminded people of that, walking onto the stage with his new band, enriched by Darryl Jones and Shankar, in addition to the greats Manu Katché, David Rhodes and David Sancious to sing, not by chance, "Games Without Frontiers," a true international anthem that the audience sang with force. Communication, commitment and genius were fused in a giant symbolic representation in Gabriel's set, in songs like "Family Snapshot," "Shock the Monkey," "Don't Give Up," and "Sledgehammer," through to the true, unique emotion of "In Your Eyes" and especially in "Biko," spectacularly whispered by thousands of voices, in a powerful whisper that transformed as it went along to end in an emotional shout. Just a few minutes later, Tracy Chapman arrived on stage, alone with her guitar. She said few words and then let her songs speak for themselves: "Across the Lines," "Behind the Wall," the splendid "Fast Car" and "Talkin' 'Bout a Revolution" in a half hour of pristine simplicity. As evening fell, the stadium slowly warmed up and a roar welcomed Sting and his band for an elegant, timely set that opened with "King of Pain" and continued on with other songs, including "If You Love Somebody Set Them Free," "Fragile" and "They Dance Alone," to the grand finale with a splendid version of "When the World is Running Down, You Make the Best of What's Still Around." But if it was rock and the myth of it to bring the dream of this tour to life, Bruce Springsteen was its hero. The Boss got on stage and the concert entirely changed. Introduced by Jack Healy and a video clip made by Stephen Johnson for the occasion, Springsteen offered up a scorching, lively set, putting dreams and reality, music and the art of yearning, commitment and passion together, lining up some of his masterpieces in an hour: "Born in the U.S.A.," "The Promised Land," "Cover Me," "Cadillac Ranch," "The River," "Spare Parts," "War," "My Home Town," "Thunder Road," "She's the One," "Light of Day" and "Born to Run." It is an unstoppable song of freedom, charged with the force that the event required and that Springsteen emitted without fear. But the final moment is the greatest and most moving of the night, when the barriers finally fell between the musicians and they all took the stage to sing a beautiful version of Bob Dylan's "Chimes of Freedom," concluding with a homage to Bob Marley and a slogan, "Get Up, Stand Up." Stand up and fight for your rights. It's a fantastic moment for music and for engagement, a small brick in the monument to freedom that rock has always tried to build.

On the Venice Lagoon: History Watches Pink Floyd

[*July 15, 1989*]

P erhaps as many as 300 thousand people – the biggest concert recorded in Italian rock concert history. Pink Floyd, playing in that mirror of water in front of the Piazza San Marco. A utopia realized, a catastrophe that didn't happen, hanging in the balance for hours, those hours of waiting and then the concert. The audience was everywhere, young people climbing lamp posts on the corners of the houses, on scaffolding – colorful, barefoot, unclothed, torn, tired and happy youths, enraged by the city that did not provide toilets, adequate security or basic provisions. Under the arches of the old city, just before the concert, you could find everything from broken bottles to vomit and everything else imaginable, a swamp to wade through with great caution. The morning before, around 10am, the Piazza San Marco already looked like a stadium just a few moments before the starting whistle of the final game of the World Cup – and the Pink Floyd concert was still twelve hours away. People had slept at the train station, stacked one on top of the other, crushed in the early hours of the morning by a human sea unloading from all the arriving trains. The more fortunate ones found the open doors of the international hostel in

HISTORICAL NOTES

1987 – To promote *A Momentary Lapse of Reason*, their first album without Roger Waters, the band begin a worldwide tour consisting of 199 concerts attended by around 5 million spectators.

1988 – The European tour begins and includes 8 concerts in Italy. The free concert in Venice is telecast live throughout the world. The live recording of the concerts at the Nassau Coliseum, New York is released as the double album *Delicate Sound of Thunder*.

1990 – The tour ends at Knebworth Park to an audience of 120,000 persons.

The crowd in Venice during the 15 July 1989 concert.

the Giudecca and only a few found shelter in the porticoes of the Piazza San Marco; it was pouring with rain and the majority of them had preferred to sleep indoors. For that matter, the municipality, once again, shone by its lack of organization: no one, for example, had ordered the opening of the sports hall in the Arsenale. All the cities in the world with inadequate facilities open their buildings to the audiences of mega rock concerts. Venice did not. It didn't even provide barriers to divide the public from the water. If there were any, they were paid for by Pink Floyd and set up by the concert's organizers.

Woodstock on dry land and this party by the sea: a meeting of rock and tradition. The *vaporetto* strike hadn't stopped the preparations for the festival at Il Redentore the day before: a 1,093 foot (333 meter) long bridge of boats was assembled to connect the Zattere (the promenade) with the Chiesa del Redentore (Church of the Most Holy Redeemer), designed by Andrea Palladio in the Giudecca neighborhood. It was a votive bridge with which, along with fireworks, the city annually thanked God for having saved it in 1578 after three years of plague. There were all types of boats lining the Grand Canal: rubber rafts, motorized rafts, motorboats and yachts. Many of them were outfitted for the celebration with a pergola covered in ivy or some floral tribute, with a small, colored paper light underneath, much like those seen at the Rificolona festival in Florence, or those used for Chinese New Year in February. Festivals are the story of a population and, from that appendix to the Piazza San Marco that is almost the Riva degli Schiavoni and which overlooks the lagoon of the Giudecca neighborhood, there was a mass of people waiting to hear its story told by David Gilmour, Nick Mason and Rick Wright.

At 7pm, the audience in the water had filled the lagoon around the stage. The boats became solid ground; you could walk across them all the way to the Giudecca neighborhood on the other side of the lagoon. Around 2pm the sound check started, testing the amplification system. The three members of Pink Floyd, who in the days prior had observed the enormous floating stage from the ground or motor boats, climbed aboard the Mak III, the 295 foot (90 meters) long and 98 foot (30 meters) wide barge to test the microphones and instruments. Everything seemed to work perfectly: after all, Pink Floyd's show was a well-oiled performance machine after two continuous years of touring the world. A giant machine that was well adapted to the water of the lagoon: the enormous central screen where imagery was projected during the show didn't seem to have suffered, the clusters of reflectors controlled by an electronic mixer for their thousands of movements didn't seem to have suffered, and the laser beams were cooled by tons of water from the lagoon. Standing on it before the concert, the stage seemed like an enormous workshop for Saint Peter's Basilica: ultra-specialized technicians, each one an expert in his field, worked tirelessly. Everything had to be checked and double-checked, more often than not by massive, sweaty, shirtless men in shorts, covered in enormous, colorful tattoos. They were the types of men to be afraid of if you run into them on the street at night – but instead they were the soul of that which would be called the musical event of the century.

A perfect concert, the dream of a rock band that had left their English province to conquer the world, and that arrived to play in the middle of Venice's lagoon, in front of the Piazza San Marco, on a stage floating on the water.

The Hardest
Rock:
The Sound
of Freedom

[September 28, 1991]

The Berlin wall fell in 1989, but in 1991 the Soviet Union was still standing, even if it seemed to be wobbling dangerously. It was September of 1991, just a month before there was an attempted coup, with the "kidnapping" of Mikhail Gorbachev, which was resolved with the defeat of the coup leaders. To celebrate the victory, Moscow hosted a tour date for the hardest rock bands in the world, "Monsters of Rock," in an aerodrome located in the Tushino neighborhood, on the extreme northern edge of the Soviet capital. All the young people of the capital mobilized to listen to AC/DC, Metallica, the Black Crowes and Pantera – over fifty thousand of them, making it the largest crowd ever recorded in the USSR. It was an event not to be missed, in part because alongside the bands from the west, the most appreciated local acts were to appear, such as Electrosudorozhnaia Terapia, whose name means "electro-shock therapy."

From the day the wall fell, lots of things changed in the Soviet Union, and Gorbachev's policy of "openness" allowed for western music (which in the country's darkest days had arrived illegally from radio stations such as the BBC or the Voice of America, or more simply,

HISTORICAL NOTES

1980 – In England, Paul Loasby organizes Monsters Of Rock, the first edition of the festival dedicated to rock and heavy metal bands, attracting 35,000 spectators. Parallel editions are organized abroad.

1991 – The Moscow leg of the festival, the first major rock event in the Soviet Union, draws the largest crowd ever recorded in this country.

1992 – The video *For Those About to Rock: Monsters in Moscow*, a documentary of this historic concert, is released.

James Hetfield, the Metallica guitarist. The Moscow concert swept away the drab Soviet past and sparked a new perspective that was receptive to sharing, passion and energy.

with discs that, in a very limited number and at astronom-
ical prices, were sold on the black market) to circulate in
numbers that were unimaginable up until a few years prior.
Gorbachev's perestroika brought about a small revolution in
this field as well. In Moscow, public and private radio trans-
mitted rock music continuously, on the state-run television
channel it wasn't uncommon to catch the airing of music
videos, and western albums started to show up in stores.
The opening of the borders to a genre that was considered
a byproduct of "corrupt capitalism" created a flourishing of
Soviet groups that, singing strictly in Russian, in some cases
produced interesting material. But before September 28, there
was nothing like this. Before that day, young Russians had
never felt that mixture of energy, music and freedom that
goes by the name of hard rock. And they had arrived at that
concert despite the oppressive atmosphere in Moscow, despite
heightened supervision. Russian guards everywhere, with just
one mandate: maintain order at all costs, block the kids of
Moscow, driven by the stars of western rock, from resolving
what remained of the Cold War in their own way. To avoid
chaos, to prevent the collective craziness from overtaking the
400 thousand people present, they were ready to use their
batons. And they did – but only briefly.

By the end of the concert, the soldiers and kids were
drinking together; they were hugging, with a new social pact
under the auspices of AC/DC, Metallica and Pantera. The
concert would remain in the collective memory of an entire
generation. And, it was to the sounds of the Four Horsemen
led by James Hetfield that the miracle took place, that something changed. The frames you can watch on YouTube have

an analogue charm, the patina of history. It came during "Harvester of Sorrow": first, the guards charge, trample and try to take control without cutting anyone any slack. Then everything dissolves. Roles, hierarchies and fears fade, the plot unravels. The soldiers start to fraternize with the fans; their faces change, relaxing. Some take off their uniforms, never again to rejoin the ranks.

The riffs of Metallica and Pantera welded the cracks of a generation. For a moment, they erased the gray of the Soviet past and opened a common horizon made up of sharing, passion and energy. Everything ended with the final performance, that of AC/DC. Angus Young jumped on stage in front of hundreds of thousands of people in ecstasy. Back in Black became almost an endorsement for overthrow: don't turn back, and it all goes away – the coup, the lack of resources and the blocked political situation. Rock transformed the present; it dissolved anxieties and fears for an instant, connecting the lives of 400 thousand people to the image of a better, livable and free future. It was a Soviet Woodstock to break down the empire, only for it to return in the guise of Vladimir Putin. But the youth from Moscow learned their lesson: rock as a vehicle for freedom is an idea that immediately takes root. These roots stretch down to today, down to Pussy Riot and other kindred spirits.

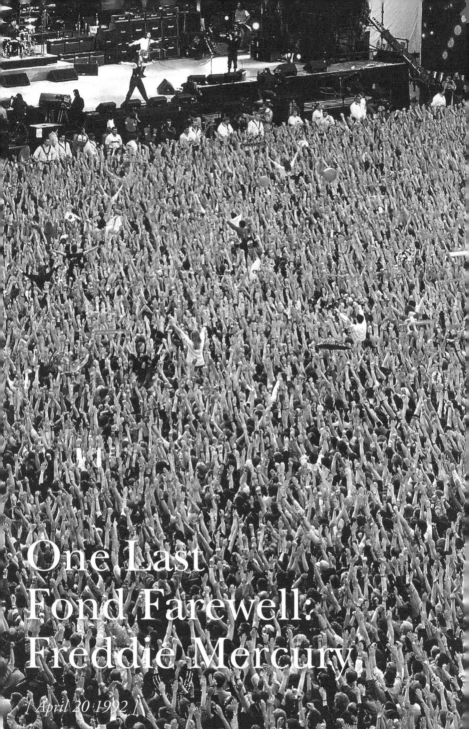

One Last Fond Farewell: Freddie Mercury

[April 20 1992]

It was a celebration that also deserves to be called a coming to consciousness. Consciousness about the drama that was beating down on the planet at the start of the 1990s and that many, too many, still were pretending didn't exist. The Freddie Mercury Tribute at Wembley Stadium on April 20, 1992, wasn't just an emotional reminder of the singer, who had died the previous November; it wasn't just paying homage to the memory of one of the most charismatic front men of recent years. On that April day, rock put the tragedy of AIDS on stage. It put the need to realize that only a common effort would be able to stop what promised to be a mass nightmare in front of the eyes of millions of spectators. And it did it in its own way: without hypocrisy or false morality, instilling in the consciousness of millions of television viewers, connecting from all parts of the world, that just the word, the information, the fact of not looking the other way would allow the planet to confront that which many would call "the plague of the twentieth century."

Remember and raise awareness, then. The concert for Freddie Mercury was divided in two. Without collapsing into sentimentality. And that

HISTORICAL NOTES

1990 – Freddie Mercury's last public live appearance, when he receives the Brit Award.

1991 – Freddie Mercury dies on November 24.

1992 – At the Brit Awards ceremony Roger Taylor and Brian May of Queen announce their decision to organize a grand event in memory of this great artist. The Freddie Mercury Tribute Concert For Aids Awareness is telecast to 76 countries and is viewed by over one billion persons. The proceeds are donated to the Mercury Phoenix Trust, an organization that fights AIDS.

The huge crowd in front of the stage during the Freddie Mercury Tribute Concert held at Wembley Stadium, London on 20 April 1992.

there was little room for melancholic nostalgia – inevitable in these circumstances – would be demonstrated in the first part of the concert, in the afternoon. Metallica and Guns N' Roses were the ones to warm up Wembley Stadium. And anyone who was there can consider themselves among the chosen few because, at the time, the two Californian bands were at the height of their ability to set the stage alight. The Four Horsemen lined up three killer pieces, all songs from their recent *The Black Album*. "Enter Sandman," "Sad But True" and "Nothing Else Matters" were devastating. Then it was Axl and Slash's turn. Guns N' Roses only played two songs that afternoon. But the two songs were more than enough: "Paradise City" and "Knockin' on Heaven's Door" were simply Guns N' Roses at their zenith. Axl especially, who didn't make you lament, not even for an instant, on what Freddie Mercury was like on stage: absolute charisma.

But the real story happened in the second part of the concert when the three "surviving" members of Queen welcomed, one by one, the best of worldwide rock and pop to cover their songs. The parade of stars was breathtaking: David Bowie and Annie Lennox – simply magnificent – transformed "Under Pressure" into a gospel for their lost friend. Elton John and Axl Rose didn't make you rue the absence of Mercury in "Bohemian Rhapsody." The same Axl threw all of the rage that he had in his body into the drumming of "We Will Rock You." A surprise came with George Michael, who was beyond being at home in his rendition of the difficult "Somebody to Love."

Until the grand finale, when they all thrilled the audience with a collective version of "We Are the Champions."

There was room for a few forgettable clamorous performances. Of all of them, there was Robert Plant. The singer of Led Zeppelin was on the stage along with Queen to sing the band's last hit: the voyage of "Innuendo," the gypsy ride turned into progressive rock that had been Mercury's swan song. Something went wrong from the start; Plant, as never happened in his career, was unable to enter into the song. He hit the wrong note; he went off beat. In short, it was a debacle to be erased. In fact, Plant has never given his approval to the publication of that song in the official concert compilations and releases. As a partial excuse, he did have the flu. But anyone who wants to see how even the gods can hit the wrong notes just has to search for the performance on YouTube. And who knows how wryly Freddie Mercury would have smiled at seeing one of his idols unable to sing one of his band's songs.

The Satellite of Love: U2's Zoo TV Tour

[November 27, 1993]

"Everything you know is wrong." Five words. Five words that, better than any others, restored the spirit of the times in the early 1990s, the years without the Wall and without ideology, the years of pervasive television, shoved into the heads and consciousness of all citizens of a world reduced to a global village. Five words shot into alienating lights, symbols liquefied by the powers that were, and techno backgrounds. These five words were what started the, by then, eighteen months and 155 concerts of U2's Zoo TV Tour. But that day in Sydney, November 27, 1993 was different. It was different because Bono, The Edge, Adam Clayton and Larry Mullen shattered the "media" par excellence. It was different because that concert was broadcast worldwide, and rock instantly became, once again, the fastest, most immediate and efficient antibody against the Big Brother that was clamping down on the ranks. Everything you know is wrong. And at the center of the upside-down world, rock became the key to its interpretation, to the restoration of logic to the disorder. Bono, especially. To the music of Zoo Station, he emerges split in two thanks to a camera

HISTORICAL NOTES

1984 – "Pride," the band's first international success, reaches 3rd place on the UK charts.

1992 – The Zoo TV Tour, aimed at promoting the album *Achtung Baby*, debuts at Lakeland, Florida. Three months later the European edition, begins in Paris.

1993 – While the tour is in Australia, the Sydney concert is telecast all over the world. Island Records releases *Zooropa*, which is cut during the tour. Seven million copies of the album are sold.

1994 – *Zoo TV: Live from Sydney* is released.

Bono at Lisbon on 15 May 1993, during Zoo TV Tour.

trick. Embodying at once all the contradictions of a divided world that after the end of the Cold War seemed to lack objectives, holding its breath, with eyes wide open waiting for what came next. Wearing black leather, dark wraparound sunglasses, moving sinuously: The Fly, his alter ego that came into existence after the release of *Achtung Baby* two years earlier. It wasn't just an album; it was a foreign body that brought the mainstream down to the newly reopened streets of Berlin, contaminating everything.

The 1990s took shape in this concert, in which U2 stubbornly wore the clothes of the latest rock heroes, still able to inspire dreams and passions. Rock to which they pay homage, revitalizing its language with electronic influences, videos and worldwide broadcasting. This is a U2 that goes on stage contemporaneously across the globe, on the television, as they are talking about television itself, exploiting the satellite dishes that signal the tour in which everything is true and false at the same time. They are both avant-garde and classic; they are visionaries that look to and imagine the future, as well as careful observers of contemporary reality, in a show that tries to artistically represent the global village. The size of the show – mammoth-like and hyper-technological – reduces the physical dimensions of the four members of the band, but at the same time makes the crowd the protagonist of the event, using images that are constantly rebroadcast on dozens of monitors, reintroducing fragmentary images of reality and fiction, images of the world that they don't know and don't want to become part of history, in a cacophony of messages that intersect, mix together and overlap in time to the music. And, to add to the confusion, Bono himself played with reality by putting live TV on the stage, changing channels on screens connected to live satellite feeds. Bono also gave life to a virtual, technology-driven duet with Lou Reed for "Satellite of Love," singing with images of the great American rocker on the screen, as if the duet was live in that moment. Reality, fiction, "everything you know is wrong," it's all a game of mirrors and screens that create the illusions we call life.

The set closed with "Can't Help Falling in Love." This time, however, it came full circle, going back to Elvis, back to its roots. The world witnessed, live on television, the baptism of a new era, society's entry into a new world that would soon be called the Internet, the digital revolution. However, it was a baptism to the rhythm of rock music; rock was a ring linking the past and present, tight around the left ring finger of Paul Hewson, aka Bono.

Kurt Cobain:
The Last Flight
of a Rock Angel

[March 1, 1994]

Not even the most inspired screenwriter could have done better: condensing all of Kurt Cobain's weakness, torment, rage and talent into a single day and a single concert. Nirvana's last appearance on a stage – like much of their story – seemed like a dark subject, resistant to being understood only with the canons of reason. It was March 1, 1994, and for the three guys from Seattle, it was only the umpteenth show, the usual tricks, the same old organizational system that for three years squeezed them until their last drop of energy. They were in Munich, Germany, and the day didn't get off to a good start. Kurt was simply destroyed. His usual habits – heroin and psychotropic drugs – were joined by a worsening case of bronchitis that had, by then, had become torturous. He didn't want to play; he just wanted to disappear, go home, try to fix his relationship with his wife, Courtney Love – a relationship that was becoming more and more difficult to sustain as the days went on. He wanted to spend time with Francis Bean, his daughter. But, the stage, that same stage that he had yearned for since his adolescence, had become a monster that detracted him from himself. If to this low state of mind you add something

HISTORICAL NOTES

1989 – Sub Pop Records releases Nirvana's debut album, *Bleach*.

1991 – The second album, *Nevermind*, is released by DGC Records and sells 30 million copies.

1993 – Concert at the Cow Palace in San Francisco to raccogliere funds for the victims of war in Bosnia. *In Utero*, the Nirvana's third and last studio album, is released.

1994 – The band holds its last US concert in the Seattle Center Arena and then embarks on another European tour. It breaks up after Cobain's death.

An exhausted Kurt Cobain on stage in 1994.

that to call it drug abuse would only be an understatement, the picture is complete. And whoever witnessed those eighty minutes at Terminal 1 defines agreement when calling the show "absolutely terrible." For Cobain, the stage had become nothing more than the setting, every night, for his sacrifice at the altar of show business.

That evening, Cobain seemed to want to get it over with immediately. The first songs on the set list immediately gave off the feeling of a wall of sonic violence that the singer had built between himself and the world. First was a cover of the Cars' "My Best Friend's Girl," just the right song to make fun of this world and the other. Then came "Radio Friendly Unit Shifter," "Drain You," "Breed" and "Serve the Servants," driven and more distorted than usual. Cobain, in a white shirt a few sizes too big, was thin – too thin – with his hair in his face and without a trace of a beard. And like every other night, the miracle was the same: amazement at just listening to a voice of indefinable beauty as it came out of that obviously suffering body. Then Dave Grohl and Krist Novoselic attack "Come As You Are," and Cobain starts to sing, but he seems absent. Halfway through the song, the power goes out and it's like a black hole had swallowed up Nirvana instantly. A few seconds of absolute silence, then the light returns. Cobain seems almost serene for a moment, as if he had been embracing that silence. Novoselic approaches the mic and jokingly says some words that, to hear them now, would send a chill up your spine. "We're not playing the Munich Enormodome tonight. 'Cos our careers are on the wane. We're on the way out. Grunge is dead. Nirvana's over..."

The concert did start up again, however, and Cobain's

final public show would be twenty-three songs, eighty minutes, in total. It is pure conjecture, but the last part of the
concert seemed almost made to say goodbye: "The Man Who
Sold the World," Cobain struggling with all the hosts that
David Bowie encapsulated in that song; then "All Apologies,"
with "I'm married / Buried / I wish I was like you / Easily
amused;" then the last song, "Heart Shaped Box," or, how to
squeeze one's painful condition into just under four minutes.
A goodbye. After Munich, Nirvana canceled the rest of their
European tour. Kurt flew to Rome to recover, to regain some
energy. But he would slip further into his demons. Slipping
into a coma and being rushed to the hospital would prove
to be but a dress rehearsal for what would happen a month
later, on that horrific April 5, 1994, when the last brilliant
genius that rock ever had the fortune of meeting would grab
a Remington M11 to put an end to his days.

Woodstock '94: Twenty-five Years on

[August 12-13-14, 1994]

Reading the list of participants in this giant music festival, there really is nothing to fear in terms of nostalgia: the cast on the two stages of Woodstock '94 presented an extraordinary opportunity to take a credible snapshot of the "state of rock" in the 1990s. There was a bit of everything for all tastes, all ages and all generations, in a sort of giant time machine that brought together twenty-five years of rock history. Over the years, this story increasingly became a container of diverse music and sounds, that today carry symbols and names that do not even closely resemble rock, but without which its "revolution" might be different today or, in a few cases, would not have happened at all. The twenty-fifth anniversary celebration presented a cast that mirrored, in some way, the variety that was the original Woodstock, starting with global sounds: the gospel of an "all-star band" that included Thelma Houston, CeCe Peniston, Mavis Staples, Phoebe Snow, and Lois Walden; the Jamaican music of Jimmy Cliff, with Rita Marley, Toots Hibbert, Eek-A-Mouse, Worl-A-Girl and Diana King; and of WOMAD, the touring festival organized by Peter Gabriel, that made a stop at Woodstock, presenting Xalam from Senegal, the

HISTORICAL NOTES

1994 – Woodstock '94, a three-day music festival celebrating the 25th anniversary of the original event, is held at Winston Farm, at Saugerties, about 110 miles from New York. It is attended by 350,000 spectators and pays a tribute to three greats of rock music who died while very young: Hendrix, Joplin and Morrison.

1995 – Polygram releases a video of festival and the A&M Records a CD, *Woodstock '94*.

1999 – The third edition of the festival is marred by serious acts of violence.

Hundreds of thousands of young persons went to Saugerties, New York, to see the second edition of the Woodstock Festival.

Justin Vali Trio from Madagascar, the great Geoffrey Oryema from Uganda, and Hassan Hakmoun from Morocco. A non-sectarian spirit arrived from Senegal in the person of Youssou N'Dour, one of the biggest stars of African music. The spokesman for world music, Peter Gabriel, also took to the stage, chosen to close the festival, not by chance but because of his work which has unequivocally contributed to keeping a non-sectarian spirit of music alive, open to influences and communication between diverse worlds and cultures.

Of course, they couldn't do without a few old heroes from the original Woodstock. After all, it wouldn't have been possible to imagine Woodstock without them, especially the three "debut acts" from the original festival: Joe Cocker, Santana, and Crosby, Stills & Nash, who played live for the first time at that Woodstock. Of the rock of yesteryear there were the best that memory offers: the Allman Brothers Band, with their Southern Sound; the Band, featuring Bob Weir of the Grateful Dead, Bruce Hornsby, Rob Wasserman, and Hot Tuna; the part re-united members of Traffic, Steve Winwood and Jim Capaldi; Aerosmith; on to the Rock and Blues Revue, past and present, that brought together Paul Rodgers and Andy Fraser (of Free), Slash (of Guns N' Roses), Brian May (of Queen), and Jason Bonham, son of the late Led Zeppelin drummer John Bonham. But the bridge between past and present was once again Bob Dylan, the only one among the greats to never have abdicated his poetic unrest, absent from the original festival but ready, on this day, to hold high the flag of unconditional visionary rock.

The majority of bands on stage at Woodstock '94 represented the modernity of American music, the sounds and the moods of younger generations. To escape nostalgia, to link the dream of the past to the reality of today, Woodstock '94 offered up all the various spirits of rock at the time, starting from rap, which, carrying on the combative, rebellious spirit of music from the 1970s and given rap's ability to become the immediate and understandable language of the streets, had become the emblem of the era. Hard, combative rap represented by Cypress Hill, sexy and danceable rap from Salt-N-Pepa, up to the "roots rap" of Arrested Development.

The harder bands, the ones that could mix the tensions of metal-rock to those of punk, the rules of adventure with those of the cutting edge, weren't missing either. In fact, there were the electric, noisy sounds of Nine Inch Nails, the unforgiving rock of Henry Rollins and his band, son of the punk rock of the 1980s, the avant-garde Primus, the rock of Porno for Pyros, fronted by Perry Farrell, the organizer of Lollapalooza, a true alternative rock festival that had dominated the scene in prior years. There were also many bands of the most recent generation: Blind Melon, the Cranberries, Candlebox, Green Day, Kings X, Collective Soul, and the English band James, alongside more noted groups such as the historic champions of new wave, the Violent Femmes, as well as the Spin Doctors. And that's not all. To complete the picture of a genre-less festival, there were the Neville Brothers, Melissa Etheridge, Sheryl Crow (one of the most beautiful voices of new American music), the Italian star Zucchero, and heavy rockers Metallica, who were the farthest, musically, from the spirit of the original Woodstock. It also had the spirit of a great "rave party," with all the kids at Woodstock dancing all Saturday night to a long series of DJ sets and the participation of three of the most psychedelic and "zippy" house and techno bands around: the Orb, Orbital and Deee-Lite.

Nostalgia? Very little. Fun? Lots, including the revival of mud, just like the first festival. Peace and love? A lot, everywhere, in an atmosphere that seemed to revive the glory of the past, updated for the end of the millennium. Woodstock '94 was the last of the "old" rock festivals. After this, everything was different.

Radiohead: English Rock Changes Its Sound

[June 28, 1997]

The concert that ferried rock into the twenty-first century didn't start in Glastonbury, 25 miles (40 kilometers) south of Bristol, at dusk on June 28, 1997. Or rather, it did…sort of. In reality, it started twelve days before, on June 16, when *OK Computer*, Radiohead's third album, arrived in UK record stores. That was the real moment in which thousands of people felt like they were at the gates waiting to be let in: adrenaline and curiosity grew day by day. The reason was simple: if this last album from Thom Yorke and his gang was immediately perceived as something that transcended fashions and trends, as something that injected a new mutation into the heart of rock, the live show would be the essential litmus test to measure the distance between intention and reality.

The fact is that on that night in June, Radiohead were simply aliens from outer space. They were a thousand light years from the frivolous decadence that the whole world of Britpop seemed to be sliding into, a genre that the band was still filed under. For a little while, just a few seconds more, and no longer would anyone dare to compare Radiohead to Oasis & Co. The lights on the stage descended upon

HISTORICAL NOTES

1992 – The band releases the first single, Creep.

1995 – The second album, *The Bends*, is a great success in the UK. Radiohead goes on tour as a support band for R.E.M.

1997 – *OK Computer*, a visionary and psychedelic rock album, sells almost 10 million copies and immortalizes the band. It plays the last set of the Glastonbury Festival to an audience of 45,000 persons in pelting rain. Besides the tracks from *OK Computer*, the band plays earlier songs.

The Radiohead band at Capitol Records, Los Angeles in 1997.

Thom Yorke, alone with his Fender in front of hundreds of thousands of people. He began with "Lucky," a little wonder of a song inspired by the war that continued to devastate Bosnia at the time. Yorke sings of a man who survives a plane crash. And, metaphorically perhaps, it is about the accident with celebrity from which Radiohead was able to save itself thanks only to the music. Thom takes everyone by the hand and begins the journey. When the chorus begins, the ice becomes lava and, welcome to the dimension in which music, a collective ritual, is only about the ineffable.

But one can't go on like this; your arteries won't hold up and your eyes can't stay peeled open looking towards the future. So, you turn back, see-sawing with songs from *The Bends*: furious versions of "My Iron Lung" and "Planet Telex" are tangled with "Airbag" and "Exit Music (For a Film)." Thirty minutes felt like the passing of decades, and that was hardly anything at all. The show entered the history books with tracks 8, 9 and 10 of the lineup. That night, like many after, "Paranoid Android" was uncanny. "Turn on the lights, I want to see the audience," York said into the microphone before starting to play. Face to face, a smile and then he got serious. "This is a song about chaos," the singer often repeated, and in Glastonbury that chaos was addressed, checked and given to the public.

Then came "Karma Police," and here the only thing to do was to look for that version, sit down and listen, swaying all the way to the finale, "For a Minute There \ I Lost Myself." And to give credence to the case, the "there" is the song that follows, "Creep." Because if Radiohead had continued with a decade of fake "Creeps," they surely would have become anything but billionaires. And likewise, they surely would have lost themselves. Their first international success was simply let go, played with too much emphasis, more than sounding like something of their own. They would play it live very few other times.

The abandonment of "Creep" had just one effect on that concert: the lightening of a load, the release of tension, Radiohead's ship sets sail definitively. If you had to choose the moment in the career of a group that changed things, for Yorke and his band, this was unquestionably it. From that point on, a new equation would be established in the physics of rock: that of Radiohead concerts and collective hypnosis. Everything came more into focus: Jonny Greenwood's and Ed O'Brien's guitars, and the rhythm section from the other Greenwood, Colin, and Philip Selway. Radiohead's script is written; they'll change only the colors that, from time to time, they decide to use in their dance around the fire of rock.

Rock dies and is born again; it changes its skin and becomes something new. There are still guitars, but they become unrecognizable. Electronics transform sounds but also souls; language is denser, darker, but no less emotional, no less passionate. Radiohead opened the door to the future; they followed the path that others had started on earlier in the decade, and they crossed over the last river, setting fire to the ships behind them. They could no longer retrace their steps; there was no way to be linked to the past, and the audience at Glastonbury let go, let themselves be transported towards the new millennium on a wave of music that no longer had clear outlines, capable of taking on different shapes, extraordinarily mutant, wonderfully imperfect and elusive.

Love Parade: Dancing in the Heart of Old Europe

[July 12, 1997]

"Let the sunshine in your heart." The slogan, simple and clear, rang for weeks in the cities of Europe. It was the signal that rallied all the kids of the Old Continent that convened in Berlin on July 12, 1997 to celebrate the Love Parade, an extraordinary outdoor dance party, and a political protest, to the sound of techno music. The year before, there were 750 thousand attendees reunited by the drums of the underground, of the subterranean communication that linked discothèques and nightclubs across Europe, of that independent rumbling that has always ensured that the signals of youth culture moved faster than any official means of communication. In 1997, they would total more than a million. One million people that marched from 2pm in the heart of Europe, in the street that leads from the Ernst-Reuter-Platz to the Brandenburg Gate, invading Berlin with their sounds and colors. German, French, Italian, English, Slovenian, Belgian, Russian, and Swiss youth to "express their joy for living," as the founder of the parade, dj Dr. Motte said, stressing that "the Love Parade is the gathering of all those who have an open heart." The Europe of the Maastricht

HISTORICAL NOTES

1989 – Four months before the Berlin Wall is destroyed the Berlin DJ Dr. Motte organizes a free musical pacifist event that will be held every year until 2003.

1997 – During the ninth edition more than one million persons parade through Berlin, accompanied by ear-splitting techno music.

2006 – After a two-year interruption Love Parade is revived with the slogan "The Love is back".

2010 – The last edition is held at Duisburg, Germany, but the event turns into a tragedy as 21 persons die and about 400 are injured.

A photograph of the Berlin Love Parade: hundreds of thousands of young people dance around the Victory Column.

Treaty, of a single currency, of meetings between Prime Ministers, was still far in the future. However, in the center of Berlin, on this day, there was already a united Europe, the one dreamed about and lived in by a generation of young people who didn't care for borders and who spoke a single language: the language of music. "We understand each other through the common language of music. This is the music of our time and it has its roots in house and techno. This is the kind of music that expresses our vital consciousness," stated Dr. Motte. And he was right, because more than any other demonstration, the Love Parade with its din, its rhythm and its warmth, put an entire generation on stage through its music. No, it wasn't Woodstock, the Isle of Wight, or Glastonbury. The Love Parade was a 'tribal gathering,' a meeting of the tribes spread throughout the world of young Europeans that, only in appearance, lacked a center; it was a giant rave where dancing reigned supreme, where the rhythm was obsessive, pulsating and unstoppable, and where the messages were fused and confused in the music itself, incomprehensible to many, unbearable for adults. It was the Europe of young people united by techno, music that is neither English nor American, but the offspring of the provinces of the empire of pop, music that speaks English only out of habit but that, in reality, doesn't speak at all, basing its communicative capability only on the rhythm of electro and techno. It is music that works, and has worked for years, growing exponentially in its success among young people, just as the Love Parade has grown.

In the beginning, in 1989, there were only 150 kids dancing in Wittenbergplatz to the sound of techno coming from the amplifiers of a Volkswagen bus. But, by 1990, there were two thousand, six thousand the following year, fifteen thousand in 1992, finally arriving at the oceanic masses of the two years prior: 250 thousand in 1995 and 750 thousand in 1996. So, it was a party, but it was also officially a "political" demonstration, with slogans like "The Future is Ours," "The Spirit Makes You Move", "Peace on Earth," "My House Is Your House and Your House Is Mine," and "We Are One Family" that recalled the old slogans of "peace, love and music," but were moved by new images, new sounds and new hearts. It was an optimistic and pacifistic youth that assembled in Berlin to give shape to their dreams with an extraordinary collective celebration. The underground organization of the early years, then, made way for a worldwide mega-event. The turnover expected for Berlin's Love Parade was around sixty billion, and half the world's media were there to transmit the event to the world, the image of a city that, just ten years earlier, had been a symbol of division and separation from the world but that now wanted to be the symbol of a new unity. But those who really made the party were not politicians from Berlin, not the German tourist board, not sponsors or TV channels, but the hundreds of thousands of young people that crowded the city from the day before and that, in spite of those who painted them as insensitive or senseless, gave life to the largest and most peaceful celebration of life that the continent had ever seen. "A few years ago, people gathered before the Brandenburg Gate to ask for the demolition of the Berlin Wall. Today we ask for the demolition of your walls, those of prejudice," announced the organizer. And with him, on July 12, 1997 in Berlin, a million young Europeans asked as well, dancing on floats to the rhythm of techno music.

Live 8:
The Global
Concert

[July 2, 2005]

The dream of Bob Geldof, that of making sure that music can be a direct and positive agent for change, had already been realized in 1985 with Live Aid. Twenty years later, Geldof dreamed of more, that is, to influence even the G8, or the governments of the richest and most powerful countries in the world, to make sure that they forgive the debts of the poorest countries, improve and increase their aid and put fairer trade rules in place. In short, make sure that poverty became a thing of the past; "Make poverty history" was in fact the campaign slogan. And thus Live 8 was organized, a giant, global concert, that came to life in ten cities around the world at the same time, on the day before the G8 summit in Scotland, on July 2, 2005.

Live 8 was, without a doubt, one of the great moments in which the story of rock took the stage in its entirety, with its past, present and future. And perhaps it was, at least up to today, the last great moment in which the dream of rock once again became real, with all its experience in dizziness, hope and passion. There was rock, all of it, represented by the faces of the old, great stars such as Paul McCartney

HISTORICAL NOTES

2005 – May 31, Bob Geldof announces the organization of the event.

June 11 – The G8 leaders announce they have agreed to cancel the debts of 18 countries.

June 13 – 66,500 pairs of tickets for the concert at Hyde Park in London are awarded to the winners of an SMS competition.

June 17 – The Live 8 List, with over 30 million names, is presented to Tony Blair, the G8 president.

July 6-8 – The G8 summit decides to increase aid to developing nations.

The Live 8 logo shown at the press conference in which Bob Geldof explains the details of his second charity concert.

and Elton John, young bands trembling with electric passion such as Green Day, furious rappers like Kanye West, or a queen like Annie Lennox who could sing alone at the piano while images of children mangled by poverty scrolled behind her. Or Ligabue, Pelù and Jovanotti who together reaffirmed that "Il Mio Nome È Mai Più" (My Name Is No More), or Sting who sang "Every Breath You Take," while the faces of the leaders of the G8 scrolled across the big screen. An infinite list, a live encyclopedia of the music of the world, and in this Babel there was history: Pink Floyd, Brian Wilson and the glistening echo of the Beach Boys, Stevie Wonder, The Who, Pet Shop Boys, R.E.M., Green Day, Deep Purple, Coldplay and George Michael, a mile a minute references to the Beatles and Bob Marley, summoned obviously also by his wife Rita and his son Stephen, who were surprise guests during the performance by the Black Eyed Peas, in Philadelphia. The lineup is almost impossible to list in its entirety.

A story thrown violently into the playing field from the start of a duet that fans of rock music could only have dreamed of: U2 and Paul McCartney, in a splendid, fortuitous earthly coincidence that made the lyrics to "Sgt. Pepper's Lonely Hearts Club Band" the perfect epigraph for the event. "It was twenty years ago today [from Live Aid, obviously]... We'd like to take you home with us...We hope you will enjoy the show." In the background, the "band of lonely hearts" was also a sweet metaphor for what had happened, sweet and exciting like only the Beatles knew how to be. The planet of lonely hearts was united there, at Live 8.

Twenty years or so was also the amount of time that the members of Pink Floyd had been estranged. Not even the fall of the Berlin wall was enough to reunite them and to celebrate *The Wall* with the reunification of Germany: only Roger Waters would go. And their noisy, fabulous reunion alone, after years of arguing and distance, is a piece of history. At Live Aid, Madonna came to us as a mischievous adolescent, at Live 8 she started by saying: "Are you ready for a revolution?" More mature, elegant, singing alongside the girl that at Live Aid was the image of the suffering of African children who now in 2005 was a marvelous twenty-five-year-old. She, the living symbol of concrete results, was saved, grown up and graduated thanks to a big rock concert like Live Aid.

The ten cities of Live 8 produced an enormous, impossible quantity of music, difficult to follow even, with many simultaneous performances and obligatory zapping between channels, with a choice between Sting in London and Roxy Music in Berlin, between Ligabue in Rome and The Cure in Paris, with a few artists that went from one city to another, such as Zucchero from Rome to Paris, Dido and Youssou N'Dour from London to the Eden Project in Cornwall where the African musicians brought together by Peter Gabriel played as a group. Moscow, Tokyo and Johannesburg with smaller representations, in comparison with Philadelphia, imposing, more youthful in terms of its cast with many rappers (which were not at Live Aid) and an unrestrained Will Smith who created the "click spot" live – the snapping of the fingers every three seconds to represent the interval of time that represented the death of a child in Africa – that was on television on the days of the concert with other famous faces, from Claudia Schiffer to Sophia Loren, presenting the click to all viewers with clear collective emotion. Will Smith was one of the few to unite the complicated and unfathomable event, calling upon all the cities: Berlin, packed with people; Paris, festive and multi-ethnic; Rome, deployed in full force with all or almost all its important singers. "We don't want charity, we want justice," was the theme of the day.

But Live 8 was also an extraordinary event for a digital age; it marked a turning point in regards to broadcasting live events. Traditional TV suddenly appeared old, incapable of accounting for what was happening around the world in any sufficiently extensive way. And whoever was able to follow the concerts via satellite or the Internet, or on their cell phones, had a completely new and different experience, being able to see all, or almost all, of the concerts at the same time. The satellite channels took advantage of a technology already widely experimented with in reality shows such as Big Brother or the direct broadcasts of F1. But if in the cases of Big Brother and F1 channels offered various angles a of a single event, digital television providers made one channel, 109, available to their viewers where the audience could choose what to watch, London or Rome, Berlin or Paris. They could pass from one square to another, from one concert to another, from one star to another, in a continuous pinwheel that had no other direction than their own curiosity. And America Online did even more than that, allowing those who didn't have a satellite TV to follow the six concerts contemporaneously online, also allowing for the alternation between sets as the user wished, guaranteeing high quality audio and video as well. TV and the web, however, are household devices and those who were traveling or on the road would have had nothing to follow. But the latest generation of phones resolved that problem and anyone with a video smartphone could watch and hear, even if in a miniscule format, the most beautiful and moving moments of Live 8. Traditional television, the not digital, not interactive kind, even if it had been obviously important because it allowed the public at large to follow the concert live, seemed old and gasping for air in comparison to the new media. It didn't make us leave our house, it didn't make us go beyond the borders of our country, in an event that instead, for the first time in the world, had made it clear to everyone that the world of communication today was no longer what we once knew.

A Farewell To The Thin White Duke

[January 10, 2016]

He turned 69 two days before his death, on the same day that *Blackstar*, his last album and what will remain as his testament, was released. Two weeks earlier he had announced his "definitive and irrevocable" retirement from the stage (in any case he had not performed live since 2006). David Bowie died in New York on 10 January 2016 of liver cancer. His death was announced on his official Twitter and Facebook profile: "David Bowie died peacefully today surrounded by his family after a courageous 18 month battle with cancer."

It is difficult, if not downright impossible, to imagine 20th-21st century culture without David Bowie's fundamental contribution. In the last fifty years the English artist revealed his genius as an innovator, constantly intent on experimenting with a variety of styles, changing his repertory and his persona, always offering his public the possibility to view the world with different eyes and from a different perspective.

If it is true that rock is not a genre, but rather a "way of doing things",

HISTORICAL NOTES

1947 – Bowie is born in Brixton, south London.

1969 – "Space Oddity" is the best-selling single in England.

1976 – The release of *The Man Who Fell to Earth*, the first of the fifteen films in which he acts.

1985 – He takes par in Live Aid at Wembley Stadium.

1996 – Bowie is inducted into the Rock and Roll Hall of Fame.

2001 – He opens The Concert for New York City for the victims of the September 11 tragedy.

2006 – His last concert, a charity event at the Black Ball in New York, is performed with Alicia Keys.

2016 – His last album, *Blackstar*, is released.

Musical memorabilia in the studio of Mike Garson, who collaborated with Bowie from 1971 on.

Bowie was the rock artist par excellence. His 'way' was eclectic, surprising, innovative, theatrical and popular. Every shift in his musical approach, every image, helped to forge our collective imagination, make our dreams and phantoms come to life, inspire and arouse us. He has demonstrated that true art must be free, and that rock, whether one likes it or not, has been one of the basic art forms of our time. And then there are his songs, true pearls of an infinite necklace, irreplaceable jewels, works that have left a lasting mark on the history of music. Again, there are his fundamental albums, which in a normal world would be played in schools. Such basic ones as *The Rise and Fall of Ziggy Stardust and the Spiders from Mars, Low, Heroes, Young Americans*, just to mention a few, have become a historic watershed. Rock, but not only music.

David Bowie's contribution to contemporary culture is simply inestimable. He is one of the few artists to have left his mark in a different way in every period of his career, in his quest to remain at the cutting edge, never following what is trendy but rather reinventing himself and breaking new ground, always blurring the difference between art and life. He wore many masks, but never had a preference for any one of them; he had his characters live and die as only great actors are capable of doing; he celebrated life, love and sorrow – and death in his last album, death without ever hiding behind his public persona.

Whoever loves music can only grieve for the loss of David Bowie. Because Bowie is much more than a musician and singer; he was the perfect personification of everything we love in art, music, creativity and freedom. Yes, freedom, the freedom represented by his many different masks and personas, by his desire to always be 'elsewhere', his inability and refusal to be pigeon-holed or labeled, his continuous, intense and overwhelming curiosity about everything the culture of his and our time has expressed. David Bowie never gave up when faced with failures or illness, not even when he was confonting death itself, finishing his last album well aware that it would be the last chapter of an extraordinary story.

It's hard to imagine a world without David Bowie. What is certain is that this void can never be filled.

Index

311

317

Ernesto Assante, began working in journalism in 1977 and in his thirty-plus year career, he has collaborated with numerous weekly and monthly Italian and international publications, including Epoca, L'Espresso and Rolling Stone. He conceived of and oversaw the "Music", "Computer Valley" and "Computer, Internet and More" supplements for the Italian newspaper, "La Repubblica". He is the author of books on music criticism, a few of which were co-written with his colleague Gino Castaldo. In 2005, the two created "Lezioni di Rock. Viaggio al Centro della Musica" (Lessons in Rock. A Voyage into the Heart of Music) with the intention of delving into the stories of those who have gone down as legends in rock history, making use of guided listening and demonstrative videos. From 2003 to 2009 he taught "New Media Theories and Techniques" followed by "Analysis of Musical Languages" at the Sapienza University of Rome in the Communication Science Department. Among his numerous publications about music are *Legends of Rock, Masters of Rock Guitar, 5 Seconds of Summer* and *U2 - Past, Present, Future*, all released by White Star Publishers.

Photo Credits

page 14: Michael Ochs Archives/Stringer/Getty Images; page 20: Keystone/Getty Images; page 24: Michael Ochs Archives/Getty Images; page 28 Michael Ochs Archives/Getty Images; page 32: Gilles Petard/Redferns/Getty Images; page 36: Hammond/V&A Images/ Getty Images; page 40: © Keystone Pictures USA/Alamy/IPA; page 44: David Gahr/Getty Images; page 48 Michael Ochs Archives/Getty Images; page 52 Michael Ochs Archives/ Getty Images; page 56 Rowland Scherman/Getty Images; page 60 CBS/Getty Images; page 66: David Gahr/Getty Images; page 72 Lawrence Schiller/Polaris Communications/Getty Images; page 76: Herve GLOAGUEN/Gamma-Rapho/Getty Images; page 80: Val Wilmer/ Redferns/Getty Images; page 84: Andrew Whittuck/Redferns/Getty Images; page 88: Paul Ryan/Michael Ochs Archives/Getty Images; page 92: Hulton Archive/Getty Images; page 96: Bob Dean/The Boston Globe/Getty Images; page 100: Ralph Morse/The LIFE Picture Collection/; Getty Images; page 104: © Trinity Mirror/Mirrorpix/Alamy Stock Photo; page 108: © Pictorial Press LTD/Alamy Stock Photo; page 112: © INTERFOTO/Alamy Stock Photo; page 116: Reg Burkett/Express/Getty Images; page 120: Hulton Archive/Getty Images; page 128: Bill Owens/20th Century Fox/Hulton Archive/Getty Images; page 132: David Redfern/Redferns/Getty Images; page 136: Jorgen Angel/Redferns/Getty Images; page 140: Thomas Monaster/NY Daily News/Getty Images; page 144: Universal Pictures/ Getty Images; page 148: Evening Standard/Getty Images; page 152 Michael Ochs Archives/ Getty Images; page 156: Jorgen Angel/Redferns/Getty Images; page 160: Bernard Gotfryd/ Getty Images; page 164: Ellen Poppinga - K & K/Redferns/Getty Images; page 168: Michael Ochs Archives/Getty Images; page 172: Richard E. Aaron/Redferns/Getty Images; page 176: David Corio/Redferns/Getty Images; page 180: Michael Montfort/Michael Ochs Archives/ Getty Images; page 184: Richard E. Aaron/Redferns/Getty Images; page 190: Ronald C. Modra/Getty Images; page 194: Val Wilmer/Redferns/Getty Images; page 198: © Olycom/ LFI/Photoshot; page 202: David Redfern/Redferns/Getty Images; page 206: George Rose/ Getty Images; page 210: Virginia Turbett/Redferns/Getty Images; page 214: Hulton Archive/ Getty Images; page 218: Michael Ochs Archives/Getty Image; page 222: ©MGM/Everett Collection/Getty Images; page 226: Ebet Roberts/Redferns/Getty Images; page 230: Frank Micelotta/ImageDirect/Getty Images; page 234: Blank Archives/Getty Images; page 240: Denis O'Regan/Getty Images; page 244: The LIFE Picture Collection/Getty Images; page 248: Garcia/Stills/Gamma-rapho-Keystone; page 252: Ebet Roberts/Redferns/Getty Images; page 258: © Olycom/Retna/Photoshot; page 264: Marco Sabatini; page 268: Mick Hutson/ Redferns/Getty Images; page 272: Phil Dent/Redferns/Getty Images; page 276: Martyn Goodacre/Getty Images; Page 280: Frans Schellekens/Redferns/Getty Images; page 284: The LIFE Picture Collection/Getty Images; page 290: Jim Steinfeldt/Michael Ochs Archives/Getty Images; page 294: Pohl Henrik/IPA; page 298: Dave Hogan/Getty Images; page 304: Jay L. Clendenin/Los Angeles Times/Getty Images

WHITE STAR PUBLISHERS